Television Producers

From live sports coverage to situation comedy, British television is producer-driven. *Television Producers* focuses on the individuals in control of seven programming categories across British national television. The working practices of producers of 'quality' drama are contrasted with those of producers of cheap game shows and people shows. Documentary film makers are compared with producers of news, current affairs, sport and 'infotainment'. Each genre is a separate world with its own distinctive use of TV technology and money, pattern of recruitment and careers, and world view.

Television Producers looks at the work of individual producers, schedulers and network barons. Over 250 producers across the range of British television – BBC, ITV, Channel Four and the independents – were interviewed for the book. Considering future possibilities for British broadcasting, Tunstall argues that television's recent industrial revolution has greatly reduced producer security, while leaving producer autonomy largely intact.

Jeremy Tunstall is Director of the Communication Policy Research Unit at City University in London. His previous books include *Journalists at Work*, *The Media in Britain*, *The Media are American*, and *Media Moguls* (Routledge).

Communications and Society
General Editor: James Curran

Television Producers

Jeremy Tunstall

London and New York

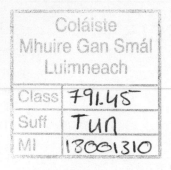
First published 1993 by
Routledge
11 New Fetter Lane, London EC4P 4EE

Simultaneously published in the USA and Canada
by Routledge
29 West 35th Street, New York, NY 10001

© 1993 Jeremy Tunstall

Typeset in 10/12pt Times by
Ponting–Green Publishing Services, Chesham, Bucks
Printed and bound in Great Britain by
T J Press (Padstow) Ltd, Cornwall

British Library Cataloguing in Publication Data
A catalogue record for this book is available from the British Library.

Library of Congress Cataloging in Publication Data
Tunstall, Jeremy.
    Television producers / Jeremy Tunstall.
        p.   cm. – (Communication and society)
        1. Television–Great Britain–Production and direction.
    I. Title.   II. Series: Communication and society
    PN1992.75.T86   1993
    791.45'0232'092241–dc20   93-7178

ISBN 0–415–09471–2
ISBN 0–415–09472–0 (pbk)

Contents

Acknowledgements

This book is based on interviews with 254 British TV producers (including a few senior executives). These producers were generous with their time and remarkably open in what they said. I am deeply indebted to the trusting and generous way in which they responded; their insights, observations, anecdotes and humour contributed to an enjoyable research experience. All producers were promised anonymity, but a few individuals subsequently agreed to have their names attached to a longer quotation.

My thanks are due also to the Economic and Social Research Council (ESRC) which generously funded a broader enquiry, also encompassing newspaper executives.

Mark Dunford and David Wood were my research assistants and colleagues on this study; both proved to be effective and imaginative research workers and between them they completed 131 producer-interviews (while I did 123 interviews). David Wood was primarily involved in the newspaper study but he did a number of TV interviews, including those with the producers of the main British TV soap operas. Mark Dunford completed all or most of the interviews in several sub-fields, including game or people shows, drama and youth programming. Mark also completed 27 interviews with producers of regional TV news and current affairs; these latter interviews are not directly analysed in the present book, but were valuable as background material. Mark is also the co-author of Chapter 8.

The following people very generously read and commented on a preliminary draft of this book: Richard Barron, Mark Dunford, Stuart Macdonald, Graeme Salaman, Howard Tumber, David Walker, David Wood and my daughter Rebecca Tunstall.

This project has involved massive quantities of word-processing and most of this labour has been skilfully done by Maggie Brough, who was ably backed up by Catherine Gale and Jane Morgan.

I am also indebted to the active support of various other people at City University – especially to my Social Science colleagues, to the efficient and helpful staff of the University Library, to Susan Griffiths, and to the University's additional financial support in transcribing interviews.

Last, but not least, love and apologies for my TV habits and conversation over three years to Sylvia, Rebecca, Helena, Paul and William (the dog).

J.T.

List of tables

Also by Jeremy Tunstall:

The Fishermen
The Advertising Man
Old and Alone
The Westminster Lobby Correspondents
Journalists at Work
The Media are American
The Media in Britain
Communications Deregulation
Studies on the Press (with O. Boyd-Barrett and C. Seymour-Ure)
Media Made in California (with David Walker)
Liberating Communications (with Michael Palmer)
Media Moguls (with Michael Palmer)
Media Sociology (editor)
Sociological Perspectives (editor with Kenneth Thompson)
The Open University Opens (editor)

Chapter 1

Producers in British television

The 'series producer' or 'series editor' in British national television is the main focus of the book. Each TV programme is a collective enterprise involving between twenty and a hundred people; producers are the individuals in charge of these programme teams.

British television is, however, 'driven' by producers in additional ways. It is sometimes said that the British tradition of PSB, 'Public-Service Broadcasting', would stand more accurately for 'Producer Self-Service Broadcasting'. This latter assertion, at least, is an over-simplification; but the practice of 'public service' in British television (made up of education and information as well as entertainment) has required the individual producer to create the TV service that the public has received.

Former programme producers have gone on to run not just the BBC's two national TV channels but also the entire BBC (with its 27,500 employees in 1991–2). Even in the advertising-financed ITV companies, former producers have always been prominent in management; and since Channel Four began in 1982 it has been dominated by former producers and 'commissioning editors' with a programming orientation. From 1982 independent production companies made much of the programming for Channel Four, and since around 1990 increasingly also for the BBC and ITV channels; almost all these independent production companies were again run by producers. People with advertising backgrounds have played a much smaller part in running British television.

PRODUCERS IN PRIVATE WORLDS

Public Institution and Private World was the subtitle that Tom Burns chose for his book about the BBC in the early 1960s and early 1970s.[1]

His study focused on senior management and the producers of just two types of programme output. The present book is about producers in seven different genres or TV programme categories; it suggests that each programme genre – sport or drama or news – has its own distinctive 'private world' that stretches across all the channels.

This study covers a wide range and omits a few categories, such as purely educational programming. However, an important characteristic of British television is its tradition of covering a wide range of different programme types, and of carrying this range within the high-audience hours of the evening. Part of the traditional 'public-service broadcasting' project is that both popular and less-popular programming should be scheduled in the most popular hours on the main channels. It is also characteristic of British television that several of the genres are factual – including not only news, current affairs and sport, but also documentary and mixed-goal or 'edinfotainment' programming (this latter unlovely term is intended to underline the heavy emphasis placed on a large mixed bag of factual programming, which seeks to deliver education and information entertainingly – or is it to deliver entertainment educationally and informatively?).

Each specific genre has its particular requirements and working cycles, which tend to cut its producers off from producers and others working in different fields with different timetables. Most British producers spend between 4 and 6 months each year locked into the intensive effort involved in meeting deadlines for a series of programmes; during this intensive phase they may well work 7 days a week for many weeks in succession. The other half of the year includes vacation time and perhaps 5 months of less intensive work. During these other months the producer may be supervising writing, casting supporting roles, engaging in research, looking at locations, seeing possible interviewees, talking to actors' agents, and so on. Producers spend much of the time out of their offices – in the studio, at the location, viewing the raw rushes and, later, the rough edited film or tape.

Even at the quieter times of the year most producers do not arrive home until after the London rush-hour. They often take home with them scripts and programme outlines to read, as well as cassettes of programmes submitted by available writers, directors or performers. Much of their domestic TV viewing is of programming in their own genre. Thus producers tend to be locked into a genre-specific world even when at home.

Each of the genres is located within a department or departments; and even independent production companies specialize, so that here also producers are locked into the private world of a single genre. Each genre has its own specific goal or goals; it has a characteristic style of production – location film, or live studio, or the 'outside broadcasts' of sport. Each genre has its own internal system of status and prestige, its own values and its own world-view.

Departments and genres also function as career-ladders. There is continuing movement between organizations: many producers have started in the BBC, moved to ITV, then back to the BBC, only finally to go freelance or to set up as independent producers; but such job-moves all take place within one small world which shares one broad career-ladder. It is common for a producer's career to have involved several job-moves, each move following one particular senior colleague. Producers also in turn tend to be surrounded by production team-members with whom they have worked on several previous programmes and projects.

Thus the producer's own work-career advances within the private world of a particular genre whose peculiar work-mix of timetables, goals, production schedules and world-view largely shuts its members off from the members of other private genre-worlds.

WHERE THE PRODUCER CAME FROM

The producer role (like television itself) has multiple origins. The British TV producer historically is derived from the civil servant, the radio producer and the film producer, as well as from show business and the stage.

The BBC in the 1920s emerged from the Post Office, which was a department of government. The producer role in the BBC and in advertising-financed television derives from an inter-war civil service which still had colonial responsibilities; there are echoes of the district officer, gallantly attempting to administer one small corner of a vast empire. There is also a military element in this history: the BBC was set up in the 1920s by men who had served in and survived the first world war. British television in the 1940s and 1950s was built by men who had served in the second war or had done two years of post-1945 military service. Many young producers of the 1950s had been 'national-service' officers, and the television producer was seen as a leader of men (not women).

Political neutrality was a key element. The producer, like the civil servant and the army officer, avoided partisanship. In contrast to France or Germany, the British producer role was not, and still has not been, politicized. In Britain the BBC gradually evolved the tradition of being non-partisan while quietly patriotic. This non-partisanship has also been supported by the BBC's early reliance on neutral news agencies as a model for radio news. The non-partisan tradition acquired in 1955 a non-commercial element; when advertising was introduced with ITV, the relevant legislation and regulatory authority required producers to be sheltered from any direct advertising connections.

The BBC, modelled on the Post Office with its monopoly of post and telephone, was a vertically integrated monopoly. This conception of vertical integration was only modified by the ITV and its cartel of fifteen regional companies. The British TV-producer role developed within a pattern of two large systems – BBC and ITV – both of which made the bulk of their own programming and also transmitted it to a national audience.

This pattern, which reached maturity in the 1970s, involved two large cultural bureaucracies with an occupational hierarchy. Like the civil service, television had three main occupational categories. At the top were the managers, amongst whom former and current programme producers were the largest subgroup; producers mingled with general administrators, accountants and senior engineers, constituting a managerial elite. In the middle was a large category of TV skills and crafts; there were the men (and a few women) who operated TV studios and the outside broadcasts, the outdoor filming, the post-production and editing functions and other craft skills. Third and last were the clerical and lower service functions, in which women predominated. These latter two groupings were again reminiscent of the civil-service executive and clerical levels.

Another crucial civil-service-style feature in the 1970s was job security. It was required by the trade unions, and accepted by both BBC and ITV, that 70 per cent or more of the employees were in permanent and pensionable employment. In the 1970s a substantial minority of producers and directors were freelances; but many of these had been in staff positions previously and had chosen to go freelance. At the skilled levels and above in both the BBC and ITV there were very low rates of employee turnover, and 86 per cent of BBC employees in 1989 had been in the BBC for all their broadcasting work-careers.[2] The numbers of producers and other personnel employed in British television expanded steadily – buoyed up by expanding revenue – in almost every single year from 1946 to 1988. Producers were integrated into general management. Within this broad category, several levels of programme decision-making can be identified in 1990s terms:

Channel Heads

Departmental Head (BBC); Director of Programmes (ITV)

Executive Producer (BBC); Department Head (ITV)

Series Producer; Editor

Producer; Assistant Producer.

In this study we are focusing primarily upon the series producer or editor; this is the highest level of person who is in regular daily editorial or 'hands-on' control of the content of a series of programmes. At the executive-producer levels and above, the responsibility is typically for more than one series and has a lower 'hands-on' component.

Many producers are hesitant about accepting promotion out of the series-producer level; they often express their dilemma by referring to parallel cases of people promoted above the core-activity level – the teacher who is too senior to teach, the sailor who is too senior to go to sea. The tradition in British television is that the producer is part of management. The producer is made aware of what the senior people are thinking; the producer receives a flow of advice and guidance – much of it spoken, some of it written. Words such as 'guidance', 'guidelines' and 'consultation' are heavily used.[3]

The emphasis placed on 'flexibility' and the avoidance of rigid rules in turn reflects the vague collection of goals towards which British broadcasting traditionally strives; each one of the public-service trio 'education, entertainment and information' is fairly vague, and how these can, or should, be mixed together in a particular series of programmes is very uncertain indeed.

There is inevitably a substantial degree of tension in such a system. From time to time conflicts between creative autonomy and organizational hierarchy surface into press publicity and political controversy; this may involve a channel controller vetoing the work of a series producer. However, much more frequently these tensions are managed quietly within the system; often the disciplinary intervention takes the form of a 'Don't do that again' retrospective memo, rather than an actual veto.

Many, or most, difficult decisions for the producer focus, in fact, on logistics and money. If television is an art-form, it is a cumbersome and expensive one. If the producer is an auteur or author, he is an author who needs the active involvement of thirty or forty other people, expensive equipment, studio space and – not least – a network to transmit the end-product. Few people who have not been involved in television recognize how much work, energy and time in programme preparation go into polishing and refining small details; dotting the 'i's and crossing the 't's is an elaborate undertaking in this thousands-of pounds-per-minute medium.

The producer role encompasses elements not only of the civil servant but of a latter-day Renaissance Man, capable of playing all the parts. The producer ideally should be good with both words and pictures, the two main building blocks of television. He or she needs some basic grasp of TV technology, of tape against film, of sound, lighting and sets; requires (usually extensive) specialist knowledge of the particular programme genre, such as drama or news; needs to be able to juggle ideas against finance; needs plenty of sheer energy; needs some performance skills – the ability to enthuse and activate others during a long working day; and needs diplomatic skills to smooth ruffled egos and to persuade outsiders to do things at different times and for less money than they would prefer.

This civil servant, macho-military, Renaissance Man, creative manager was in practice usually a man – a white, responsible, British male who could be trusted to do a decent job in difficult circumstances. Some of this tradition has now changed in ways favourable to women – if not to ethnic minorities – but the point remains that the producer role was traditionally conceived as male.

FROM INTEGRATED-FACTORY PRODUCTION

Until 1982 British television consisted of just two vertically integrated organizations (BBC and ITV) which each made the bulk of the programmes in its own factories (or studios), assembled the schedule and transmitted it over a national network. This 'integrated-factory' approach derives from BBC radio, where the radio studios could be tucked quietly away in the basement. In the case of television the studios were larger, but were still placed at the lower levels of buildings; above ground were the programme-makers' offices and on the top floor were the senior managers. British television was vertically integrated both as an industry and within its own buildings.

There are two other possible production systems which in the 1990s are both increasingly important. In 1982 Channel Four introduced the 'publisher' concept to Britain; it 'published' (assembled and transmitted) programming commissioned and acquired from other producers. By the early 1990s, on government direction, this publisher model was also increasingly followed in both ITV and BBC television.

There is also a third model, that of the 'packager', which prevails in cable and satellite systems. Cable did not get far in 1980s Britain, but from 1990 satellite offerings did attract customer-households in increasing numbers. These satellite and cable channels are typically themed to one specific genre such as news, sport or movies. The cable or satellite provider typically packages the channels with programming acquired in bulk from large suppliers of news, sport, movies, and so on.

By 1990 the Channel Four publisher model was well established and, along with it, a distinction between, on the one hand, 'commissioning editors' inside Channel Four, and, on the other hand, outside producers who actually made the programming. The packager model was also starting to become entrenched; the packager, of course, only directly employs very small numbers of producers.

Up to about 1990, however, the integrated-factory system of production remained the normal and dominant pattern. In the 1970s the British TV producer had been largely insulated from fierce head-to-head competition and from harsh financial pressures. For a period of eighteen years (1964–82) there were just three channels, with the audience in effect amicably shared 50/50 between one ITV channel and two BBC channels. The audience was offered large rations of educational and informational programming as well as entertainment. There was plenty of money – with all the booming advertising revenue supporting just one channel, and a steadily growing licence fee (as consumers switched to colour sets) going to the BBC; British television in the 1970s was much more generously funded than was western Europe's television overall.

Television producers lived a sheltered life within a system based on consensus and cartel. There was a consensus between the political parties and between broadcasters schooled in the BBC and ITV versions of public service. The trade unions also played a central role, favouring good-quality British programming, a broad mix of programming genres, and strict quotas of cheap programme imports. The unions got secure employment for their members, with extremely generous levels of manning and overmanning.

The ITV network was a cartel of non-competing regional companies which had a monopoly on TV advertising; the regulatory body, the Independent Broadcasting Authority, required it to carry quotas of non-entertainment, mainly factual, programming. Each of the ITV companies bargained fiercely to keep its share of programming airtime, which meant that even ITV's entertainment programming was supplier-driven and less than 100 per cent market-orientated.

British TV schedulers were required by the system to seek both audience ratings and prestige. Schedulers were expected to put some 'serious' programming into the high-audience times; buttressed by generous finance, and perhaps 'hammocked' between a previous popular programme and a following popular programme, some serious programmes did quite well in both prestige and audience terms. However, both BBC and ITV deliberately spent heavily on some programming (such as serious drama and arts features) which had quite modest ratings appeal. British television cautiously adopted cheap-but-popular American formats such as the quiz or game show and the soap opera and placed a quota of these into high-audience and early-evening times. Consequently, there were huge differences in cost per million of audience, with one programme costing – in these terms – ten or even twenty times as much as the adjoining programme in the schedule.

While a few established (popular or prestige) successes might run for 25 or 35 weeks per year, most British TV series conformed to a mini-series pattern of as few as 6, and no more than 13, programmes per year. Popular situation comedies, for example, could take 15 years to accumulate 100 episodes. This mini-series emphasis fitted both ITV cartel-bargaining and BBC deference towards TV writers; it fitted also with the producers' perception that quantity often led to reduced quality.

This mini-series system of short runs – but lengthy preparation and extended filming/recording – reflected producers' interests. The performers (such as actors) were not very highly rewarded in British television; nor were the army of (mainly women) clerical and support staff. The people who did well were the producers and their teams and the highly unionized technicians; they were fairly well paid, securely employed, not over-worked on very long series runs, and provided with interestingly varied work.

One consequence of these 'public-service' arrangements was that the British TV audience was fairly undifferentiated. The main determinant of the audience was the time of day and the availability of people at home to view. All programmes on at a particular hour had broadly similar audience profiles. This did not completely eradicate any concerns about the audience. The total size remained important, as was the 'share' of the viewing audience that watched the particular programme.

Many producers in the early 1990s still did not know the proportion of men and women in their audience; many believed – against the research facts – that there was, for example, a characteristic 'Channel Four audience'. However, given that the audience profile for most programmes is much like the audience profile for any other programme transmitted at the same time, the total audience size is indeed much the most significant number. Producers always know this total ratings number and they also know that the number is greatly influenced by the competition in the same time-slot.

British producers, as late as 1990, still lived in a world in which cash and specific sums of money were not the effective currency. A producer in practice worked primarily within a budget, not of money, but of resources. These resources would involve people – such as researchers, reporters, actors, the design people and the studio crew; second, there would be the studio spaces and the use of outdoor film or outside broadcast units; and third, there was the time for which these people and resources were allocated – often very generous by international standards. In addition, the producer would have some cash (for travel, staying in hotels and so on) but knew that the cash element was only a fraction of the total cost. The producer had little idea of the real cost and often suspected, or knew, that the ITV company itself or the BBC also did not know the real cost: so why should the producer bother? Even the concept of 'over-spending' the budget was a vague one, because – in these vertically integrated organizations with their permanent facilities and staff – there was no agreed cost that could be attached to, say, one extra day for forty people and a studio.

With many short runs of 6 or 7 programmes, the producer might have only a hazy idea of the intended audience, the real cost, or the real goal (from the company's viewpoint). Given this degree of vagueness, the producer was also likely to be unclear how 'success' could be defined.

In keeping with this traditional lack of concern for financial detail, producers – despite being managers – were given little or no management preparation. Indeed, the recruitment process, which focused broadly on artistic skills and education in the humanities, selected and promoted some people who were not good at arithmetic. Finance was seen by some producers as a tiresome chore which could safely be entrusted to a unit manager or some other member of the production team.

AROUND 1990: BRITAIN'S TV REVOLUTION

Producers interviewed during 1990–2 saw this as a period of revolutionary change in British television. Many used terms such as 'commercialization', 'casualization', 'deregulation' and 'break-up' to describe this revolution. The majority of producers criticized the Thatcher government policies and the Broadcasting Act of 1990 as based on ideology rather than insight; most producers, however, agreed that some change was necessary and a significant minority welcomed the broad thrust of the changes.

Most producers would agree that the precursor to the 1990 Revolution was the launch of Channel Four in 1982. This change was, however, also in keeping with the traditional slow advance of British broadcasting policy which had now created new channels in 1955, 1964 and 1982. Channel Four was, however, radical in that it created a new industrial model: it marked a move from integrated-factory production to the publisher model.

The publisher element in British broadcasting gradually expanded in the decade after 1982. Initially, Channel Four only had a few per cent of the British TV audience; by the late 1980s both it and the independent-production sector were getting larger. The Thatcher Government then set a 25 per cent independent-production target for ITV and later (in the 1990 Act) for the BBC. During the early 1990s it became increasingly clear that both the BBC and ITV would contract out more than 25 per cent of the production to outside producers. The four new ITV companies which in 1991 won new franchises from the previous incumbents all began broadcasting in 1993 using the publisher model. By 1993 the four conventional British channels were operating two production systems alongside each other. The two advertising-financed channels – Channel Four and ITV – now operated predominantly the publisher model. The BBC still operated mainly as an integrated factory but was also moving towards the publisher model.

What made the changes around 1990 indeed revolutionary – compared with normal British slow evolution – was that around 1990 not only the second publisher system but also the third system – the packager – was arriving on the British scene. This was a move not just to one additional channel but to multiple additional channels.

The Thatcher Government, in effect, made several efforts toward multi-channel television before any such system had made a successful take-off. In the early 1980s the Thatcher Government embraced both direct broadcasting by satellite and cable television but neither achieved a successful launch. Then in 1985 the Peacock Committee was set up to consider BBC finances including advertising; Peacock reported against BBC advertising but in favour of new channels and subscription payment per channel. Peacock's attack on the 'comfortable duopoly' was taken up in the Government's 1988 White Paper which criticized in particular the ITV channels' internal cartel arrangements. The 1990 Broadcasting Act toned down some of the White Paper rhetoric but retained much of its spirit. Alongside, but separate from, the 1990 Act, Mrs Thatcher undoubtedly encouraged Rupert Murdoch's Luxembourg-based (and regulated) Sky satellite offerings in competition with Britain's official British Satellite Broadcasting (BSB) offerings. These two systems announced a merger in late 1990; the resulting BSkyB subsequently began to achieve significant rates of household penetration for its service. The packager model had arrived.

Compared with the changes in several other European countries, these British changes may appear modest. Indeed, not everyone would even agree on what were the key events or dates. 1990 is a convenient date because it includes the Broadcasting Act and the emergence of BSkyB; but much of the significant change occurred before 1990. The entire ITV system took fright in 1988 – mainly over the White Paper – and the ITV companies decided to confront the trade unions and to act tough in other ways. Yet all the years from 1985 to 1993 included important changes; and, in retrospect, historians may see the entire period from 1982 (the launch of Channel Four) to 1996 (the new BBC Charter) as another example of British gradual change.

If so, most workers in British television would probably disagree. For most of them there was indeed a period of revolutionary change in the two or three years around 1990. Preliminary interviews for this study began in mid-1989 and several producers then referred to 'casualization' as a major current trend.

'Casualization' had several aspects. First, there was a massive reduction in regular employment. In 1987–8 the ITV companies were employing 17,000 people to run a single national channel (with some regional programming); by 1993 ITV employed 6,000 fewer. The BBC – especially from 1990 – began cutting staff, although it favoured many small bites of a hundred or two hundred redundancies rather than the ITV big-bang approach.

Second, there was a marked shift towards employing people on short contracts, usually for a few months. Consequently in the early 1990s some people (mainly aged over 40) were permanently employed on the old life-long basis; some senior people were on contracts of a few years; many producers were on contracts of one year or six months; more junior production personnel were often employed for the few months of the series run. In the technical studio areas there was a similar range.

Third, another major facet was the closing of studio buildings. In their vertical factories both the BBC and ITV companies had too much production capacity, too many buildings and too many studios. With the move towards contracting production out to independents it gradually became evident that this over-capacity was on a massive scale. In late 1991 the BBC announced a 40 per cent cut in its capacity for studios and facilities.

Fourth, there was a quite overt attack on the trade unions. This had been a repeated theme in Thatcher Government rhetoric and policy documents in the 1980s. The broadcasting trade unions – in the 1970s of legendary strength – now saw their power rapidly reduced. There was a spate of trade-union mergers, resulting in one main union, BECTU (its full name – Broadcasting, Entertainment, Cinematograph and Theatre Union – indicates its genealogy).

These numerous changes and forms of casualization had multiple impacts on British TV producers. Many producers interviewed for this study had entered television in the 1960s or 1970s when it offered extremely secure employment:

> If you were any good, they expected and wanted you to stay there for life.

By the early 1990s producers felt themselves to be in a fairly insecure job, which now involved working here for a year or two before moving on to some other organization.

The 1990 changes also involved various forms of slimming-down and speeding-up. The slimming-down affected not only the number of people on a camera-crew but the number of people responsible for researching, filming and editing a programme. Speeding-up took different forms in different genres; but in drama, for instance, a producer who in the mid-1980s might have had 15 days to film an hour's drama would by the early 1990s have been reduced to 10 or 11 days.

PRODUCERS DEPENDENT ON THE PRESS

In contrast to their private world of genre, work and career, producers are aware of being in some respects dependent on the public forum of the British national newspapers.

Producers know that newspaper coverage of television is read by the general public, by other print journalists and by politicians. The producer's colleagues comment on press coverage in corridor conversations; the producer also knows that the barons at the top of the system see a daily digest of press comment from all newspapers and specialist publications. The barons themselves anxiously scan the press because they know that press comment helps to establish the public image of their channel.

The producer eventually receives several kinds of feedback on his or her series. Audience ratings only become available a week or so later; even letters take a day or two to arrive; the opinion of the controllers upstairs also takes time to filter down; the press coverage, however, is not only public but also immediate.

Most producers have a low opinion of most press comment. They claim that most press writers on television display their ignorance of the subject; nevertheless, producers are eager to receive positive coverage. Producers especially welcome 'preview' comment in the daily press in advance of that evening's television; this is welcomed not least because it is believed to increase the ratings. 'Post-views' – pieces about last night's or last week's television – are widely dismissed as both unfair and unable to affect ratings. In addition, there is massive publicity in the TV pages (which greatly increased in the early 1990s) – much of it being show-biz-style coverage, mainly about stars, presenters and on-screen personalities; this coverage varies from adulatory, press-release, material to scandal about the TV personalities' private lives. Finally, there are stories with possible political and policy implications, some of which are seen within television as deliberate attacks on the channel in question. The Murdoch press was seen by many producers as aggressively promoting its Sky satellite TV interests. Many producers see much of the national press as continually searching for anti-BBC stories. All producers are aware of a common pattern: every few months one newspaper publishes a TV scandal story which has political implications; politicians take up the press story; other newspapers, other politicans, radio and television itself engage in follow-ups of the 'biggest TV crisis since . . .'.

All producers must accept that publicity is one of their job functions. Producers are, indeed, asked to provide material for insertion into the main programme guides such as *Radio Times* and *TV Times*. Before a new run of the series, the producer supplies additional publicity material – often about new presenters or new actors – to the in-house publicity department. There is also a general recognition that to obtain 'preview' coverage the producer needs to get a videotape to the preview journalist several days before the programme is transmitted. Each week hundreds of motorcycle-messenger journeys are involved in carrying tapes across London to previewers. This is only possible for programmes completed several days before transmission; producers assert that this pre-availability requirement is why previewers mainly cover drama, documentary and current affairs, and (they say) ignore programmes transmitted live or near-to-live.

Producers are aware that many audience members only 'discover' the series by, say, the fourth or fifth episode, when the short run is nearly finished. For this reason, and because the press is believed to relish novelty, publicists and producers tend to focus on the first programme in a new series run. This leads the producer to place his or her potentially most popular or sensational programme at the start (while hiding 'weaker' episodes towards the end).

Many producers, having focused their promotional efforts on the first programme, decide that their publicity work is now completed. Other producers continue to battle away at the promotional effort, sending out fresh publicity material (and fresh motorcycled tapes) for each programme in the series. The height of such publicity efforts is found in some of the factual TV areas; some programme teams include a high proportion of personnel from journalism who spread the word to their newspaper friends.

In the 1980s factual TV producers in general (and perhaps independent producers of Channel Four programmes in particular) increasingly offered newspapers background articles linked to a TV programme scheduled for that evening. The newspaper gets a solidly researched article, perhaps based on several weeks of preparatory investigation by a researcher and a producer. It might be said that investigative journalism in the British press is alive and well and based on TV programme research.

This multi-faceted dependence on the press serves to underline for the producer the fleeting nature of television: press cuttings are part of the industry's available record, whereas most British TV programmes in practice fail to register in the industry's collective memory. This dependence upon newspapers, which are regarded as covering television in such an amateurish and unsystematic manner, also reminds the producer that the industry's overall system for awarding prestige and recognizing 'quality' is itself highly uncertain or – as some producers say – 'whimsical'.

PRODUCERS: LESS SECURITY, MORE RESPONSIBILITY

Very few people in British television today would deny that producers are now less secure than they used to be. It is also widely agreed that producers now carry additional responsibilities.

In the past the producer was simply required to make a batch of programmes in an integrated factory, within which a large range of back-up services were available on tap. Today many producers are out in the independent-production world, running small businesses in which nothing is provided on tap. Even the producers within the large organizations have additional tasks: today many series are made primarily in-house, but also contract out, say, 3 or 4 of a run of 13 programmes to outside producers. The in-house producer thus has to learn the skill of commissioning programmes out to other producers; this activity also brings with it extra tasks in the form of a flood of supplicants looking for finance for their programme projects.

In some of the more expensive areas, such as drama and documentary, producers are also increasingly expected to arrange co-production finance. A US or Australian channel may be willing to pay one-third of the cost but this involves additional diplomatic-entrepreneurial tasks for the producer.

More generally, the tightening-up of budgets and programme finance has meant that producers spend more time talking about, and working on, budgets and money.

Increasingly also producers are required to make choices over what technical facilities they use. The 1970s practices – always making the programme in the integrated factory's downstairs studio, or always using a company film-crew for outdoor filming – no longer automatically prevail. The BBC in 1992–3 introduced its 'Producer Choice' initiative which encouraged producers to 'choose' between using in-house studios and facilities or using outside specialists. Again, sizeable sums of money are involved; again, there are new work-tasks, and new expertise is required.

Producers, then, have in recent years become less secure, while acquiring more responsibilities. Have they become more, or less, autonomous? That is one of the questions this book seeks to answer.

Part I

Factual

Introduction

This short introduction to Part I makes a few general points about factual programming and its producers on British television. The sheer quantity of factual material on British television is indicated by Table 1.1. Only one conventional channel (ITV) in 1991 devoted much less than half its output to factual television. The 'minority' channels, BBC2 and Channel Four, both carried a higher proportion of factual programming than did the large-audience channels, BBC1 and ITV. BBC1 also spends about twice as much as BBC2, and ITV outspends Channel Four by a larger margin.

Table 1.1 Factual programming on British television, 1991–1992

Programme type	Percentages on each channel			
	BBC 1	BBC 2	ITV	Channel Four
Documentary, features and current affairs	16	22	14.8	21.4
News	17	7	15.0	9.8
Sport	10	13	6.5	7.9
Other factual (education, religion etc)	5	24	3.3	11.6
TOTAL FACTUAL	48	66	39.6	50.7
Fiction and entertainment	35	28	53.1	40.5
Children's	13	3	7.3	8.8
Continuity and trails	4	3	–	–
GRAND TOTAL	100	100	100	100
Total hours (weekly)	123.5	119	144	139

Source: BBC and ITC.

Factual programming overall is indeed cheaper to make than is fictional and entertainment programming. The two major non-factual types of output, drama and light entertainment (including comedy), are much more expensive to produce than are the main factual categories. Factual programming is cheaper primarily because it does not need to employ the large numbers of actors, performers and related staff involved in fiction and comedy.

British broadcasting's traditional broad spread of programming – now referred to as 'public-service broadcasting' – has always aimed to provide a substantial dose of informative and educational programming. Table 1.2 indicates one important reason why these substantial doses have continued – factual programming is cheaper; it represents good value for money. Factual programming is also seen as virtuous in another way – it is overwhelmingly home-made, British-made; 'programme acquisition', which is extremely cheap, largely involves importing fiction and comedy.

Within British television the audience ratings are always of some importance; but prestige within the TV industry does not correlate closely with popularity. Let us look at our four factual fields in turn.

The more ambitious documentary programming – such as that which involves large amounts of foreign filming – is fairly expensive to make and only achieves modest audience numbers. In terms of cost per viewer this is the most expensive of the factual genres. It carries high prestige within the TV industry.

News and current affairs, or TV journalism, covers a wide range.

Table 1.2 Selected programme categories: costs per hour of BBC1 and BBC2 network productions, 1992

Programme type	Percentage of total hours produced	Percentage of total cost	Average cost (£000) per hour (first showing)
Drama	4	21	481
Light entertainment	8	13	161
Features and documentaries	17	18	94
Average of all network first showings			90
News	7	6	77
Current affairs	17	11	59
Sport	15	7	40
Acquired programmes	21	9	38

Source: *BBC Facts and Figures, 1992.*

News costs more per hour but is also much more popular than current affairs. If TV journalism is taken as a single field, it is average in audience popularity and below average in cost per viewer. Its prestige within television and outside is high. This favourable combination of cheapness, popularity and prestige is unique.

Sport is, or has been, one of the cheapest of all TV programming genres; its overall audience popularity is average and its cost per viewer is low. This favourable combination is not enough to avoid sports producers carrying rather low prestige within television; but sport is nevertheless recognized as an essential component of the public-service project – especially by the BBC.

Our final 'other factual' category is not fully represented in Table 1.1. The study incorporates not only adult education and religion, but leisure, youth, cooking, gardening and consumer programming. This large miscellaneous category includes a bewildering range, but it tends to be programming which aims at large minorities and appears mainly on BBC2 and Channel Four. Overall it is average in terms of cost, popularity, cost per viewer and prestige within television.

POLITICAL ORIENTATIONS

Each of these genres has its own distinctive orientation to politics, partisanship and neutrality.

Documentary has traditionally defined itself as a non-political art-form. By leaving news and party politics to TV journalists, the documentary-makers have largely escaped the attention of politicians and regulators. British TV documentary is often highly opinionated, and one-sidedly ideological; it is able to escape the formal requirements of neutrality by choosing non-party or cross-party approaches, such as supporting environmental and Green causes. The documentary-makers are also committed and ideological on specific foreign issues, which again often tend to involve preserving the environment, or indigenous peoples and their culture.

It is in news and current affairs, of course, that political constraints are most obviously present. There is, indeed, a legal requirement to be neutral and non-partisan. Although this does cause TV journalists some anxiety, the standard rituals are derived from those invented by Victorian new agencies and then followed by radio, long before TV journalism began. Television (and radio) journalists have, in effect, taken the vows of objectivity and non-partisanship; they automatically think in terms of 'balancing' government and opposition views. Television journalists and producers are typically more anxious, more often, about the cumbersome logistics of news-gathering.

In sports television party politics plays only a fairly small part. Sports producers are, typically, very much more concerned with the internal politics of the sports they cover.

'Other factual' programming deals with some highly political and publicly sensitive topics, such as education, employment, consumer, health and gender issues. This is where some of the most politically uninhibited programming is shown. The scrutiny of politicians and regulators tends, however, to be experienced by producers as much less of a threat than is the scrutiny of company lawyers challenging consumer and other critical programming.

GENRES AND PRODUCTION SYSTEMS

The next four chapters deal with four different factual genres, each of which has its own set of production arrangements.

One fundamental difference is the speed at which different genres are produced. Much sport is live, whereas a single documentary programme may take a year to complete. News is partly live, and mostly generated within a few hours.

Documentary, with its long gestation periods and emphasis on high quality, is found amongst the prestige output of all four conventional channels, and on public-service grounds it has usually been scheduled in mid-evening. Documentary producers see themselves as film-makers and they tend to prefer to work on film, which is more expensive than tape.

News and current affairs, with its very short gestation periods, operates on a large scale in terms of hours per week and in the scale of editorial and technical back-up staff. All channels carry some of this material, but in Britain it appears mainly on the major BBC1 and ITV channels and in high-audience times; both major channels build their schedules around their main early-evening and later-evening news programmes. The major weekly current-affairs programmes *Panorama* (BBC1) and *World in Action* (ITV) both have a long history of being scheduled on Monday mid-evening and have become flagship programmes for their networks.

British TV journalism switched from film (and its cumbersome developing and editing requirements) to videotape in the early

1980s. News is presented live from a studio with edited 'packages' (typically a staffer with a location report) and live or near-live inserts from 'our correspondent' at the site.

Sport specializes in lengthy live reports of sports events; all British channels carry some live sport, mainly in daytime, and they also carry 'edited highlights' and magazine compilations of several events, typically in late evening. Sport has its own specialized 'outside-broadcast' technology, which involves taking to the site of the sports event not only a multiple-camera system but a mobile version of the entire technical back-up and studio-editing apparatus normally found in a permanent studio. This large collection of equipment and personnel is expensive to get to the event but becomes quite cheap per hour when used over the long time-spans which the BBC, in particular, gives to live sport. Thus live sport becomes a convenient way of filling empty daytime hours at modest cost.

The costs and finances of programming increasingly absorb the time and energies of producers and each of these genres has its own distinctive financial complexities.

Documentary, as a fairly expensive genre of fairly modest audience popularity, is increasingly dependent on 'co-production' finance; this means, in practice, sharing the cost with one or more foreign networks. The long lead-time makes these negotiations possible, and the negotiations in turn may lengthen the overall production timespan. Dependence on US, Australian or Japanese finance also inclines the subject-matter towards more international topics and less 'parochial', British, topics.

Television news organizations in some respects resemble newspapers, but instead of the traditional print-journalist's notepad, pencil and telephone, these TV journalists and their teams carry around the impediments of camera, sound equipment, lights and electronic news-gathering. Behind these advanced troops, there is a massive base-camp army of 'post-production' skilled personnel. Increasingly in news these personnel are cutting, editing and re-editing videotaped material for potential and actual use in an endless sequence of weekly, daily and hourly outputs. The costs here are large per day and the technology continues to change rapidly.

In sports television one strategic cost-factor has unique salience. This is the contracted fee which a network pays in order to televise a popular sports event.

The mixed or miscellaneous or 'edinfotainment' fields present a mixed pattern overall. These gardening, cooking, consumer or educational programmes are a mixture from several different viewpoints. They vary from the live outside broadcast to the long-gestation documentary approach. They appear on all channels and at all times of the evening as well as daytime. In financial terms they also vary from cheap to expensive. Many of these programmes are studio-based; often there is a live discussion in which several experts or celebrities comment on a prepared film report. Many of these programmes are also mixed in another sense: they may be 'magazine' programmes, a mix of several different items. Sometimes there may be one entertaining item intended to hook the audience, then an educational item, which the production team may see as the 'core', and finally a more newsy informational section perhaps about events that have happened (in the field in question) during the last week.

HOW AUTONOMOUS ARE FACTUAL PRODUCERS?

Anyone who works in an organization, and within an occupation or profession, must accept many constraints. The lawyer in court and the surgeon in the operating theatre are both constrained in obvious ways. The British television producer is also located within an industry, an organization and an occupation, and must accept many constraints. In particular, this book argues, TV producers are subject to strategic decisions about commissioning and scheduling programme series. Much power is located at the level of the channel baron who sanctions finance and places programming in the schedule.

Once the go-ahead for the new series or the new season has been obtained, the producer has a substantial level of autonomy. Much of the guidance that comes down from above is indeed guidance; much of it says, in effect, obvious things about not breaking the law and not over-spending the budget. Another (perhaps unspoken) piece of guidance is to maintain last season's audience level, or at least to do roughly as well in relation to the relevant competition. A final piece of guidance requires the producer to stick broadly to the approach agreed when the series run was commissioned; often this involves a target audience, a specific time of day on the particular channel and an agreed sub-genre style.

Unless the series producer is a total novice, he or she is typically left in day-to-day and programme-to-programme control. The broad subject-matter of the projected programmes needs to be known higher up − not least to avoid clashes with the output of other producers and other programmes; but typically the series producer does not show scripts to a superior and is trusted to be the person in charge, whose day of reckoning comes only at the end of the series run.

The factual-series producer has a budget to spend – varying from hundreds of thousands to millions of pounds – and is typically left very free to decide how this sum will be spread between the programmes in the series. Many series combine some expensive programmes (and distant filming) with some cheaper studio-based (stay-at-home) programming. It is the series producer who decides the actual combination and the topics to be covered.

The producer also chooses the production team. Especially in the first season there may not be a free hand, because some personnel are inherited from the previous season or assigned by a departmental superior; but after two or three series runs, the producer can re-shape the team or acquire an entirely new team – new directors, writers, reporters and presenters.

This team-building autonomy also allows the producer to decide precisely what kind of producer to be. In factual television the series producer often has a team of several directors, each of whom is responsible for supervising the filming and editing of two or three programmes. In some cases the series producer personally also directs one or two programmes.

The director role varies greatly between genres. There is a sharp difference between the studio director who oversees several cameras simultaneously operating on a studio floor and the outside location director, who, working with one camera at a time, provides the main artistic input to a documentary film.

The producer in factual television is often a 'hyphenate' – most usually a producer-director; but the producer may (or may not) also be actively ('hands on') involved in writing scripts, in editing film and tape, as programme publicist, and so on.

In British factual television an important decision for the producer is whether or not to have one 'presenter' – a single face which will become identified with the programme – and whether to use a famous or an unknown face; other alternatives are to have no presenter (common in British documentary) or to operate as producer-presenter (like Melvyn Bragg in *The South Bank Show*) or to adopt some other radical hyphenate solution such as the researcher-presenter. These decisions rest with the producer and often lead to extended agonizing and indecision.

Factual television involves a myriad of small details. The team's producers or producer-directors in charge of specific programmes will have the fullest knowledge of those details. Only the series producer, however, will have broad insights into the whole series. The series producer, for example, may regard some programmes as potentially stronger as well as more risky than others. The series producer often must ponder a proposed foreign-filming story which is potentially the best programme in the series, but which is also the most costly and may seem to have only a 50 per cent chance of reaching the screen. Because of the risks of losing money here, the series producer may have decided to make several much cheaper and safer programmes in the series.

Producers who have been in charge of programmes over several years typically list the major changes that have occurred in them. These changes can include a nearly complete change in personnel, a different set, different opening titles and so on. The producer may also have changed the programme series in more fundamental ways: these changes can include reshaping the programme in its general goals; the programme may have become much more orientated towards entertaining a younger audience – perhaps with the use of appropriate music, graphics and presenters. Or the programme may have been steered in a more educational direction – with a greatly increased emphasis on associated printed material. 'The book of the series', the related consumer magazine, or 'Write in for the Fact-sheet' can have major impacts on the production team's work-effort and on the character of the series.

Autonomy, in TV production as elsewhere, also depends in part on the potential availability of alternative career-moves. One consequence of the pursuit of a distinctive production style may be the enhancement of the producer's reputation within television; but the career implications of this – like so much else – may differ from field to field.

In documentary the producer-director can make a reputation as a film-maker, which may or may not lead on to employment outside television. In news and current affairs there are big hierarchies up which to advance and career-paths which lead into TV general management as well as outside employment in journalism, public affairs and public relations. However, the successful sports producer is not typically aware of many colleagues who have moved on to much higher things.

Chapter 2

Documentary: film-makers

Documentaries are a slow art-form within a TV daily industrial system which delivers round-the-clock entertainment and information. Within British television documentaries not only carry considerable prestige, but also exist on a substantial scale; this scale varies somewhat with definition, but British television's four conventional channels offer about 20 hours of documentary per week, mainly in the evening hours. These thousand hours per year of documentary include repeats and some imports, but British television certainly makes several hundred hours of new documentaries each year.

This flood of material is made by about two hundred producers, directors and producer-directors who see themselves as factual film-makers. Each of these currently active film-makers will make between 1 and 3 hours in a year; 90 minutes (or three half-hours) would be a typical year's film-making.

Documentary-making encompasses ordinary people in real-life situations of drama and pathos; but British documentary also covers science, the arts and religion, as well as natural history and the environment. Across this huge range of the ordinary and the extraordinary, documentary-makers see the acquisition of high-quality film – and its shaping into an original final form – as central. Documentary television, because of this high-quality tradition, has generous rations of expensive filming time. The slowness of the documentary form derives partly from this lengthy filming time, but also from lengthy editing and preparation. A short series might involve 20 weeks of filming, 30 weeks of film editing and perhaps a preliminary 6 months of preparation and research. By normal TV standards, however, the core team would be very small, perhaps just three or four people.

What may sound like an incredibly slow and leisurely pace to outsiders, including other TV producers, is often experienced as a demanding, and sometimes hectic, schedule by the documentary producer. Often the subject-matter is complex and access to some delicate social (or animal) area is not easily achieved. The filming phase can often be demanding – it may involve exhausting travel, climatic extremes and many emotional highs and lows. Finally, the editing phase is no less demanding; it involves the director or producer-director sitting beside an editor crouched over a small screen in a claustrophobic editing suite, gradually editing down a mountain of material into a lovingly crafted final product. There may well be other tasks, such as the 'book of the series' which must be completed at high speed before the film-editing stage (if it is to be published as the series is transmitted).

Given that the documentary has a slow production system, some producers – especially of short series – deliberately slow the whole process down still further. Some natural-history documentary series are deliberately conceived to allow a return to the film site at the same season next year. Other (human) documentaries focus on a year-in-the-life-of the prison, the school, the family, or the terminally ill hospital patient. In addition to these subject-definition requirements, a producer-director may see an extended schedule as an additional opportunity to impose creative vision on the entire series; over, say, a two-year period, a producer can personally do most of the preparatory research, can personally direct all the filming, and can also supervise all the editing. Such producers argue that this represents an efficient use of the series budget; it also, of course, adds credibility to the notion of the documentary as an authored product, with the documentary producer as film-maker/author.

Many documentaries are one-off programmes devoted to a single subject; these 'single' documentaries in British television mostly appear within an anthology general series under the editorial control of an executive producer. A well-known executive producer now speaks about the directors he commissions:

> I employ film-makers first of all who aren't just jobbing film-makers; they are very interested in the subjects. They are keen to explore the means of disseminating information in the film form; they are prepared to take chances. The trust they create with their subjects and the amount of research and effort and energy they devote to the better understanding of those people's lives mean

that in the end they are rather like the wedding-guest in *The Ancient Mariner*. You need the ability to listen; your subjects clutch your arm and they tell you things. The lack of fear must be achieved by giving a great deal of yourself to them. You are a chameleon and it is very difficult to know who you are at times. The key question is 'Why?' A film director must want to know why this is happening and, in order to find that out, he has to be assimilated into that community. It can play hell with your private life. But you must maintain an individual way of assessing; you can't be completely taken over by them. There are some who say that my directors fall in love with their subjects; I refute that, I think they have got extremely close and still managed to retain an individual authority which gives them the ability to make authored accounts. They have been questioning the subjects to the point of quite painful revelations but the subjects have willingly given of those revelations. I am encouraging ... film-makers who are extending the language, the visual and oral language, to the public and making assessments that I think will survive for some time, that aren't bland. This is an area in public-service broadcasting which needs to be addressed – to tell the story of our country through the words and actions of those who live in it.

(Paul Watson)

DOCUMENTARY AS INDUSTRIAL SYSTEM

In 1989, the high-point in employment numbers, British television employed over a thousand full-time people on documentary production. The BBC Documentary Features department employed about seventy producers and a programme staff of 265; this included some non-documentary people but excluded additional documentary staff in several other areas. As BBC staff numbers have been reduced, the number of independent producers in this field has expanded and their work now appears on all four conventional channels.

British television offers three main types of documentary output: continuing series, short series and special series. Amongst the continuing series the BBC's major series are traditionally the backbone of British TV documentary. The 1992–3 line-up is given in Table 2.1.

The ITV system has always carried fewer documentaries; ITV has focused on a small number of very high-quality prestige series, such as *First Tuesday* and *Viewpoint*, and the arts programme *The*

Table 2.1   BBC major documentary series

Series	BBC 1	BBC 2
General series	Inside Story	40 Minutes
Science	Tomorrow's World Q.E.D.	Horizon Antenna
Arts	Omnibus	Arena Bookmark The Late Show (4 times weekly)
Natural history and environment	Wildlife on One	The Natural World Nature
Religion	Everyman Heart of the Matter	
History		Timewatch

Most of these series ran for between 10 and 26 programmes per year.

South Bank Show. As in other areas Channel Four's policy on documentary and arts programming has varied greatly but from around 1990 it strengthened its documentary reputation with *Cutting Edge* and other mid-evening series; on its own count, Channel Four in 1991 carried 494 hours of documentary (including repeats) or over 9 hours a week.

The major continuing series are typically overseen by a series editor or executive producer, who employs a usually sizeable team of individual producer-directors to make the separate programmes. This executive producer is often also responsible for overseeing one or more series of the second type, the short series. This latter is typically a one-off series of perhaps 6 programmes on a single theme. An executive producer will normally leave a trusted series editor of short series largely to his or her own devices; and the short series becomes, in practice, the longest documentary form capable of being dominated by a single personal vision.

The third and final type of documentary output is the special series, which is a grander, longer and more expensive version of the short series. Examples include the 26-week series *World at War* (Jeremy Isaacs for Thames Television) or the various BBC natural-history special series fronted by David Attenborough.

Within the different types of subject-matter, different styles prevail. Historical documentaries typically rely on archive film and interviews with participants. Natural-history programmes obviously engage in location filming and often use cameramen who specialize in birds, or underwater filming, and so on. Arts documentaries tend to focus on individual musicians, artists or writers with appropriate filming. Science documentaries face the challenge of putting research findings on screen, but also focus on the scientists, their teams, dilemmas and controversies. Many single documentaries in the big general series use the fly-on-the-wall technique – essentially getting the camera into a hospital, a police unit, a civil war or a family, and then waiting to film what happens.

PRODUCER PASSION . . . AND STAGEFRIGHT

'Passion' is not a word much used by other producers, but documentary producers quote passion as an essential ingredient of their work. They talk about balancing ideas and passion. One executive producer said that his three key ingredients were 'the idea, passion, and correct casting' – matching the producer with the idea and the right cameraman and film editor.

Deep involvement – and not least the sense of intimate human involvement with the subject-matter – goes along with commitment to the individual programme and to the documentary enterprise more generally. The series editors also emphasized the enormous fascination and the multiple attractions of their work. One said simply 'I love it.' Another could think of no 'worst' aspect of his job apart from the journey to work:

> The best thing is the sheer freedom; I discuss ideas all day long, the people around me are pleasant to be with; we get praised, we are established, we've got a supportive boss, we have plenty of would-be co-producers, there are lots of talented people who want to work here.

Nearly all these series producers had experienced a precocious entry to film-making. By the age of 25 most of them already had experience of directing camera-crews. They had achieved their precocious starts via several entry-gates. Almost half had followed the elite entry-pattern of direct entrance from university (Oxford being the most usual) and/or a BBC traineeship. Several others had made their first films at university or at film school. Nearly all had worked on one or more prestigious programmes in their twenties, including BBC current-affairs programmes such as *Panorama*.

Documentary series editors tend to stress the supreme importance of the 'basic idea'. Their key tasks, they say, are first to sift out, from the many on offer, an idea which will make a good documentary; then they must choose a film-maker to turn the idea into a film; finally, the series editor must see that the film-maker sticks to the basic idea and the agreed story line.

During the filming (or taping) phase the film-maker is normally alone at the film location with a camera-crew; the series editor keeps away from the filming itself, both because of time scarcity and also to allow traditional directorial freedom. Series editors sound somewhat nostalgic when describing the creative excitement of the filming phase; this is the heroic phase – the days and weeks of truth suspended between planning and editing. Some series editors have themselves worked recently as producer-directors on a programme, or even a whole short series. They talk about the 'creative buzz' which they derive from grappling with technical film problems, while trying to extract dramatic and forceful material from their amateur performers. The film-maker must establish emotional rapport with these subjects; a close and trusting relationship between film-maker and subject will show on the screen.

All these producers agreed on the importance of emotional commitment, both to the particular subjects and subject-matter and also to the documentary enterprise more generally. Along with the emotional highs, there also go emotional lows. Documentary seems to induce a greater degree of producer stagefright than is found elsewhere. Documentary film-making involves the creation of an artistic product out of human materials which are often insufficiently malleable. These producer-directors lack the events and statements of news; they lack the contests of the sports producer; they lack the scripts and actors of drama. The documentary-maker has to make it happen, to create an art object out of a factual, free-floating reality. These producers seem to see themselves as performing a kind of conjuring trick – turning reality into an art – which may just refuse to happen. This conjuring trick must be performed during the filming phase:

> The fear I have half-way through the series . . . I think 'This is just not going to come off', the whole thing is a rather ridiculous trick; directors have deep insecurities, it's a ghastly thing, and you have to whip it up as some sort of blancmange, because you know how easily it could all collapse.

Another producer referred to 'that terrible mixture of nerves and exhilaration you get on location', and mentioned being sick behind the crew bus.

In short series especially, but in documentary-making generally, these film-makers become willingly imprisoned within film-related timetables. Such timetables exist in many occupations; here, however, we find a timetable that focuses on distilling and recording reality-on-the-hoof. This seems to induce in documentary producers a sense of multiple realities and multiple time-systems.

BRITISH TRADITION: DOCUMENTARY AND APOLITICAL PUBLIC SERVICE

British documentary film-makers see themselves as heirs to two great traditions – one in public-service broadcasting, the other in 1930s documentary film-making. These are both fields in which Britain can claim to have been a leader. Under John Reith in the inter-war period the BBC did indeed develop actuality radio broadcasting and located it in a department called 'Talks'. The BBC differentiated two strands of television which emerged from radio 'Talks'. 'Current affairs' was radio's feature or weekly journalism, and like daily-news journalism, it focused on politics, the neutral and non-partisan reporting of government and party politics.

Documentary was defined negatively as neither news nor current affairs: while these two dealt with politics, documentary was apolitical – it did not deal with politics, and politicians seldom or never appeared on documentaries. Initially, in post-1946 BBC television, documentary was in some respects close to drama, because reality was often presented by actors – for example, in series based on the lawcourts.

British documentary film became well established in the 1930s and then moved centre-stage in wartime with its depiction of British service personnel in action. Although during the war many of these films were shown in cinemas, the documentary film could here also be defined negatively – it was not the commercial film; it was neither Hollywood, nor did it compete with the Hollywood showbiz feature-film. When documentary-making, after 1955, was also taken up by ITV, it became one of the chief elements in that vaguely defined concept, 'public-service broadcasting'. Documentary aimed to inform and to educate but it attempted to do so with absorbing filmed images.

Documentary-makers claim that theirs is an art-form that gives voice to, or gives volume to the voices of, the ordinary people. There is a 'let the people speak' element in documentary which dates back to the war years under Churchill as well as to the post-war Attlee years. Of course, documentary cannot be totally apolitical. Indeed, some documentary-makers evince strong political views, but these are predominantly centrist views. 'Green' or environmentalist views are expressed not only by natural-history and science producers but by producers in general documentary strands. Numerous ITV and BBC documentaries since the mid-1970s have been sceptical on nuclear power and other Green issues, and broadly against big business.

Many British-based documentaries focus on the public sector, such as hospitals, prisons and the police; many programmes about housing, unemployment, transport and race depend upon the active help of state and local government agencies. These programmes are typically critical from within a reformist perspective.

Such caution and neutrality on the home front is not required from foreign-based documentaries, which often present highly critical accounts of current events in central America or central Europe. Many such documentaries achieve their emotional appeal by identifying with the weak against oppressive governments and the workings of the world economy.

The prestige aspect exists at every level of British documentary television. This prestige aspect has several elements. Documentary seems to perform some of those difficult spannings of opposites much favoured by British tradition in general and 'public-service broadcasting' in particular. Documentary is both ancient (in broadcasting terms − dating from the 1930s) and modern (it deals with contemporary people and issues). Documentary contains elements of the informative/educational as well as of popular entertainment. Even more remarkable, it is both costly and relatively cheap.

These two last combinations entail a certain amount of discreet help. Documentary achieves middling-size audiences, partly because documentary producers 'balance' more and less serious material; the arts series may profile a classical-music virtuoso one week and a rock group the next. Documentary also achieves its middling audiences because it has traditionally been scheduled in higher-audience time-slots than its intrinsic audience appeal would dictate.

The high-and-low cost combination comes about in this way: documentary is fairly expensive to make, mainly because of the generous costing which allows lengthy research, filming and editing. In some published data, however, documentary is shown as having only average costs per hour. This is because more expensive documentaries mostly rely upon co-production and other foreign funding. This, of course, is seen inside the networks as a happy combination; prestige actually translates into cash and helps to finance the enterprise.

Thus while most documentary series are moderately cheap for the British network to fund, there is really a dual system. There are expensive international documentaries which film abroad – often for lengthy time-spans in very remote places – and are co-funded by foreign networks. Second, there are cheaper documentaries, not intended for foreign sales, which target the British audience with British subjects. Many of the British documentaries deal especially with the poor but also the rich of London; this comes about because most documentary-making is based in London and uses London-based personnel. Rather than film in Liverpool or Newcastle, it is cheaper to concentrate on London prisons and mental hospitals, on race in Brixton, rats in Hackney and sleeping-on-the-streets in the West End. Considerations of filming costs have led to massive documentary coverage of present-day Dickensian low life in London.

DOCUMENTARY AND NETWORK HIERARCHY

Documentary programme production, with its emphasis on film-maker autonomy, is nevertheless located within the steep hierarchy of a TV network. The senior producer, responsible for a substantial number of documentary programmes, has two key work-relationships within this hierarchy. One key relationship is, of course, with the working producers within the senior producer's team.

The other key relationship, looking upward, is not with the departmental boss, but with the baronial controller – in the BBC case, the individual controller in charge of either the BBC1 or the BBC2 channel. Documentaries, being prestige programmes dependent on 'quality' rather than simple popularity, require patronage, and in the British system the main location of patronage is at the very top of network decision-making. Once the patronage is supplied, the autonomous film-making can take over; while the patronage is still being considered, the future of any documentary programme or short series lies in the hands of the network baron.

The network baron's power encompasses several linked decisions

– programme remit, finance, scheduling and proposed editorial content. Programme remit involves the general mission of the programme within the network's total output; the network controller might ask the producer to make the programme more or less serious, to alter the number of programmes in the series or to change between a single story and a multi-story format. Finance, obviously, is crucial: the controller decides how much finance will be available. The controller also decides the time-slot in which the programme is aired; this scheduling power, of course, greatly influences the size and type of audience that will be obtained. Finally, the controller must approve – and can demand changes in – the proposed editorial approach.

These standard baronial powers have added salience in the documentary field, which lacks external guidelines such as the national news agenda provides in news and current affairs. Nor does documentary provide the continuing characters (and relatively predictable audiences) of drama and comedy series. Documentary is much more a one-off enterprise, consisting of single documentaries (within strands) or short series; this one-off character of documentary gives special significance to the switch-off and switch-on powers of the network baron.

The series producer is aware of being uncomfortably dependent on the baron's decisions. There is a strong sense that this dependence is unsatisfactory, but also inevitable: 'One man is better than a committee' is the prevalent attitude. Nevertheless, this one man is seen as making decisions on the basis of personal 'whim' (or 'gut feeling'), rather than with detailed knowledge of the project. Producers who have recently fared well point to the benefits of such a system:

> If you come to them and you are enthusiastic about something and they know your background and they know your track record, they like to go with it because they think 'This person's enthusiasm will carry this through'; it may only need one side of an envelope, it's your vision they go with and that's good and that's what you want, you want that sort of creative people in positions of power.

Other series producers, who have been less favourably treated, use terms such as 'whim'. These producers tend to repeat the controller's verdict – which they have usually heard only at second hand, via their departmental head's attendance at a committee meeting. As reported at third hand to the outsider, the controller's verdict tends to sound somewhat terse, ill-informed and often couched in highly emotional language:

He hated this voice I'd used in the commentary – he actually used the word 'hate' at a Heads of Departments programme review board; and it's quite interesting when you get that strength of attitude from a guy who effectively gives me my next job, especially compared with the press response which was terrific and the quite-good audience figures.

The main weight of controller power is exercised in the financial go-ahead for the series. If a continuing series has adequate audience numbers and baronial approval, the discussions about next year's output may be quite brief, perhaps focusing on the precise number of programmes compared with last year; and in budget terms the controller may well indicate a pro-rata figure such as a 5 per cent overall cut or a 5 per cent inflation factor.

The 'yes or no' decision on a proposed new short series exemplifies controller power in its starkest form. For the offering producer the decision will trigger or veto total expenditure of one or two million pounds and will determine the working life of the producer for as long as two years. With the money and outline agreed, the series producer switches immediately from a situation of dependence into a phase of creative autonomy which in turn includes its element of patronage. This 'idea' phase leads to the selection of the producer-directors and other key team-members. Then the producer-directors of particular programmes in their turn become supplicants, dependent on the series editor's permission to go ahead.

Throughout the lengthy middle phase of research, filming and editing, the series producer is relatively independent of control from the top. At the end of the series production cycle, the series producer or executive producer is again dependent on the baron's network powers. The key power here is scheduling. The series is already destined for a particular channel, and an evening showing. Documentary producers dislike slots as early as 7.30 p.m.; the best times for documentary are seen as between 8 and 10 p.m. Day of the week is crucial, because this determines the competition on other channels; producers of documentary series on BBC1 and ITV are especially aware of their exposed position, in a high-audience time-slot on a major channel. Documentary producers see these as shark-infested waters, and they fear especially being scheduled opposite one of the most popular entertainment shows.

Documentary producers seem to pay less attention than any other category of producers to the audience data which are available.

Documentary producers claim to know of certain programme formulae within their remit which will attract an unusually big audience. These include scientific programmes about human sexual behaviour; underwater filming of a shipwreck; anything about ancient Egypt; scientific whodunits; arts programmes on current entertainment and movie superstars; documentaries involving Prince Charles. There are also sure-fire low-audience subjects such as 'any artist (except Hockney)'.

Documentary producers believe in programmes which will make difficult ideas and remote topics accessible to millions of people. Certain basic assumptions are widely held and widely acted upon – for example, the appeal of human interest and drama in real life presented through a strong narrative. Unlike some other producers, the documentary-makers do not see research as providing data for fine-tuning. Fine-tuning expertise would be difficult to apply to one-off programmes or short series, in contrast to programmes with a repeated format. It would also conflict with the film-making definition of the documentary as an artistic whole, based on an original idea, and assembled through filming spontaneous human behaviour.

TWO PRODUCERS: WHOSE AUTONOMY?

Apart from the senior producer's relationship with a distant channel controller, the most crucial relationships are with the producers, or producer-directors of particular programmes within the series. In the majority of cases the series producer will be in charge of between three and ten working producer-directors. Typically the series producer is in charge of between 5 and 26 programmes, while several programme producers are each in charge of between 1 and 3 programmes or hours of screen-time. The programme producer or producer-director is (like the series editor) heir to the British documentary tradition of producer autonomy and programme-authorship. The individual producer-director starts work with very few programme staff – perhaps a part-share in a researcher and a production assistant. All this serves to encourage authorish ambition. Quite often, also, it is the individual producer-director who had the idea for this specific programme or who at least fleshed out an idea initially proposed by the series producer.

The relationship, then, between the series producer and the small team of programme producers provides possibilities both for artistic co-operation and for artistic conflict. In the most common case the co-operation probably greatly outweighs conflict; but this is not always the case, especially at certain points in the production sequence.

From the series producer's viewpoint the first step is to assemble the programme team in general and the small inner ring of film-makers in particular. The series editor may be in competition within the department:

> There is always a marshalling of producers and it's a bit of a tug-of-war over who can stay on what programme and who wants them to move on and also the decision has to be made what's going to be good for them and what's going to please them as well as what the editors want; and all editors want some of the same people, so there may be some bartering.

For the independent producer there may be no stock in-house producer-directors. This gives the selection of film-makers a different flavour:

> There are only a limited number of people out there who've got tried and proved track records, but there's up-and-coming talent – the big trick is being able to spot fresh talent, which must, of course, be a gamble: that's my biggest problem.

Having acquired the team, different series producers operate differently; but there is always a process of writing and agreeing outlines for each programme. Some series producers insist on a written script as necessary for costing the programme. A key item on the costing is the number of days and the location of filming plus related variable costs such as lighting, travel and subsistence. A 30-minute programme may have 12 or 15 days of filming; but other expensive items are additional weeks or months of research, the use of archive film and perhaps 5 weeks of film (or tape) editing.

Some series editors are sticklers for these preliminary phases of idea–script–budget and the film-maker may have to return with numerous successive paper offerings until go-ahead permission is finally granted. At this point, however, the series producer steps back and the programme producer's phase of greatest autonomy commences. Again, practice differs greatly in detail. An experienced film-maker who has the confidence of the senior producer is likely to be left very much alone; no news is taken to be good news. The senior producer will watch more closely the performance of a less-experienced or less-accomplished film-maker; this watching can be done via looking at daily 'rushes', the complete footage shot by the camera crew.

Documentary series editors normally look at the complete rushes, at least before the editing phase begins. For a 30-minute programme there may be 6 hours of shot film, which, multiplied by the number of programmes in the series, makes looking at rushes a major time-consumer for the series editor. A series editor who is especially anxious about a particular film-maker may assign that person to a physically proximate location which allows daily viewing of rushes; but often the filming is in some remote location which in practice minimizes senior-producer control and maximizes the autonomy of the working film-maker.

The two producers agree on a general strategy for editing the rushes; the film-maker then disappears for some weeks to sit beside a film editor who gradually assembles the rough-cut version of the film. This rough-cut stage usually reveals at least some differences of opinion between the two levels of producer. These differences of opinion can lead to quite bitter conflicts. The underlying reasons for this are the strengths of the autonomous film-maker tradition in documentary, plus the high degree of ambiguity as to which of two producers in conflict should excercise how much autonomy.

A long-established film-maker may have security of employment, which encourages creative intransigence (as seen by the series producer). A freelance producer, employed for a few months to make a single film, may be just as insistent on maintaining film-making autonomy; such a producer may be inexperienced not only at making films but at accepting someone else's creative judgements. The series producer often argues that the film is not sufficiently clear and has wandered from the agreed story-line; a common request is for the film to be re-assembled with a different emphasis and in a different sequence. Series editors say that most working film-makers are willing to accept a good proportion of 'suggestions' from someone with a much longer track record. A common approach of the series editor is to be satisfied if the majority of the total suggested changes are accepted.

In documentary, the series editor feels reluctant to insist that all changes be accepted; such severity is seen as contravening the canon of creative autonomy. There is also the sheer emotional strain involved in conducting film-editing battles with several different deeply entrenched programme producers. It may be a matter of deciding how much energy to invest in which fights. However, series

editors believe that their lesser involvement in the details of filming
– and the related on-site emotional experiences – leaves them in a
more objective position to decide on essential editing changes:

> If I feel 'That's got to go' I try to persuade them. I find that even
> if I say 'Listen, I'm sorry, that seems to me simple-minded and
> stupid, I just can't possibly leave it in' the programme-maker
> often fights back. Nothing that goes absolutely against the grain
> with me can I tolerate, but of course the producer or the director
> can't tolerate my doing something that goes absolutely against the
> grain with him. So then, one has a difficult time and sometimes we
> argue for two or three days about one small item. If I can't stand
> something in, and he can't stand it out, then we have a battle. If
> you're on a daily newspaper you haven't got time for that, the
> editor has to say 'Sorry, I'm the boss, we cut it out'. In our process
> you just have to make time for that; it costs money, you've got
> people sitting around waiting while the two of you argue, and so
> you try and argue through the night if you can, and one of us may
> get persuaded. But I find that every time I've allowed something
> to stay in a programme which my guts told me was wrong, I've
> regretted it. So now I don't let it happen – I really hold out and
> people find me very obstinate and unreasonable at times like that.
>
> They say I'm being stupid. Yeah, there's one of those per
> programme, sometimes two per programme. Somebody who is in
> a dozen ways very good and talented disagrees with me about
> something, and you just don't know, maybe my judgement is
> wonky, but you just have to back your own judgement; it's the
> only way you can operate.
>
> (Brian Lapping)

It might seem that on the general documentary series these conflicts
would be greatest; after all, these one-off programmes can be about
almost anything, and the common denominator of human drama will
have its main emotional impact on the programme-maker who has
become close to the subjects. This emotional closeness is undoubtedly a real factor in editing conflicts. In the specialist documentary
there are yet other factors that show up what the series producer may
see as film-maker intransigence. These specialist programmes also
involve a strong emotional element, because the subject-matter is
often an individual – a scientist, an artist, a prisoner or a religious
missionary – with whom the film-maker has established emotional

rapport. Some producers on specialist documentary series also have significant professional qualifications, such as a higher degree in a relevant science or experience in arts criticism. This combination of emotional rapport and professional expertise can result in formidable resistance to the series producer's editing demands.

INTERNATIONAL DIMENSION

The documentary-film movement since the 1930s has always been very international; so also today, in British television, documentary remains international at all levels. Its subject-matter – human interest and human drama as well as science, the arts and natural history – crosses national frontiers. Many British documentaries deliberately do not use a celebrity presenter or anchor-person; this facilitates acceptance by foreign audiences. Documentary is also international in terms of co-production, which in practice means co-finance.

In British television senior documentary producers get involved in two main types of international activity. The first type is exemplified by the BBC co-production tradition. One producer's recent short series had been financed with three roughly equal slices: one million dollars from US public television, an equivalent sum from the BBC programme department, and a final one-third from BBC Enterprises on the basis of other anticipated foreign sales. The details of these arrangements vary, but typically the BBC obtains the largest single slice of external funding from the USA – from the big public stations WNET (New York) or WGBH (Boston) or from a cable channel such as Discovery or Arts and Entertainment. Other advance money comes primarily from Australia, Canada or (increasingly) Japan.

Normally the BBC (or ITV company) will put up the largest single slice of the finance and will also take editorial control. 'Co-production' in practice involves merely consultation; but since this occurs early in the planning process it can affect the subject-matter of entire programmes. US co-producers are known to regard most domestic British subjects as 'too parochial'.

These co-productions add not only to the finances, but also to the glamour and prestige of documentary production. Documentary producers exude financial as well as artistic self-confidence ('The Americans can't get enough of our stuff' and 'It went down well in Japan'); and winning international prizes is regarded as commonplace. Documentary co-production also fits well with network goals at home – serious programming, financial realism and success, with British documentary apparently taking the lead in the world.

There is another international aspect to British documentary that attracts less prestige and publicity. British television is also a significant importer of documentaries. Some imports are promoted as such; *The Civil War* US special series which aired on BBC2 in 1991, was quite fairly publicized as a Public Broadcasting System (PBS) classic (although British producers thought its use of professional actors' voices old-fashioned). Many other documentary films are imported and Anglicized in one of several ways. A British series of, say, 17 programmes may include two Australian or US programmes. Some of these imports are US-made programmes which involve supporting British co-production finance. Sometimes small adjustments are made to match the different running-lengths of PBS, BBC and ITV 'hours'; in other cases some British-accented commentary is added.

Around 1990 there was, however, a growing trend towards more radical re-structuring and re-editing of imported series. Two or three Australian films may be cut down into a single British programme, with the items linked by fresh commentary. A long NHK (Japan) series is cut down into a radically shorter British version; NHK benefits not only because it enters the otherwise difficult British market, but also because the British version has much more sales-appeal in a world market used to buying documentaries from English-language producers.

Not all purchasing of documentaries is from large US or Japanese producers. There are many freelance documentary film-makers (and camera-people) around the world; some specialize in particular topics (Alaskan natural history or Brazilian environment). London-based documentary producers who have themselves filmed in many countries have their own favourite unknown (but talented) film-making friends in Australia, Brazil or Canada. These film-makers are already there and filming; sometimes a relatively small financial advance (and some raw film-stock) is enough to trigger some high-quality film, which can be incorporated into a new British documentary series.

All these developments have added a major new dimension of international entrepreneurship to the role of the senior documentary producer. This entrepreneurship has both a high and a low end in terms of finance and prestige. The high end is represented by the short series which attracts prizes, million-dollar deals and sales in thirty countries – all at modest cost to the home network. Such a visible achievement adds to the prestige and self-confidence of the currently successful producer.

There is also a low-end pattern. Here the series producer, perhaps a highly experienced man in his fifties and past the peak of his career, is heavily engaged in 'versioning' – making a British version by cutting, re-editing and re-voicing a mixed bag of films from a variety of networks and freelances around the world.

Some series involve both types of international activity. The series producer may do a deal with a programme producer – 'you can make one programme above our normal cost-level if you will also "version" another programme cheaply':

> I say, 'OK, you can do your big expensive project, so long as you do me that on a balancing factor'; we had an excellent programme recently which got over 10 million viewers and most people didn't realize it was a Japanese film – we bought it cheaply, topped and tailed it with a British case, and it looked like a British-made show which had done some filming in Japan.

YOU'RE ONLY AS GOOD AS . . .

'You're only as good as your last series' is a much-repeated saying. Documentary producers believe that, in their case, the criteria for deciding how good that last series really was are themselves unclear. Reputation and 'success' depend heavily on controller 'whim', the intended (and unintended) consequences of scheduling, and the inexpert opinions of newspaper TV pundits. A decent level of competence, these producers believe, is not enough. These producers believe that the documentary form, as practised in British television, requires some element of originality; and this is not easy because today's producers typically had their precocious start some twenty years ago and have been trying to pursue originality ever since.

It is widely believed that several years in charge of a major series are more than enough for even the most talented and energetic individual. The long series runs make for a hard grind:

> Everything that I do is multiplied by 22; seeing each producer and deciding what they are going to do is multiplied by 22 . . . reading their treatments is times 22, seeing their rough cuts is multiplied by 22; it multiplies up, and you begin to lose your energy to

grapple with the next one; my predecessors all say the same thing, you can't do this job for more than five years.

When such an executive producer stops running a major series, there is the obvious question of what to do next. The usual answer is to create an innovative and original short series. However, running a short series is no less demanding and is certainly more insecure. Whereas the continuing series has an existing team of producer-film-makers which may only need some annual adjusting, the short-series producer must assemble a completely fresh team. The funding must be raised, many outlines, treatments and proposals must be written; and then, if the project at last gets the go-ahead, the series producer's future career and destiny are closely linked to the ultimate success or failure of the current project.

Increasingly, also, the more free-floating new arrangements – fewer staff producers, more freelances and independents – mean that the series producer now often lacks a single continuing close colleague. Even the major continuing series draw upon a floating group of producers who are employed by the department and assigned only to make a specific single programme for a particular series.

Most documentary-series producers seem to be self-confident and self-assured people; some clearly use their strong personalities, self-confidence and track record to persuade and dominate their working producers. Others clearly pursue the same ends in somewhat subtler ways. All these producers also openly admit to a high degree of uncertainty and insecurity. All documentary producers require a wide range of TV talents; they also face unusual demands in terms of 'quality' and 'originality'. The new requirements of farming-out work to independent producers also impose additional burdens; documentary is a major focus for independents, meaning that the documentary-series editor tends to be deluged with programme proposals, 'all of which have to be read and separately answered'.

The special salience of the international element in the senior documentary producer's work extends the required talents in an entrepreneurial direction. It emphasizes the distinction between those senior producers who are, and those who are not, adept and successful at co-production and entrepreneurship. Success at putting together one co-production deal seems to lead to subsequent deals; contacts are developed, the entrepreneurial appetite is whetted, further deals are proposed and some are consummated. Given that co-production finance is so important in the sanctioning of series, this has heightened the distinction between the producers who are seen as currently successful and in demand, and those who are currently seen as less successful. The successful category focus more on co-productions; the second category are more likely to find themselves in the less-prestigious import or 'versioning' business.

Some documentary producers are anxious about their own careers, as well as deeply suspicious of what they see as the new forms of both domestic and international co-production finance. British involvement in funding for Russian and other former Soviet filmmakers – such as the Central Television/Channel Four funding of Juris Podniek's *Hello, Do You Hear Us?* – is universally welcomed. However, producers say, there are growing numbers of increasingly murky deals in such areas as popular-music documentaries; here the co-producer can be a music star's record label, which can potentially involve producer control being lost to commercial-music promotion.

Hands-on control of a sequence of short series, while making one or two programmes personally – this remains a common ambition for documentary producers of all levels and ages. Some executive producers of a major series would be happy to move back to the short series, especially if they could create or find a successful one. Other seniorish producers try to avoid going too far up the executive-producer ladder in the direction of departmental head, or deputy head. A common solution is to go independent.

One senior producer described his career tactic as 'to tread water'; he wanted to continue to run smallish series in a way that enabled him to make one complete programme himself per year. Another attractive career-move is a small diversification, such as into the drama-documentary area; this appeals to the documentary-maker's restless search for something new, something which will extend the career track record and present new challenges. Drama-documentary is a complex subject in itself, whose own history goes back to the early days of television. It enables the producer-director to direct actors and thus to broaden his range. Producers who have done one or two drama-documentaries typically then wish to move on to full-blown TV drama. This is a logical progression in many ways: it broadens the producer's creative base; it is a move from one high-prestige and expensive field to another; documentary and drama would be an ideal base for an independent production company.

This drama-documentary ambition also re-emphasizes the artistic, creative and film-making orientation of documentary producers.

Chapter 3

Journalist producers

Television news shares with documentary a concern with facts and everyday reality, but is in most other respects at the opposite end of the spectrum from documentary. Television documentary involves an individual film-maker with two or three team-members crafting an artistic product over a period of many months. Television journalism operates at high speed; little TV news is more than a few hours old and much of it is live or 'near-live'. Television weekly journalism – called 'current affairs' in Britain – tends to have a turn-round time of several weeks, but even these programmes are much closer to British Sunday newspapers than to documentary.

Television news, of course, runs several times a day, resulting in a massive total output; the BBC's regular daily TV journalism adds up to well over a thousand hours a year. In 1990 Independent Television News (ITN), responsible for TV news (but not current affairs) on ITV and Channel Four, had 1,219 employees, before making large cuts. If one includes all channels, news and current affairs, national and regional, there were some 2,200 TV journalists in Britain in 1988.[1] If one includes non-journalist technicians and others, the total journalism work-force was much larger.

Its requirement for political neutrality and objectivity also distinguishes TV journalism. In sharp contrast to documentary, the prevailing broadcasting law places a legal requirement of political neutrality on news reporting. These neutrality requirements do cause anxiety for producer and reporter, and the accusations from politicians – which surface in the press from time to time – are indeed threatening. However, the objectivity requirement causes less anxiety for producers than do the normal complexities of journalism, overlaid by cumbersome television logistics.

Certainly politicians – especially senior politicians – sometimes bargain over conditions, areas of questioning, and which other guests may be on the programme; but this occurs mainly outside the daily news programmes where speed is of the essence. Moreover, most politicians are much more eager to be invited than they are to complain about being interviewed. House of Commons traditions ensure that British politicians tend to be quite robust at political repartee. Several producers – especially of current-affairs programmes – did say that Cabinet Ministers were often extremely choosy in placing conditions on their TV appearances. However, the same producers also said that certain commercial companies and their chief executives were more choosy and also more prone to legal threats, complaints to the regulators and legal action.

On the specialized political programmes the relationship with most politicians seems to be quite relaxed. One important ingredient here is political humour: both producers and politicians have a common purpose in trying to avoid viewer boredom, and humour is to the fore. This is especially noticeable in the Channel Four programme *The Week in Politics*, where politicians enter into the combination of joviality and sharp questioning. Meanwhile, the most genuinely controlled kind of political coverage is the live (and recorded) coverage of Parliament: the agreed rules restrict the coverage to an uncritical record of Parliament rather than political analysis.

Television journalists have all, in effect, taken the vows of public neutrality and objectivity. A few of these journalists are well known among politicians for partisan views of either left or right. However, it is also well understood and agreed that experienced journalists are quite capable of following the ancient news-agency and BBC-radio tradition of steering a central course between the two main political parties.

It does not escape these producers' notice that politicians-in-power and public-relations personnel are always thinking up new ways to obtain soft media coverage. An example is the practice developed in the last Prime Ministerial years of Mrs Thatcher, of Prime Ministerial 'impromptu' press statements in the street outside 10 Downing Street. This practice, echoing the White House Rose Garden routine, seemed to enable the Prime Minister to offer a short sound-bite before stepping quickly off-stage through the front door. However, news values are always double-edged. Yes, the government gets more coverage, some of it very soft; but, yes also, news values emphasize the negative, the government in trouble.

This proximity to political power is one factor in news and current affairs being an elite field – as well as a private world – within television. This is also an elite field in terms of entry. Of the thirty-three journalist producers we interviewed, almost one-half had gone straight from university (Oxford outnumbering all others combined) into television at the national level. This elite-entry pattern has often involved a BBC traineeship and quick attachment to a national news or current-affairs programme. One-third of all these producers had worked on the BBC *Newsnight* programme; one-third had worked on either *Tonight* (and its successors such as *Nationwide*) or *Panorama*. The London element in this elite grouping is emphasized by one-third of these journalists having worked at Thames Television on *This Week* (in its various versions) or in other Thames journalism; one-third had also worked at London Weekend Television (LWT) on *Weekend World* or other programmes. The local regional programmes of both London ITV companies had been significant staging-posts; this London local element contrasts sharply with the fact that few of these thirty-three producers had had significant experience in regional television outside London.

News producers tended to have stayed for many years within either BBC TV news or ITN, because these two relatively large organizations offered ample career-ladders. Of the total group, the majority had worked for at least two of the London-based elite production units. Several had worked for three or four of the six mentioned.

However, it is possible to exaggerate the elite element in British TV journalism. While a large minority did attend either Oxford or Cambridge, the majority did not, and another sizeable minority did not attend university. Also important as an entry-gate was a previous career in newspapers, and the large minority who had started in print journalism had mostly begun on newspapers outside London and in several cases outside Britain.

The influence of newspapers is seen in many other ways, sometimes in a rather arbitrary mix of newspaper tradition with TV logistics. Even a senior TV journalist who had never worked in newspapers described TV current affairs as based on 'traditional methods – making phone-calls and meeting people'.

In some respects news and current affairs match quite neatly the peculiar British divide between daily and Sunday newspapers. Indeed, the weekly current-affairs programmes tend to be scheduled on Sunday and Monday, meaning that Friday and Saturday are often the most hectic days for current-affairs producers, just as for Sunday-newspaper journalists. In both daily newspapers and TV news the most hectic work-period is the early evening, before the premier deadline at 9 or 10 p.m.

TV PASSPORT JOURNALISM: THE HEROIC TRADITION

'I've worked as a field producer in about thirty-four countries' said one senior news executive. This is the heroic tradition which spans all TV journalism in Britain, but which historically derives more from current affairs than from news.

For many years British TV news was fairly anaemic; the first half-hour news (in reality, 25 minutes) was *News at Ten*, launched by ITN in 1967. For two decades after 1945 TV news was restricted in time, weighed down by cumbersome 35-mm (movie-style) cameras and six-person film-crews; because the film required lengthy developing as well as editing, most evening-news film was shot before midday.

Until about 1970 the weekly current-affairs programmes achieved higher audiences than the news and carried higher prestige. *Panorama* (the BBC's long-time Monday-night flagship) began in 1953; in the 1960s *Panorama* and its ITV competitors – such as *This Week* (1955) and *World in Action* (1963) – were the undoubted leaders in TV journalism. While they did cover for the first time many domestic British topics which later became TV staples, these programmes engaged heavily in short visits of two to three weeks' filming, especially to situations of colonial and post-colonial war from Algeria and Aden to Vietnam, Zaire and Zimbabwe. The current-affairs programmes were prestige offerings with generous budgets; the crew and its heavy equipment would travel by plane and bus to the location, film the fighting, interview one or two Presidents or Prime Ministers and return to London. Back home, the film was carefully edited into a polished combination of dramatic film and judicious news analysis. Initially, the news journalists could not compete.

A peculiarity of British TV journalism was that the daily and weekly categories of journalists were kept apart. The BBC's current-affairs department was located in an old film-studio at Lime Grove in west London; the BBC news department until 1970 was an hour's journey away in north-east London at Alexandra Palace from whence BBC TV had been launched in 1936. Even when TV news moved, it moved to a separate building, and retained a separate existence from

BBC current affairs. ITV followed the BBC pattern. ITV's network news provider was ITN, which operated entirely separately from network current-affairs programmes made by individual ITV companies.

ITN attempted, often successfully, to be a pace-setter in TV news; but especially in the years 1955–67 it was quite a small organization with quite a modest weekly output. Even after the 1967 *News at Ten* introduced longer news programmes, ITN still had a total output of only about three hours a week. ITN had very few staff correspondents outside London, let alone outside Britain. It relied mainly on foreign 'fireman' trips of a few days for its coverage not only of the world, but also of Europe. The BBC TV news was not greatly different, and it also used the 'fireman' approach.

Passport or fireman visits continued through the 1970s as the main way in which both TV news and current-affairs programmes covered the world.

1982–3: EVERYTHING CHANGES, AND STAYS THE SAME

In several respects the changes of late 1982 and early 1983 transformed British TV journalism. Channel Four was launched and it offered Britain's first 50-minute news (at 7 p.m.); it also introduced a number of fresh current-affairs programmes, which broke new ground in terms of mixing news and opinion. The BBC launched its (initially fairly soft) breakfast news in January 1983; and two weeks later a completely new advertising-supported breakfast show (initially rather weighty) was launched by the new TV-am company on the ITV network.

Other important developments in technology were helping to transform TV news and enabling the daily news to challenge the prestige and supremacy of the weekly programmes. Live satellite feeds from distant locations were becoming cheaper, providing a better supply of quick material both from 'our own correspondent' and from video agencies. Electronic news-gathering (ENG) had not only arrived but also been accepted by the trade unions, allowing the evening news to carry live and near-live inputs which competed with the following morning's newspapers.

By 1983 these developments had indeed produced major changes in the organization of news. In particular, the numbers of hours of output per week were greatly increased and the scale of the BBC and ITN operations was transformed. By 1985 the BBC and ITN together were transmitting about 22 hours of national TV news per week; ITN had 32 ENG camera-crews and BBC news had 19 ENG crews in London, while still using some film and also having access to the BBC's substantial regional news operations.[2] No longer could either ITN or BBC journalists realistically think of themselves as involved in some small-scale heroic activity; they were working in large news bureaucracies.

This latter simple reality was, however, in several respects not fully accepted. For much of the 1980s both the BBC and ITN were presided over by TV journalists whose journalism experience derived from the earlier heroic period. At ITN there was David Nicholas, the third in a succession of TV journalists with newspaper experience who functioned both as chief executive and editor-in-chief. At the BBC the Director-General from 1982 to 1987 was Alasdair Milne; he had achieved success in the BBC as Deputy Editor and Editor of *Tonight* (an early-evening news magazine) in the late 1950s and early 1960s. Milne, as Director-General (chief executive) of the BBC, also carried the title of Editor-in-Chief of the news and current-affairs output.

In practice, both BBC news and current affairs continued on their separate ways – in which, to say the least, journalism came before management. In the case of ITN, the owning ITV companies carried financial responsibility but lacked power; ITN continued through the 1980s as a producer-run enterprise in which journalism was in the forefront, while financial and management considerations followed behind.

Since ITN was providing the main news on both ITV and Channel Four, the BBC/ITN duopoly remained dominant, and heroic traditions remained in place. In 1983 a serious challenge to this duopoly was attempted by TV-am. Licensed by the Independent Broadcasting Authority (IBA) to provide serious news, TV-am had the disastrous opening traditionally enjoyed by IBA innovations. In this first disastrous phase, TV-am was led by five star presenters – Peter Jay, David Frost, Angela Rippon, Anna Ford and Michael Parkinson; these front-of-camera faces won the licence but lost the ratings war against the BBC breakfast offering. The basic problem at TV-am was very simply the lack of appropriate producer experience and direction. An additional problem was the adoption of the Peter Jay/ John Birt 'Mission to Explain' at the most inappropriate possible time of day.[3]

TV-am survived various other tribulations. These included the actors' strike which starved it of early advertising revenue; its 'recovery' phase led by Greg Dyke as programme controller from May 1983; the re-orientation towards soft news and toy advertising; and the lock-out of the technicians and their trade union. Later in the 1980s TV-am's televised tabloid-newspaper approach achieved high audiences and profits. During 1991 it finally achieved credibility as a news provider, but TV-am nevertheless lost its licence and was condemned to die at the end of 1992.

In retrospect, TV-am was itself a shining example of everything changing, yet staying the same. TV-am in the 1980s already belonged to the past. It had a fashionably architected building in Camden Town and studios which were idle most of the 24 hours. In January 1991 it employed 423 people at an average salary of £29,000, the highest in British television.[4] In the winter of 1991–2 it tried, but failed, to impress the Independent Television Commission (ITC) by sending a number of journalists and crews to the Middle East to cover the Gulf War; thus the last hurrah of TV-am conformed to the old heroic tradition of passport journalism.

BBC: BUREAUCRACY, BIRT AND COMPUTERS

The BBC's TV journalism was comprehensively reorganized from 1987 onwards. These changes became known in the BBC and by journalists outside as 'The Birt Revolution'; John Birt was brought in by the BBC Governors and their new Director-General, Michael Checkland, to be Deputy Director-General with the specific task of re-shaping the BBC's journalism. Although John Birt did indeed lead a major re-shaping of BBC journalism, any other experienced TV news executive – especially one coming to the BBC from outside – would probably have carried out the reform remit in a fairly similar way.

All large organizations go through major changes from time to time, and the BBC has seen many such changes in its history. This particular set of changes could be called the Bureaucratic Revolution, rather than the 'Birt Revolution'. The key reform was to turn the BBC's journalism into one organization, rather than several fragmented separate enterprises.

By the early 1990s BBC1 had four daily news programmes at 6.00 a.m., 1 p.m., 6 p.m. and 9 p.m.; BBC2 had two daily parliamentary programmes at 8.15 a.m. and 3.04 p.m. (on three days a week) when Parliament was sitting, plus the news analysis of *Newsnight* at 10.30 p.m. The weekly current-affairs programmes included BBC1's

Panorama, Question Time and *On the Record* and BBC2's *Public Eye, Assignment* and *The Money Programme.* In addition to this total of eight daily and six weekly programmes the BBC had a massive national radio news output; it also had a large regional output in terms of daily regional news in both television and radio, and local news in radio. This domestic BBC journalism output had a budget of £150 million in 1992–3.

This massive BBC operation in 1987 was still fragmented along three deep fault-lines. There was relatively little integration between national and regional news (and this still continues); radio and television were almost entirely separate; and there was still the old division between daily news and weekly current affairs. The latter two divisions were gradually reduced after 1987.

Before John Birt's arrival in 1987 there were many examples of bureaucratic organization within, for example, the separate entities of TV news and TV current affairs. Especially in news, a number of bureaucratic organizational elements were shared with large newspaper organizations. Senior TV news executives attended a daily series of meetings focused on the day's main deadlines, which could mean a senior producer attending 20 scheduled meetings (journalists do not like 'committees') per week. BBC and ITN news also operated a series of 'desks' similar to those found in newspapers which co-ordinate particular areas of coverage and particular programmes; these desks use newspaper terms such as 'up the table' or 'down the table' to denote seniority. These desks, and TV news generally, have long operated a series of shifts; an 'editor of the day' may work two or three shifts of 12 or 14 hours and then have several days off. Another traditional feature of news bureaucracy is the files – both of past output and of material relating to future output. The BBC news operation by 1987 already operated a computerized newsroom system which enabled items on the bulletin to be shuffled and which speeded up access to archive material. Another standard device of news bureaucracies – specialization – was also well advanced along several dimensions; there was specialization along conventional TV division of labour lines, by subject division and between news-gathering (or input) and news-processing and presentation (or output).

By 1987, then, there were strong elements of separate bureaucratic organization which encompassed TV news, TV current affairs and radio. The lack of overall organization, however, had in the mid-1980s been evident in the BBC's muddled response to several highly publicized differences between the BBC and the Thatcher Government.[5] These problems of political response derived from a wider organizational and management problem.

When John Birt was asked in 1987 by the BBC Governors and Director-General to reorganize the BBC's journalism, he was Director of Programmes at LWT. John Birt's career in television had two main themes. First, his career conformed to the standard precocious and fast-track pattern of the elite current-affairs producer. He was an Oxford graduate who had started in current affairs on Granada Television's *World in Action* and had been the youthful editor in charge of LWT's prestige *Weekend World* current-affairs programme in the 1970s. Here at LWT he became associated with a particular emphasis on news analysis.

The second theme in John Birt's well-publicized career was organization, management and pre-planning. Unusually for a current-affairs producer in British television, he had followed not an arts or social-science degree course at Oxford, but engineering. His approach to current affairs was one of meticulous planning. As the youthful Controller of Current Affairs at LWT, John Birt had in the late 1970s his first experience of management above the programme-editor level. In July 1980 he applied for the Chief Executive post at Channel Four (the post went to Jeremy Isaacs, who also had a current-affairs producer background). During the years 1981–7 Birt was LWT's Director of Programmes; for nearly six years he was a member of the committee that planned the ITV network schedule and its supply of programming. The LWT executives also took the lead in the detailed planning of the Friday–Sunday schedule. Those years were the heyday of the old ITV cartel arrangements during which the five largest ITV companies carved up the cake between them on the basis of an agreed formula related to company revenue. Throughout this period John Birt tried to persuade his network-planning colleagues to run the ITV network on more rational managerial lines. He argued, for example, that the 1981 practice of making detailed planning only six months ahead was inadequate.

Linking together these two themes of the TV journalist and the TV manager was a third theme of John Birt, the image. His office at LWT was virtually within sight across the Thames of Fleet Street, where the national newspapers still resided. The theme of Birt the manager was less interesting to the press journalists than the theme of John Birt the whizz-kid eccentric genius of Sunday midday TV news analysis. This line of press coverage followed John Birt during

his 1987–9 reorganization of BBC journalism. Again, Birt the
eccentric theorist (and militant reformer) made good copy, while
Birt the boring bureaucrat was less enticing.

John Birt first attracted press attention during the launch of
Weekend World by LWT in 1972. Unlike the 25-minute weekday
prime-time current-affairs offerings of Granada and Thames, LWT's
current-affairs flagship had an unambiguous prestige goal; it was
there to placate the regulators and the establishment. It was deliberately serious, long (varying between 60 and 90 minutes) and
scheduled on Sunday midday. After some early experimentation, it
became a single-topic programme which attracted very low audiences
(around 500,000 or a 1 per cent rating) and a high reputation for
serious journalism. *Weekend World* also became identified with a
particular approach to TV journalism which emphasized words and
ideas and saw video as secondary. Critics claimed that this dogmatic
approach was merely a radio talk (or a lecture or a printed article)
with video illustration. John Birt, the programme's young editor,
insisted on agreeing a detailed script before filming could begin.
This could, some said, lead to reporters and camera-crews trying to
find an 'expert' willing to say what the pre-written script required to
be said. John Birt was, perhaps, only taking the conventional 'word-
led' view of current affairs to its logical conclusion. He was
consistent also in recruiting programme personnel from non-visual
areas such as print journalism and the civil service. He surely
succeeded in showing that *Weekend World* was, if not the way, at
least an interesting way, of doing TV journalism.

When John Birt moved to the BBC in 1987, the BBC journalists
who were about to be reorganized expressed their natural anxieties
to their opposite numbers and friends in the printed press. Press
attention initially focused first on the party-political dimension, and
second on Birtist journalism, while the underlying theme of Birt the
boring bureaucrat was ignored.

John Birt's arrival in 1987 did indeed follow the sacking of
Alasdair Milne as the BBC's Director-General; the BBC Governors
clearly had lost confidence in their Director-General, and this was a
politically delicate time for the BBC. The BBC Governors had
chosen in John Birt a man whose whole adult life had been focused
on TV journalism and who had long ago taken the TV journalist's
vows of neutrality and objectivity. Not one producer interviewed in
this study accused John Birt of political partisanship, but some did

see him as the obsessive propounder of the editorial theory that TV journalism should be heavily pre-scripted.

The BBC Governors were obviously aware that Mrs Thatcher was antagonistic to both the BBC and certain elements in TV journalism. The Governors will also have been aware that criticisms of 'left-wing' and 'oppositional' could more accurately be applied to Channel Four, or even ITV, journalism than to the BBC's. The Governors, however, advised by their new Director-General, the accountant Michael Checkland, probably did believe that BBC news and current affairs were 'out of control', not politically or editorially, but in a management sense. The BBC's journalism was not as fragmented and lacking in structure as the ITV and Channel Four competition; but the BBC's journalism (including radio) was on a larger scale – employing over 2,000 people – and also was amenable to overall reorganization.

John Birt's reorganization took several forms. He did bring with him a few people from LWT, and a few others arrived later, but the 'Birt Revolution' left long-time BBC personnel still in most of the senior positions. There was also an increased tendency for scripts to be drafted at length in advance; some of this, however, would have happened anyway as part of the BBC budget revolution, its attempts to introduce budgets which revealed total costs. More detailed financial planning inevitably requires more detailed editorial planning.

Much of the initial agitation among the BBC's journalists focused upon the establishment of a new command structure for news and current affairs. Characteristically, John Birt, before even arriving at the BBC, designed a new organization chart which created a number of completely new senior-executive posts. Several of these jobs were filled by people who followed John Birt from LWT; others came from elsewhere, including newspapers. Most of the senior slots on the new organization chart, however, were occupied by long-established BBC people; some of these latter were given major promotions. Certainly, some producers who had been moved side-ways, and were encountered in this study, still felt bitter two or three years after the changes; but other old BBC hands – including some who had received accelerated promotion – were enthusiastic.

The 'Birt Revolution' involved several levels of reorganization. Many changes were at the middle level and focused on particular programmes: these tended simply to take further the previously well-pronounced bureaucratic themes. There were yet more meetings for senior producers and more attempts at co-ordination and cross-consultation. In pursuit of a clearer command structure, named individuals were placed in charge of particular news programmes; previously, a flagship programme like the *Nine O'Clock News* had not had a single individual boss. Another predictable managerial move, to strengthen these programme executives and their teams, was to give each programme its own budget; lack of a programme budget had been a marked feature of the old regime. All of this was, of course, made easier by the background events, such as the decline in trade-union power.

There was a strengthening of the newsroom computer systems and a continuing increase in the access all BBC journalists had to each others' current stories. There was also a strengthening and reorganizing of the entire range of specialist correspondents. In addition to the individual TV foreign correspondents, specialist groupings of correspondents – covering foreign affairs, social affairs, and business and economics – were established.

More radical were the strategic efforts directed towards linking TV news with current affairs and linking both with radio. The new specialist-correspondent units were intended to appear both on daily news programmes and on existing current-affairs programmes such as *Panorama* and *The Money Programme*. Two new weekly programmes were also created: *Public Eye* to specialize on domestic British social policy and *Assignment* to specialize on foreign affairs. All this was designed to use the BBC's journalism more rationally; it also involved each programme editor focusing on an agreed area and engaging in more negotiation and discussion both with other producers and with individual specialist correspondents.

Some current-affairs producers definitely missed the more free-wheeling style of the heroic tradition, and disliked being located within a more managed, costed, and bureaucratic framework:

> There's a hierarchy in BBC news and current affairs that doesn't allow their journalists the same freedom that I can enjoy here . . . My argument with the Birtists was over cutting-room journalism. After John Birt arrived it became a rigid process. Everything had to be planned in advance and costed before you ever went out and did the film. The process was stifling and didn't suit my kind of journalism. It wasn't the way I felt I could operate at my best. It was obvious that it was going to be a different sort of *Panorama*.[6]

Another strategic Birt theme was the bringing-closer-together of BBC TV and radio journalism. The term 'bi-media' described this policy of gradually persuading reporters and correspondents to appear on both radio and television. This was especially relevant to foreign reporting and the BBC's previously three separate teams of foreign correspondents, working for television, for domestic radio and for World Service radio.

A final strategic Birt point is perhaps the most important and it is another fact which actually pre-dates the arrival of John Birt. He was brought in not only to reorganize, but also to expand, the BBC's journalism. Against the background of the 1986 Peacock Committee Report the BBC Governors had decided to invest more money in journalism; they also wanted to ensure that BBC journalism was more weighty than that of ITN and the ITV network. More BBC money was duly spent. John Birt was thus the news builder as well as the news bureaucrat. Not only was BBC journalism reorganized according to a fairly predictable management plan; but, despite some resistance from producers and much press agitation, the reorganization proceeded quickly and fairly consensually, not least because of a major new injection of finance.

JOURNALIST PRODUCERS AT WORK

Producers of weekly journalism are in many ways similar to other TV producers in factual areas. It is the daily-news journalists who are most completely shut off from the bulk of television. At ITN, for example, an entire company is dedicated to daily news with only minimal involvement in weekly programmes.

Within this range of journalism output there is variety also in the different types of producer. One type of producer accompanies the reporter and camera-crew on stories. In the case of a senior foreign correspondent, the correspondent may be an established star while the producer may be a relatively junior unknown; but the normal practice is for the producer and reporter to act as equal partners, with the producer operating as an all-purpose 'fixer'.

A substantial number of such producers will contribute towards a major news programme. The producer/editor of such a team presides over a much bigger total team of perhaps a hundred people. The number who contribute to such a daily programme in a given week may be well above one hundred, while the core staff is much lower. The editor is supported by a small management team, including a deputy editor and a unit manager (in charge of finance). Then there is a second main layer of perhaps five producers called 'output editors', or 'editors of the day'; these may work two very long days, the first day in preparation and the second day in running that day's programme. In addition to programme presenters, sub-editors, junior producers and researchers, there are three technical teams who also work on such a daily programme: the studio team under the studio director; the crews who go out on stories; and the post-production/editorial people.

Daily programmes pursue stories in several time-frames: some stories are known about and activated several days in advance; many stories, such as domestic politics, are covered on the day; other stories are carried live or near-live. These live and near-live items often involve the presenter in live interviews via ENG crews as well as via satellite to other countries. The heavier types of TV news especially (such as *Channel Four News* and *Newsnight*) now make big demands on the presenter, who may be asked to interview live two politicians, one in, say, Moscow, the other in Washington. While satellite interviews elevate the importance of the live presenter, these and other uses of technology also place additional options and decisions into the hands of the programme editor. The satellite and studio bookings for such interviews are quite cheap; sending a fireman crew–reporter–producer team to a distant country may cost ten times as much; sending a larger team, including the programme presenter, say, to cover a foreign election might cost twenty times as much. The programme editor must make such decisions.

The live satellite interview and other now-established capabilities of daily news programmes, however, are regarded as a threat by producers of some weekly current-affairs programmes. Increasingly during the 1980s TV and print journalists disputed as to whether the weekly current-affairs programme had a future. ITV programmes lasting only 25 minutes – and scheduled at 8.30 p.m. – were increasingly seen as outdated; how could 25 minutes on Russia or Romania this Thursday add to daily 10- and 15-minute live interviews, film packages and analysis from the same locations?

The trend from the 1980s into the 1990s has been towards 'auteur current affairs' – high-quality single-subject programmes, which in some ways are closer to documentaries than to the multi-item format followed by *Panorama* and other current-affairs programmes in their early years. Several versions of 'auteur current affairs' present themselves. *Panorama* continues with its recent practice of some 40 programmes per year, of 40 minutes, each on a separate political subject. There are also the specialized current-affairs programmes focusing on a broad area such as social policy or foreign affairs. A variant on this is a model pursued by Channel Four, for example in *Dispatches*; this approach dispenses with the big production team and uses a succession of one-off programmes each made by a separate independent production company.

As the established BBC series accept more individual programmes from independent producers, it becomes increasingly possible for some producers to make a number of such one-offs. Meanwhile, the editorship of one of the BBC's continuing current-affairs programmes is still regarded as one of the best jobs in British broadcasting. Running such a major current-affairs series – and making 30 or 40 high-quality programmes per year – is a demanding task; the BBC has continued its tradition of appointing a new *Panorama* editor every two or three years.

One unintended consequence of the changes in recent years may be that senior journalist producers are over-worked to the point of inefficiency. While members of the editorial production team work shifts and have extensive time off, the assumption seems to be that the man or woman in charge is in practice available seven days a week. These senior journalist producers not only work very long hours but even when at home talk to editors of the day and others by telephone. They are also doing what by most comparative standards is high-pressure, high-excitement, work. They must worry about a crew currently filming in a dangerous foreign location, legal threats against a forthcoming programme or negotiations to entice a reluctant Cabinet Minister to be interviewed. Despite the ingrained habits of neutrality and objectivity, there is often a distinctly aggressive macho note. A producer can state that she likes to 'get the boot in' in the tradition of the *World in Action* programme. A male producer spoke of how his present budgetary concerns must be balanced with an aggressive news-gathering attitude:

> Management and journalism is a curious blend; when you're gathering a story . . . you feel yourself as a bit of a fighter-pilot or a bomber-pilot . . . you regard yourself as the guy who struts around and gets it on the air against adversity and always comes out with something that's pretty respectable.

There are continuing nagging worries about the balance of weighty against popular subjects:

The pressure, for audiences, is towards the personal and the visual; immediately you have analysis, you lose audience. If you do the human impact of toxic waste, you'll get 8 or 9 million; but the economic problems of East Germany are worth only 3 million.

Collectively these producers suffer from two obsessions – they are hooked on news and on television. Most of them are heavy consumers of the print media, work long hours and weeks in a buzz of news and television, and then return home to watch a sequence of news and current-affairs programmes in the evening. BBC's *Newsnight* programme seems to be especially popular, not least because by its 10.30 p.m. transmission most even of these hard workers are at home. Before arriving at work most have already listened to solid doses of BBC Radio 4 (and in some cases BBC World Service radio).

These journalist producers have a powerful commitment to their work. The speed of TV journalism gives these news executives the sense of being present, in live or near-live form, at the making of history. Major events in, say, eastern Europe, are emotional for many people; but the journalist producer in London has additional emotional inputs – for example, live, unedited, pictures appearing on a screen plus a direct conversation with 'our own correspondent' on the spot. In such conversations and in such decisions, these producers have a sense of interacting with great events and deciding how history-on-the-hoof will be portrayed.

The kind of autonomy experienced and sensed differs considerably between news and current affairs. The news producer has a sense of a broad flow of news material already generated by the overall organization which he or she, the producer, can stir and dip into. It is the current-affairs producer who experiences the greater sense of autonomy:

It satisfies my every megalomania to think that for these successive weeks things that interest me or worry me are put onto other people's agenda, just by my ability to get them on air.

The TV news operation is not simply a large internal machine with many inputs and many programmes per week; any news operation also runs on extended guidelines set by the day's and the week's news agenda – the competing TV news, the radio, the newspapers, the news agencies. The weekly current-affairs editor reports to an executive producer or departmental head; but once the broad remit is agreed, the editor of the current-affairs programme typically has a huge degree of autonomy in both the choice and the treatment of subjects:

> There is an absence of interference, which I think is absolutely fundamental to doing this kind of job. I consult with my boss but I don't submit scripts and I don't have wrangles. For better or for worse, if the programme succeeds or fails, it's largely me that carries the can . . . Running this show requires you to be a Jack-of-all-trades. It's a bit of administration, basic numeracy and being sensible about budgets; the old definition of being a journalist – hunches about what might be important, interesting; also managing people; and being able to write.

Along with this degree of control, and a range of required skills, goes a high level of responsibility. Current-affairs editors have a sense of being on trial; these are high-profile jobs within television and 'one big mistake is remembered longer than are several successes'. It is also well known that the higher levels of television include many former editors of current-affairs (and news) programmes.

In career terms journalism can be a fast career-track within television. The early or mid-thirties was the commonest age at which to have become editor of a major programme (and a few had become editors before the age of 30). Editors in their mid-forties had already been in charge of a sequence of two, three or four separate programmes. It seems to be widely agreed that this is a high-pressure job, best done by people under the age of 50. By the age of 50 most journalist producers have been promoted to run a department, or have become independent producers or freelances, or have taken early retirement.

NEWS BUREAUCRACIES AND PRODUCERS

The early 1990s saw the strengthening of the BBC news bureaucracy and the Broadcasting Act of 1990 ensured that ITN continued throughout the 1990s as the other half of the old TV-journalism duopoly. This preservation and strenthening of the two vertically integrated news factories runs counter to the 1990s trend towards a publisher model.

The main example of a publisher-style TV journalism is still in

Channel Four, as it has been since 1982. However, some elements of it are creeping into the BBC.

There is also, in the form of the satellite Sky News channel, one major example of the third industrial model – the themed 'packager' model. Sky News started out in early 1989 with some rolling news and large dollops of US ABC news and other imported packages. The news staff was small, but most had previous TV-news experience in Britain or Australia.[7] Four years later, Sky News was still rolling out 5 hours of US ABC news per 24 hours, including an hour of *Good Morning America* in the early afternoon. Sky News was also, however, gradually increasing its own rolling news offerings.

Sky News also quickly made an impact within the BBC and ITN and, along with Cable Network News, it was already available and closely followed in most news executives' offices by 1990. By 1991 the BBC was itself offering a satellite channel of news and factual programming on the Hong Kong-based Star satellite system to Asian audiences.

In Britain, therefore, TV journalism can be said to have jumped from the first, vertical, factory model to the third (packager) model, largely bypassing the second (publisher) model on the way. The packager model is, however, designed to fill many hours while employing relatively few journalists; most of the national journalist producers employed in Britain will continue to be those in the BBC and ITN news bureaucracies for some years yet.

Chapter 4

Sports: live events

The BBC's sports producers for many years shared a building with the documentary department; one sports producer said that he was responsible for two or three hours of television per week, while a documentary producer would take a full year to fill the same amount of screen-time.

The contrast with news and current affairs is also sharp. Whereas most TV journalism consists of either short news items or longer critical news analysis, most sports coverage on television consists of sporting events, either live or as edited 'highlights'. Television sports coverage thus finds its closest comparison in the live coverage of Parliament or in the live transmission of a musical event. Sports producers would regard the comparison with, say, the BBC's annual Promenade Concerts as fair; the sports producer shows the event, while adding a brief top-and-tail, plus some half-time expert comment. Sports producers argue, however, that unfair comparisons are made with the more critical press sports coverage or with other types of factual television.

In comparison with other genres, these sports producers occupy an unusual or extreme position on a number of TV dimensions. Sports television is extreme in the quantity of live material which it transmits to viewers; not for the sports producer the luxury of several weeks of editing. Within this heavily scripted medium, sports television is extreme in the huge quantities of unscripted talk which it involves. Short introductions and 'links' between items are scripted in advance, but obviously this is not possible for the event itself. Commentators and expert analysts are required to speak in the heat of the moment; considering the sheer quantity that needs to be said (and known), remarkably few mistakes, the producers would claim, are made.

Sports coverage is technically complex in several ways. Some 'magazine' programmes last several hours and cover several events – some live, some near-live, some a day or two old; the number of possible items and links, the number of on-screen and off-screen personnel, the number of factual graphics displayed on screen – all of these are unusually high. In line with this variety and quantity, sports television is unusual in the number of cameras being directed, selected from, and supervised by, the producer-director team. The London Marathon uses 26 cameras, and some multi-event programmes use substantially more. These cameras and camera-operators are backed by another phalanx of video-replay machines and operators, capable of providing instant replays from assorted angles and corners of the playing area.

With the exception of a few star news fireman and firewoman teams, these sports personnel are British television's most restless travellers. They travel frequently within Britain, within Europe, and around the world. Sports television focuses heavily on home performers in international contests. Sports producers are the heaviest users of live-by-satellite material provided by host national networks in other countries; but such provision is also heavily supported by additional on-site output from our own producers and our own reporters, interviewing our own athletes and players.

Sports television is also unusual in the complexity of its commercial and financial ramifications. The commercial ramifications take three main forms. First, there is the money paid for the right to televise particular events. Second, there is the sponsorship, and related advertising displays, which are placed at the locations in the stadium and on the players' clothing in order to reach the TV viewer. Third, there are the more diffuse commercial elements – high player salaries and high transfer fees – which are indirectly related to the overlapping of sports stardom and TV stardom (as are also drug-taking and other abuses). Programme editors and producers are not themselves directly involved in these commercial practices; but they are, nevertheless, uneasily aware of the large sums of money, and strong commercial forces, that surround sports television. They tend to see themselves as unfairly tainted by forces from which they are completely independent.

Sports producers occupy one final extreme position as much the heaviest users of 'Outside Broadcast' (OB) technology. The bulky OB equipment can be seen at any televised sporting event. Numerous cameras, many hundreds of metres of electric cable, and much else, are packed into a convoy of vehicles. One vehicle is, in effect, a travelling version of the normal TV studio gallery in which pictures, sounds and other inputs are selected by a director and a team of vision-mixers, sound-mixers and others. Separate vehicles carry equipment and personnel to perform other key functions such as graphics/captions/words-on-screen and video-replay facilities. These same OB facilities are used not only for sports events. In both the BBC and ITV the sports area has long also been responsible for certain other events, as is indicated in this passage in a 1990 advertisement for the post of 'Editor, Events Unit' within the BBC Sports and Events Group:

> The range of output contains one-offs and series, with coverage of major occasions of general public interest and other events of more particular attraction . . . including *Trooping the Colour, The Festival of Remembrance*, *The Royal Tournament, Come Dancing, One Man and his Dog, Variety Club Awards, World's Strongest Man, Farnborough Air Show* and *The State Opening of Parliament.*

This advertisement does not mention that the BBC Sports and Events Group is also responsible for such OB Specials as Royal weddings[1] and Royal funerals.

The combined effect of these several unusual factors is to shut TV sports producers off from the rest of the world of television; but these producers' world is less private than that of other producers in one important respect. These producers are closer to their audiences than are the producers in any other genre.

COMPETITION AND CONTRACTS

British TV sport traditionally conformed to the standard duopoly pattern. Of the two vertically integrated systems the BBC was always in the lead, but ITV also carried large quantities of sport. As in other genres, the vertically integrated duopoly pattern was joined in 1982 by the publisher model of Channel Four. However, Channel Four and its boss, Jeremy Isaacs, saw sport as having only a walk-on part to play:

> It seemed obvious we could not do without sport . . . I invited Adrian Metcalfe . . . to give us sport on television that was different. Since we had no contracts, and since the BBC was sewing up nearly everything in sight, that was our only course.[2]

Channel Four tried British basketball and American football ('as an exotic spectacle'); but its main early ratings success was, first, in screening some of ITV's snooker ('I pretended not to notice the hike it always gave our ratings', joked Isaacs) and, second, in agreeing to take over ITV's horse-racing contract (horse racing appealed to Isaacs because 'I wanted an outdoor feel to the channel, and liked the idea of the green of the track, the most restful of colours, on our screens in the afternoons').

Such gentle witticisms, however, were less appropriate for the competition that emerged in 1989–90 from the satellite channels. Sky's sports channel began in 1989 and for much of 1990 competed against the sports channel of British Satellite Broadcasting (BSB). The merged BSkyB gave high priority to sports in selling its service. After some initial success with an exclusive cricket contract, BSkyB in 1992 announced its acquisition of exclusive long-term rights to provide live coverage of Premier League Association Football.

Until 1989 only a minimal breach had been made by Channel Four in the sports TV duopoly; but from 1989 onwards sports television was moving rapidly into both new industrial systems, the publisher and the packager models. The publisher model became much commoner, as both BBC and ITV (as well as Channel Four) contracted out the coverage of some entire sports to independent production companies. In addition, the packager model was pursued by BSkyB as it specialized on providing an endless flow of live sport, mainly acquired *en masse* from Europe and the USA.

By the time BSkyB acquired the Premier Football contract in 1992, British satellite subscribers could receive no fewer than three separate all-sports channels: not only Sky Sports but also Eurosport and Screensport.

The BBC has always been the leader in British sports television: it got there first, signed contracts and built relationships with the major sports. ITV initially took relatively little interest in sport; when it moved into sport in a big way in the 1970s, it still tended to run second to the BBC. The BBC had the advantage of leadership in general. Also important was its lack of advertising; when both the BBC and ITV transmitted the same event, the first advertising break found the BBC attracting an increased audience-share. Advertising also imposes other scheduling problems, not least of co-ordination within a federal network. The BBC has another huge advantage in having two channels.

By running a lot of sport, the BBC solves several problems. Sport is part of the formidable factual wing of BBC television; sport appeals to both majorities and minorities. Very importantly, sport has been a cheap – or the cheapest – form of British television per hour. It employs a lot of production people but the huge numbers of hours make for high levels of productivity per person. Sport conveniently and cheaply fills up much time in the afternoon and latish evening. Many sports associations, producers say, are more interested in the publicity benefits of having a large number of hours transmitted than in being paid a large fee.

ITV's sports problems have always been compounded by ITV's own internal politics. The details of its sports coverage have been byzantine even by the standards of ITV; however, much ITV network sports coverage has involved one or both of the London companies combining with several companies outside London; the London ITV companies provide the core editorial team but the OB facilities and technicians are typically supplied by the relevant ITV company in the particular locality. A London ITV sports editor could in successive weeks be working with technicians from Granada Television, Tyne Tees Television and Anglia Television. One London producer claimed that in some weeks his biggest task was to assemble the local regional team who would be working for him at the weekend.

There has always been a heavy focus on exclusive contracts and most of these contracts still belong to the BBC. The remaining direct BBC vs. ITV competition is between the midweek late-evening magazine programmes which confront each other on some Wednesdays. Competition has largely departed from the level of the programme producer and has moved upstairs to the level of the sports department head who competes to obtain exclusive contracts.

From the late 1980s the ITV sports subgroup (chaired by Greg Dyke of London Weekend Television) decided that it could not compete with the BBC in total hours transmitted, or in head-to-head coverage of the major ('listed') events, or in numbers of sports covered. ITV decided to focus on a few popular sports and to obtain exclusive coverage of certain competitions by outbidding the BBC. In the case of lengthy events (such as athletics) ITV would focus on 'highlights', which attract bigger audiences. ITV also decided to drop sports with heavily elderly and working-class audiences (like darts and wrestling). The problem for ITV was that no popular British sport has a predominantly young and affluent audience; the cricket audience, for example, is affluent but elderly. ITV in practice focused on athletics, football, snooker and boxing; in 1991 ITV also carried the first Rugby Union world cup.

The emerging pattern of the 1990s has been a series of accommodations between the four conventional channels and BSkyB. Each major sport offers several different League and Cup knock-out competitions, as well as both home-based and foreign-based internationals; ITV in particular, as a single channel, may not have the airtime to include all these competitions and – even in its chosen sports – has been willing to share a sport with the BBC. BSkyB also has become involved in such accommodations: in 1992 it agreed to pay the bulk of the Premier League Football bill for the live coverage rights, but the BBC also obtained, at quite modest cost, extensive rights to evening 'highlights'.

These patterns and accommodations will probably be increasingly volatile. However, the 1990s pattern will continue to involve BSkyB delivering selected events live and in full to customers on a 'pay' basis. ITV is continuing its selective strategy with an increasing focus on more middle-class sports like Rugby Union. The BBC will continue to be, while less dominant, still the main place where most British TV sports viewing is done (in terms of total hours).

This is an extremely simplified summary of a highly complex reality. The top few people in TV sports are involved in a long series of complex negotiations with domestic national sports associations and with international bodies:

> The head of a sports department is more and more the Headmaster who doesn't teach any more; our main thought is programmes, but without contracts and ancillary things, you can't make programmes.

> My job is about contracts, management of people, budgets, planning and scheduling.

Recent developments in TV sports contracts involve a gradual merging of the interests of television with the interests of professional sport. This merging of major sports and national TV interests is taking place within an expanding commercial and cash framework. Playing an increasingly central role within this cash framework are agents, who now represent a variety of separate financial interests. Sports agents work for, and negotiate for, Governing Bodies or Associations; they also represent on-screen presenters, reporters and expert analysts. The same agents represent leading players and sports personalities, and any meeting beyond a very short routine interview may have to be agreed with the agent; the same agency companies create events such as recorded professional/ celebrity golf games, which are then offered for winter network showing; in yet other cases agents control the entire national and world rights to a particular sports event. Various branches of Mark McCormack's International Management Group perform all the above functions, and control the rights to Wimbledon and the British Open Golf Tournament.

Television sports producers increasingly find themselves working within a framework that defines their relationship with sporting bodies as a business partnership. A producer who covers a particular sport is likely to have at least some previous involvement with it, such as having reported it for a newspaper, or having once played the game. Then in his early career he will have been involved in production teams covering the sport. Now as a producer-director, producer or programme editor, he may be taken along to the contract negotiations at the Association Governing Body level. In terms of coverage the producer will always visit the site a week or two previous to the event. These site visits involve discussions about camera-positions, where the vehicles will be parked, where the cables will go, and other vital details; such site discussions take place at many different sports locations through a full year. On top of these discussions and negotiations, there is the shared experience of the TV coverage itself. If the event is a success and the TV production goes smoothly, the TV producer has something positive to share with the site hosts.

The TV producer is inevitably drawn into a confidential relation-ship: the sports authorities get some insight into the internal politics of ITV or the BBC; the TV producer also acquires insight into the politics and sensitivities of the sport in question. More than one producer could write an explosive book about the politics of British football in the early 1990s. Other producers know a lot about the inside story of British boxing and how the ITV companies broke the previous BBC TV boxing monopoly. The producers in question, however, are well aware of how important it is to maintain a reputation for discretion.

HIGH ON TECHNOLOGY AND LOGISTICS, LOW ON JOURNALISM AND DETACHMENT?

Other factually based TV producers tend to be highly critical of sports coverage:

> The problem with TV sport is straightforward: you can't be a journalist in TV sport effectively, because you can't afford to offend the authorities that you are buying the stuff from.

Sports producers are acutely aware of this line of argument but they believe it to be inappropriate. These producers argue that they have advantages (such as instant replay) that sports referees and umpires lack, and thus in fairness any criticisms should be cautiously stated. Both BBC and ITV producers claim that on some major delicate issues – such as drugs in athletics – they have been in the vanguard of criticism. They also claim that while avoiding strident criticism, they do show viewers the replay and allow them to form their own opinion; nor are the more obviously sleazy aspects – such as dirty play – hidden from viewers.

A basic question is whether sports television should, or should not, be regarded as journalism. If it is journalism, then compared with other forms of journalism sports coverage is indeed low on critical journalism, while high on technology and logistics. Sports journalism is unusual in the number and complexity of the links in the technical and editorial chains. In multi-event magazine programmes especially, sports producers know that things will go wrong and plans will have to be modified; but each time one person makes a mistake, the complexity of the sports programme – and its being live – makes possible the domino-effect of a sequence of ensuing mistakes and disasters:

> On these programmes the fancy openings are often put out in a live sequence of pre-recorded bits of tape, which are all very simple except that there's an awful lot of them. If you had all day it would be simple, but probably you've got 10 minutes, and then there's a crucial point where a smooth transmission depends on your sound man and with his paddles he at the right time must fade the one sound source down and fade the correct other one up – out of maybe 24 different sound sources. If that sound bloke gets in a tizz, he is going to absolutely kill your programme; but that's only one piece in one particular 10-minute jig-saw, which involves maybe a dozen other people in similar positions.
>
> (Rick Waumsley)

The analogy is made with a rattlesnake. Mostly it lies quietly in the desert clicking away to itself, but suddenly it turns round and bites you in the bum. Then you must be flexible enough to switch direction; from an editorial point of view, picture, audio, technical side, everyone must slip into a different mode. Just looking at the bank of monitors before we begin – we may be blasé about it because we've been there a few times. Suddenly all the screens light up and you've got perhaps athletics from Moscow, racing from Newbury, a satellite picture of boxing from Las Vegas and a swimming OB, and you think Logie Baird was a genius.

(John Philips)

The most demanding moment for the editor of a live sports programme is death on the screen:

It's happened to me on about five occasions now – not only football crowd disasters, but guys being killed falling off motorbikes, and car racing. This is the most difficult thing; it exercises the mind and also your common decency and humanity. That's when all your skills and sensibilities are brought together. It's what you fear, but you must be ready for it at all times.

(John Philips)

More even than other producers, these sports producers believe that they are misunderstood and unfairly criticized by the press. They are thinking primarily of the tabloid press. They believe the London tabloids to be absurdly over-critical both of people like football managers and of televised sport. They criticize the newspapers for paying sports people excessively large sums of money for negative 'revelations' about the sport in question:

Oh, he would have to say something fairly sensational, but if the manager sits down with the tabloid journalist and gives him a few juicy lines, that's it – £25,000, thanks very much; then the managers think we should all pay that too.

The sports producer has the normal desire for favourable publicity for his programme, but little such press coverage ever appears. The producer may try to interest the print journalist about an enticing item in a forthcoming programme, but the print journalist will use the item without mentioning the programme. These producers believe that the tabloid newspapers are resentful of television's central role in showing events; television has used its money to buy up the events and has acquired friendly access to particular major sports. Producers agree that TV coverage is predominantly favourable; they argue that tabloid journalists – frustrated by television's delivery of the events – resort to 'negative' and 'go-for-the-jugular' journalism.

While television does, of course, have a financial relationship with the major sports, the producers point out that the *Sun* and the *News of the World* are part of the News company that controls BSkyB satellite television and its sports channel. BBC producers tend to see the sports press as especially hostile to the BBC's strength:

> If the BBC signs a big new sports contract, it gets 2 inches in the press. If ITV had bought it from us, it might be a back-page lead; if Sky bought it from us it would be four pages inside the paper.

As elsewhere, there is a feeling here that press journalists are the only people who in practice could give public praise to the producer's work. Print journalists work and travel alongside the TV sports people; but the final imprimatur of some informed press discussion of sports television is not forthcoming.

ENERGY AND CAREERS

Sports is not an elite field within television, and there are few if any sports-producer careers which follow the elite and precocious promotion pattern found in documentary or current affairs. Most of these producers have been involved in the subject – sports – before they had entered television. The majority had worked in newspapers, where they had already specialized to at least some extent in sport. A typical sports producer, now aged around 40, had thus been a sports specialist for about twenty years.

The majority had finished their education by the age of 18 and had entered television in a lowly capacity, such as office boy, library assistant, assistant stage manager or 'call boy'. A substantial minority were graduates (especially from universities in major sporting cities such as Liverpool and Manchester) and had worked in print journalism before transferring to television.

An atypically high proportion – about one-half – had first entered television outside London and had been involved in local sports, as well as other programming, including local news. Overall, then, nearly all these sports producers had some experience of journalism, other than sports journalism. They had, however, no recent experience of journalism: none had returned for a spell in print journalism; and none had worked in TV news or current affairs at the national level. In career terms, they were ex-journalists, now firmly committed to TV sports.

These sports producers see their field as a difficult and demanding one, requiring a high level of knowledge and expertise; but they are less inclined than other producers to see it as insecure. Most of these producers have permanent staff appointments; the sports TV field has grown steadily over a long period of years. In sports, TV experience seems to be valued more than 'originality'. The only risky career-move that most sports producers mentioned was a possible move into satellite television. Several had been offered satellite TV jobs at greatly increased salaries, especially by BSB in 1989–90; they had declined but had still benefited indirectly from the generally expanded career opportunities and the upward impact on sports-producer salaries.

Producers typically had entered sports television around the early or mid-1970s, when there were still fairly few sports programmes on the air. Magazine programmes already accounted for many TV hours and a common pattern was to have worked up within the production team of one of these programmes. Tape editing was the commonest early career activity, both as videotape editor and as assistant producer. Typically, a long videotape-recorded sports event needs to be edited down to perhaps 5 or 10 minutes of 'highlights' for inclusion in a weekly sports magazine programme.

These producers had also worked in the OB 'scanner' version of the studio director's job. One of the producers describes the close links between the director's and the producer's jobs:

Obviously there is a major overlap between the director and the producer, because we sit virtually beside each other; but on transmission the director concerns himself solely with what is going out at that precise second, making sure that the viewer is getting the best possible service. As producer I am splitting myself between providing him with back-up and most importantly I am a scout, if you like, concerning myself with what's coming up next, making sure that everything is in place, and also trying to take an overview of the whole programme.

(Andrew Franklin)

On the more elaborate magazine programmes there are not two, but three, levels. First, there is the director in the parked scanner selecting pictures from the cameras at the event; second, there is the producer of the particular event overseeing the whole operation, including the connections with the sporting authorities and site hosts; third, there is an editor or executive producer back in London in charge of the magazine programme which may include several OBs. The editor/executive producer is typically in charge of a major programme and/or a major field such as football. These levels get confused; the same individual often works at one level in one sport or on one programme, but at another level in another area of sport.

AUDIENCE AND STARS

Rapid fluctuations in audience size through a multi-item programme reveal in considerable detail the popularity of specific sports. At the senior level such information is closely studied and additional research is commissioned on the popularity of specific sports commentators and presenters. Several producers emphasized that their programme did well for the time-slot in which it was located. Sport does, indeed, not get the best time-slots, and if a programme like the BBC's *Grandstand* gets a 3-million audience rating, this is an average figure across several hours; the total number of people who watched part of the programme is much higher.

Nevertheless, most sports producers cannot quote the age or gender composition of their audience, although all are aware that athletics and the Olympics attract a good proportion of women, while football and Rugby Union have heavily male audiences. Most of these sports producers still held a view of their audience's composition; one claimed that the letters he received indicated an audience mainly of boys and old men.

Such vagueness about audience data is in line with TV producers in general. The sports producers are unusual in believing that feedback from friends and acquaintances can be helpful. Producers quoted discussions in their local pub; younger producers mentioned friends with whom they played tennis or Sunday-morning football; two producers said they regularly talked on the telephone to sports friends outside London. Several claimed that these comments, added to telephone-calls and letters, could be very helpful. A sweeping criticism such as 'camera work was rubbish last week' can fit with the producer's own unhappiness with last week's too-high main camera location.

All sports producers stress the importance of using the best presenters and reporters. The success of the programme depends, they say, nearly as much on the words spoken as the pictures shown. The selection, deployment and performance of these on-screen and on-sound persons is a central concern for producers. These personalities in British TV sports belong broadly to three categories. At the bottom of the hierarchy is the 'journeyman' or general sports reporter who may have to cover a wide range of the more obscure sports and teams. The BBC, with its variegated sports coverage, needs people who can cover several sports. Even at this general sports reporter level the competition is strong; between Glasgow and London there are hundreds of sports journalists – newspaper, television and radio – many of whom have applied for one of the national TV reporting jobs.

The second level are the specialist reporters and presenters of the leading sports, such as athletics, football, cricket, horse racing, tennis and golf. They are the leaders in a much criticized profession: they typically have a formidable knowledge of the field, impressive skills in commentary, and a remarkable ability to recognize unfamiliar people and horses moving at speed and at a distance. These are the people who each year fill many hours of TV air-time with unscripted talk:

> There are set-piece links which are written by each of the presenters, but they don't work off autocue, so they must memorize these links; they are a talented bunch, strong on memory and very equable as well; they may be feeling uncomfortable if the weather is cold, wet or hot, but they do not convey that to the viewer.

These leading specialists typically work as freelances. They often have deep roots in the sport in question, sometimes including other media activities such as writing regularly for a national publication. The specialist sport presenter's agent may well preside over a wide range of activities, some of which sail quite close to what the BBC or Independent Television Commission disapproves of. The programme producer typically has strong views about the specialist presenters and will fight fiercely to retain his favourites; contract negotiations, however, probably take place upstairs between the head of department and the agent. Often these specialists are on lengthy non-exclusive contracts, but they are expected to obtain permission before engaging in comparable work elsewhere.

Finally there are the programme anchor persons, who – especially in the magazine programmes – are the vital link between the

different sports offerings; the anchor also conducts studio interviews. No other TV role regularly requires an individual to be on
live television for so long. The anchor person is central to the image
and reputation of the programme with the public. These few anchors
are regarded as being so important that they are typically on lengthy
exclusive contracts and are paid accordingly.

THE SPORTS PRODUCER IN A CLOSED WORLD

The emotional commitment felt by sports producers is very strong ('I
love it' or 'I adore it'). These producers, like many of their audience
members, have been sports fans since childhood:

> Essentially I'm a sports fan . . . I mean, there has to be a degree of
> talent and a bit of courage and bollocks, but basically I'm just a
> lucky guy.

Several said that to be in sport and to be in television had been their
teenage ambitions. This may be one of several reasons why the
emotional commitment of these producers to their work is so strong.

The live (and near-live) character of most TV sports is important
in pumping up the level of excitement. Producers tend to feel that
there is something very special indeed in presenting live to several
million viewers an event whose outcome neither the viewer nor the
producer yet knows:

> It has its own magic hour, and not only are you watching it
> happen, while you are helping it happen, but everyone else in the
> audience at the same split-second is also watching it happen . . . It
> has a life of its own, a brief incandescent life, it's there and then
> it's gone; when there, it's powerfully there and when it's gone,
> you never have to see it again . . . There is a fantastic concen-
> tration of simultaneous involvement in this thing.
>
> (Rick Waumsley)

The producer obtains considerable emotional satisfaction from the
contrast between an unpredictable sports event and his personal and
immediate control over how it is presented to an audience of
millions. The team element also is especially satisfying in the case of
sports television. As usual, there is a small team; but this team
collectively experiences many highs and lows because of its frequent
involvement in lengthy live transmissions:

> It's a bit like, I imagine, a war-effort type of feeling; you have a

countdown, then you have to go over the top, and if we've got through it together and survived at the end, and had a few laughs, that's very enjoyable.

Televised horse racing obviously appeals to horse lovers and to gamblers; the actual races are colourful, dramatic and quickly over. But between the races the viewer is also introduced to a unique world of super-rich owners and their trainers, as well as the jockeys, bookies and the general public. If one is interested in, say, football, or cricket, or golf, again these private worlds present a delectable array of information, entertainment, attractive pictures and the spectacle of skilled performers under pressure.

The specialist producer is in a unique position from which to dispense publicity and patronage within this emotionally engrossing small world. The top people in the sport want to talk to the TV producer. An office interview with a football producer, for example, is interrupted by telephone-calls from leading managers. The producer also talks to the players or the jockeys; and he communes with the ordinary followers of the sport. This special position within a particular sport, or within sport in general, does not, however, transfer into television more broadly. The sports producer does not carry high status within the TV industry. Sports producers are not seen as creating an original documentary vision; they do not perform the TV journalist's balancing act of combining neutrality with scepticism. Other producers would also probably say that sports producers tend to be technically conservative – they use large quantities of cameras and equipment, but in rather cautious and pedestrian ways.

Most of these latter criticisms may be rather unfair; but sports producers seem to sense themselves as belonging to a kind of golden ghetto. There are, indeed, few obvious avenues of advance beyond sports television; few sports producers are promoted any further or transfer sideways into other areas of television or journalism. It may be for this latter reason that competition for promotion within sports television is felt to be extremely fierce; some sports producers sense that their colleagues and competitors are waiting eagerly for a very public mistake, such as their failing to catch the winning throw or goal.

Chapter 5

The edinfotainment maelstrom

British television in general, and the BBC in particular, has since the 1950s given heavy emphasis to factual programming that is mixed in several ways. Often these programmes are 'magazine' programmes involving several items of only 5 or 10 minutes each; they are often also a mixture of genres – some live news and interviews, a carefully filmed mini-documentary, plus an infusion of entertainment, comedy and music.

These mixed programmes are a mix also in terms of goals. They are not simply 'infotainment' – entertainment delivered in a news and journalistic format, as in the 'real-life' murder mystery; in this British tradition there is also an element of education, such as some useful advice on how to get better use out of your garden, body, car, kitchen or holiday. 'Edinfotainment' is a deliberately awkward term to describe an awkward mix of programming. This is, of course, a latter-day *mélange* of the three goals of public-service broadcasting. The edinfotainment goal is effectively in operation across much of the total output of the two 'minority' channels, BBC2 and Channel Four. 'Minority' programming is no less vague a concept than public-service programming; but clearly it means something other than 100 per cent entertainment and news, and clearly in practice it involves a broad assortment of highly miscellaneous programming.

While the largest proportions of edinfotainment are to be found on BBC2 and Channel Four, the most celebrated and popular examples of such programming – *The Antiques Roadshow*, *That's Life*, *Songs of Praise* and *The Clothes Show* – have been on BBC1. *Tonight*, a BBC magazine programme which began in 1957, was not only the first of these super-successful edinfotainment programmes, but also the most influential of all programmes within British television. Its style and its personnel influenced the entire subsequent range of factual programming, not only news and documentary but also (through, for example, the work of Kenneth Allsop) the later sub-genre of environmental programming. Tonight Productions also created *That Was The Week That Was*, which had a major influence on subsequent TV comedy. *Tonight*, from its start, was an early-evening 50-minute magazine of short items, most of which ran no longer than 4 minutes. Donald Baverstock, the producer in charge, explained its approach to his deputy, Alasdair Milne:

> Donald . . . had a very clear notion of a sort of populist, non-cant dialogue with the audience. He wanted *Tonight* to be, simply, a straightforward, popular journalistic programme . . . He could see no reason why we couldn't be serious about the state of the British economy . . . and in the same programme smile about the hens that were laying bent eggs in Dorset . . . The notion then that television programmes should be either serious or entertaining struck us as false and rather insulting to the audience, actually.[1]

Tonight mixed heavy and light items, politics and humour, British and foreign stories.

Tonight was a classic edinfotainment mix. It specialized in the sharp political interview and the programme itself often thus 'made news'. It specialized also in quirky, whimsical humour and lovingly interviewed the eccentric human equivalents of the bent-egg-laying hens. Behind all this banter, and whimsical eccentricity, there was also an additional educational purpose. The three leading producers behind the early *Tonight* – Donald Baverstock, Alasdair Milne and Antony Jay – were all Oxbridge-educated and, taken together, they were a decidedly intellectual group to be running a predominantly light programme. The launch came in the year after the 1956 British disaster at Suez; it was also at a time when ITV (which began in 1955) was winning huge proportions of the potential audience with its all-out entertainment programming. *Tonight* conformed, of course, to the normal requirements for party-political neutrality, but it also contained a strong strain of young programme-makers seeking to educate their elders on the political, social and TV realities of the late 1950s.

Tonight established the BBC tradition that the light mixed programme should be a well-made programme. It had, in effect, gone through 18 months of development and testing in the form of a previous 10-minute daily programme called *Highlight*. Baverstock and Milne – with their large number of highly disparate items – recognized the crucial importance of the 'links' between the items;

much energy was devoted to writing these links and the briefings for the heavy interviews. There was an emphasis on high quality in all areas; several of *Tonight*'s early mini-documentary-makers went on subsequently to become successful film-makers.

Tonight celebrated many British qualities. Its mixture of politics and humour was very British, as was its obsession with eccentricity and whimsy. Its creators (especially Baverstock) were highly aware of contemporary US television, much of which was to be seen at the time on ITV screens; the producers were, however, making a programme that avoided US television and showbiz. *Tonight*, although a very London creation, also tried to celebrate non-London subjects; it partly relied for its supply of eccentric interviews on BBC regional personnel.

Tonight's writing habits also helped to establish other British TV practices. The huge number of items per week – and the primitive production conditions – placed enormous strains on the producers. The executive producer, Grace Wyndham Goldie, generously recognized the workaholic life-style demanded of the producers. She also recognized the producer-driven nature of this kind of television; she appointed Baverstock and Milne who then created and drove the programme.

> Styles in television programmes are the result, not of gimmicks, but of the attitudes to life of the production staff. The style of *Tonight* was the result of the intellectual integrity and the human understanding of its editors, Donald Baverstock and Alasdair Milne . . . Donald Baverstock . . . ran *Tonight* with a mixture of authoritarianism and democracy which he called leadership.[2]

SUCCESSFUL MIXED PROGRAMMING

There are some problems in defining even such established genres as documentary, news and current affairs, and sport; but each of these genres pre-dates television and each is located within well-established departments across British television. In the BBC 'other factual' or 'miscellaneous' or 'feature' programming has been produced in topical features, religion, youth, community programmes and continuing education as well as in documentary features and current affairs. Such mixed programming was made by the BBC not only in London, but also in Manchester, Birmingham, Bristol, Elstree and elsewhere.

Mixed-goal factual programming was adopted with enthusiasm by Channel Four, because it not only fitted the traditional trio of public-service goals, but also seemed to fit three other elements of the channel's remit: the requirements to 'innovate', to reach 'minorities' and to do so at modest production cost.

While BBC1, BBC2 and Channel Four were all heavily committed to such mixed-goal programming, ITV was much more committed, first, to a preponderance of programming aimed at ratings popularity, but, second, to the formal legal regulatory requirement for fixed percentages of education and information, as well as the informal requirement for some prestige output. Even within a particular category of programming the ITV offering was likely to be more committed to ratings than were the other channels' offerings. So, for example, ITV's leading travel/holiday programme, *Wish You Were Here*, adopted a popular mix of useful holiday advice for people on average incomes, plus an element of glossy fantasy (sunny beach holidays) during the January and February evenings. The BBC's *Holiday* programme had similar popular/fantasy ingredients, but covered also more expensive and ambitious holidays and did more documentary-style film reports. Other travel/holiday programmes had still stronger elements of information and advice: for example, the *Travel Show* (BBC) which offered advice and news during the summer-holiday season, and the *Rough Guides* (BBC), orientated towards individual, exotic and student travel.

The series producer of a mixed programme often deliberately chooses a production team with mixed backgrounds: for example, one or two documentary directors for well-made films; some news and current-affairs people for their 'harder-edged' and quicker journalistic style; perhaps also other team-members, knowledgeable in the subject-area, but inexperienced in television.

Those who launch a new mixed programme can choose from an almost infinite number of combinations. However, choosing a combination that will unlock success is much less easy, not least because what is regarded and accepted as 'success' in any particular case is itself highly uncertain. Producers of long-time successful programmes tend to point out that the successful formula often had to evolve over several years of experimentation and modification. Moreover, the formula typically seems to work successfully only for one unique programme; the particular mix seems to have unique elements, which often cannot be successfully copied. *That's Life* had several obvious ingredients: it grew from a successful show presented by Bernard Braden, one of whose reporters, Esther Rantzen, became the central personality; it combined several apparently simple elements (consumer reports derived from viewers' letters, humour from supporting male personalities, and vox-pop filmed street-interviews on funny topics). Yet, somehow, the show was more than the sum of its parts, and for much of the 1970s and 1980s it maintained huge audiences.

More perplexing still was the appeal of *The Antiques Roadshow*, another unique and eccentric combination of the serious and the popular. The show, produced at BBC Bristol, was an outside broadcast; it descended on some carefully chosen locality to assess and value antique objects owned by members of the local public. Obvious appeals included the greed–game-show element of the valuation, and the information/entertainment/nostalgia appeal of the jewellery, furniture and china. Both large and tiny objects were beautifully presented; there were strong elements of human warmth and pleasure – the spectacle of people discovering the cash value of their objects; it was also a people show, involving the interaction of proud owners and experts. The antiques experts (mainly imported from London) introduced an element of the wider worlds of wealth and art; some of these experts also added a generous helping of British eccentricity.

Despite their unique, and unrepeatable, formulae, these much-loved programmes have several common elements. All have managed to establish some kind of special relationship with a large audience. They involve the participation of ordinary people. Some programmes recruit their studio participants by 'trailing' future topics. Some mixed programmes receive many thousands of letters per year. *The Antiques Roadshow* and *Songs of Praise* involve several hundred members of the public in each show. These programmes often publish magazines or books and mail factsheets on request. Given the sequence of separate items each week, the producers are well able to gauge (from the continuous audience data) precisely which ingredients are, and are not, popular; producers of these programmes invariably take an above-average interest in research findings. They see research as an additional resource – on top of letters, personal interaction and rapport – to fine-tune the successful mix.

Behind the polished product, there typically lies a demanding and highly disciplined production system. Producers of travel and holiday programmes are used to being congratulated on their idyllic work-life, but the reality is of numerous rigorously timed, brief visits; after a very-early-morning start and a long filming day, the team may take an evening flight to a new location before repeating the same routine next day. After the flight home, there are additional hectic days of film-editing before transmission. In order to achieve topicality, travel producers operate on current-affairs work-cycles with late completion times.

Mixed programmes can be, and are, transmitted at almost any time in the schedule. They do not get favoured peak-time scheduling like news, current affairs and documentary; nor do they receive the typical weekend and mid-week evening scheduling of sport. The majority of mixed-goal factual programmes are, indeed, scheduled in the evening on BBC2 and Channel Four, where they achieve goodish audiences by the standards of those channels.

The most successful programmes have their success confirmed by being awarded favourable scheduling, such as before or after one of the super-popular weekday soaps, or early on a weekend evening. Some of these successful programmes have long annual runs, such as 30 or 35 programmes; in other cases the producer resists additional programmes on grounds of production complexity and the need to maintain quality. But the favourable time-slot, the generous number of programmes per year, and the implied prestige typically are matched by a budget that allows the producer to retain the same production team right through the year.

The successful and established mixed-goal and mixed-genre programme has the reputation of being a good place to work and also a good place to have worked. The producer typically leads a strong and experienced production team; when members of the team leave for promotion elsewhere, their places are taken by strong fresh talent. For a number of years success brings helpful scheduling, adequate budgets and celebrity presenters. To the producer who hath are given additional advantages.

Eventually, it seems, the fine-tuning becomes less active. The current producer is now inclined to say that his or her task is to preserve and defend the winning mix. Producers on some successful programmes have extremely firm views as to what constitutes suitable material. In some cases a programme philosophy, almost an ideology, grows from a production system that may originally have arisen accidentally; the programme ('We are more than just a programme') becomes an ambassador for the BBC and a bulwark of the British way of (eccentric) life. *That's Life*, for example, established its own Aftercare Unit intended to put thousands of its

letter-writers in touch with social services; the same programme
also established a Childline service for sexually abused children.
All this bolsters the successful programme's uniqueness, but may
also contribute to its ultimate demise after perhaps two decades.
By the early 1990s most of these established mixed programmes
were being described as dinosaurs from the 1970s. Relatively few
big successes were appearing among the newer mixed-goal programmes. One such success was *The Clothes Show* launched by BBC
Birmingham in 1986 as a run of 10 daytime programmes (on
Monday at 2 p.m.). It had multiple appeals: it carried expertise and
information on fashion; but it also focused on sensible clothes for
ordinary men and women. It established special rapport both with
the London fashion world and its own audience across Britain. It had
an unusually adventurous production team. It developed a distinctive visual style, as so often, partly by accident; because of its
frenetic production style and the common problem of presenters
being unavailable on certain days of the week, the programme in
some cases used, not human-voice commentary, but on-screen
graphics to explain film stories; the empty sound-track was then
filled with music. This was one ingredient in what quickly became a
distinctive – and heavily copied – creative mix. The number of
programmes per year rose frm 17 to 36.

The Clothes Show was an exception. Literally hundreds of other
factual mixed-genre programmes did not have such quick success;
were not pulled out of Monday 2 p.m. into a BBC1 Sunday 5 p.m.
slot; did not get awarded additional programmes and budgets; did not
launch successful magazines; and did not become a cult, copied by
others.

THE UNCLEAR MIX OF GOALS AND GENRES

Journalism is the predominant career background for the producers
of mixed and miscellaneous television. When these mixed areas
expanded in the early 1980s, Channel Four's commissioning editors,
like departmental heads in the BBC and ITV, mainly chose people
with journalism backgrounds to run the new programmes. One-half
of these producers had started in provincial newspapers or local
radio and three-quarters had worked in journalism, including radio
and TV news and current affairs.

Most of these producers' careers conform to either an elite, fast-
track, pattern or a contrasting non-elite, slow-track, pattern. The fast-

track pattern involves university and direct entry into national television, before the age of 25. The slow-track pattern involves the producer having worked up through one or more of provincial newspapers, radio, and regional television; producers on the slow track had typically arrived on the national TV-programme production-ladder after the age of 30.

Two-thirds of these mixed producers are university graduates (a sizeable minority of these from Oxford and Cambridge). They now find themselves steering across the choppy waters of mixed-goal and mixed-genre programming. Precisely where they are going to is unclear. Where they are coming from is easier to specify; as an overall group, they come from current affairs and journalism.

British television does not give these producers specific targets. They are not only unclear as to what goal-mix they are expected to pursue, but also uncertain as to the criteria by which success could be measured. When asked about goals they give a wide variety of answers, such as maintaining or increasing the ratings, 'sharpening the focus', 'getting a bigger audience than the previous producer', 'giving it a harder-edged approach' and so on. Some producers point out why a specific target audience-number is unrealistic – the vagaries of competing programmes in the same time-slot, and so on. Some producers say bluntly that 'the BBC doesn't work that way', or 'like other ITV companies, they wanted to keep the studio busy in the daytime'.

From their previous experience, producers know roughly what is likely to be expected of a particular programme. In discussions and negotiations with senior producers, or the commissioning editor, the series producer also becomes aware of various guidelines: for example, the project is to be more of a news-and-quick-reaction programme when compared with the department's other, more documentary, offering in the same field. The producer acquires a budget and may inherit some members of his production team; at some stage a time-slot in the schedule is allocated. Although these decisions narrow the possible range of choice, much leeway still remains.

Vagueness and uncertainty were greatest in the case of a producer taking on an entirely new series. Often the final commissioning decision on the new series had been left very late; here the highest priority was to get a batch of reasonable-quality programmes completed on time, rather than sticking precisely to previously agreed programme details. The new series had often been defined in terms of an existing programme; but the normal goal was to differ from the existing programme in some very broad way, such as going for a younger, a more up-market or a more specialized audience. A 100 per cent concentration on aggressive competition does not match the mixed-goal approach. Other differences between the planned new programme and the existing programme might be expressed in genre (and cost) terms: more or less hard news, more or less foreign filmed reports, sharper consumerist advocacy or a softer, more industry-friendly, approach. Thus even this competitive relationship to one specific existing programme was usually in terms of very loosely described differences. Competition was unlikely to be described in terms of audience-share or cost per audience; competition was normally expressed in terms of difference from the existing programme (they are doing this, so we will do the opposite). The predominant mode for new programmes involved aiming for a new market-niche or seeking a market-niche previously ignored. In the case of gardening programmes, for instance, the BBC in the early 1990s had programmes like *Gardeners' World* (which included famous gardens and their owners), *The Chelsea Flower Show* and the *Victorian Kitchen Garden*. Channel Four clearly analysed such BBC programmes as up-market and nostalgic, so it focused on modest people with unusual gardens (*Garden Club*) and launched a programme for young home-makers with no gardening experience (*Dig*).

The new series, after its first run of perhaps 6 or 13 programmes, probably would indeed have succeeded in differing from the established programme; the discussion would now focus on how successfully it had differed. Since no sharp goals had been laid down, it would be far from self-evident whether the new series had achieved success or not. The audience-figures might be looked at. If the new series was on BBC2 or Channel Four, it might have attracted an average audience of, say, 1 million – compared with 4 million for the BBC1 or ITV programme from which it was intended to differ. Did this performance constitute success or hold out promise of achieving success in the future? The series producer and his superiors would all know that this was yet another ambiguous case. The producer might point to certain aspects of the research: perhaps the Appreciation Index numbers were good and the audience-figures had risen slightly towards the end of the run, thus promising an audience increase. Others could point to more negative aspects: all would know that at this audience level – around 2 per cent of British adults – the accuracy of the Broadcasters' Audience Research Board ratings is limited. Consequently, discussion about the prospects for a new run would probably focus on what changes and fine-tuning to adopt – employing one new director for more programming, dropping one of the two presenters, altering the studio set, 'sharpening the focus', changing the music, clarifying the use of graphics or strengthening the writing. After inconclusive discussions along these lines, the programme might be given a second run or another 6 or another 13 programmes. After this second run, the programme would not be re-commissioned; another new programme would be dead. There would probably not be any additional research or any attempt at a post-mortem analysis of what went wrong. More probably, all concerned would turn their attention towards developing yet another new programme for next season; indeed, they would probably already have several such ideas sitting on the shelf waiting for this moment.

A different, but common, situation finds a producer put in charge of an existing series which has already completed several seasons. Often the producer has already worked within the department or has even worked on this particular programme – perhaps as a researcher or producer-director – in the past. With an existing series preliminary discussions will focus on the general nature of any desirable changes or fine-tuning. Often the new producer will just be asked to get on with it. Typically, at least some members of the production team will be in place; but the new producer may need to fill a few empty jobs. If the previous run was only say 13 programmes, most or all of the team may have left, giving the producer the opportunity to hire people that he or she knows and trusts. Often there are one or two key people whom in practice the producer must accept – perhaps a celebrity presenter admired by the channel controller and an older stalwart producer-director. Producers tend to describe their problems in taking over a mixed-goal series mainly in terms of constraints on budget and team size.

Series producers tend to assume that with mixed-goal programmes the goals and genres are not only mixed, but likely to continue in a state of flux. While this has obvious disadvantages of vagueness, uncertainty and insecurity, it also potentially has major advantages for the producer: it gives freedom to manoeuvre.

Mixed-goal programming appears on British television at almost any time in the 24 hours. Some of these programmes are scheduled in early or mid-evening and are also repeated at a less-favourable time, such as mid-morning or midnight. The evening audience will be several times that of the off-peak time. Producers also discuss at some length the competing programming. Quite a lot of mixed-goal programming is scheduled in the high-audience times between 6 and 11 p.m., but here it also has to compete with the most popular of all programming. Broadly, these mixed-goal programmes have weak audience-appeal compared with the most popular shows. Mixed-goal producers want to compete against prestige (but less-popular) prime-time programming.

The producer is aware that all producers, and all department heads, want to be in high-audience time-slots and scheduled against weak opposition. Scheduling closer to mid-evening is an indicator of organizational recognition and industry prestige. The producer will look to two other indicators: does the budget per programme rise and does the number of programmes per year rise? If all these indicators move in a favourable direction, the immediate message is one of success.

Another assumption of the mixed-goal producer is that it is still possible to be too popular. Mixed-goal programmes are expected not to switch towards popularity and ratings as the sole goal. This was especially noticeable in Channel Four with its general doctrine that programmes should terminate after a few years. ITV was perhaps an exception. On both BBC channels there were mixed-goal programmes with high ratings whose producers thought them in danger of being axed, despite their popularity. The producer of one programme with the largest audience in its sub-field was quite anxious about renewal for another season: he was convinced that both his immediate boss and the channel controller saw the programme as too popular and too exclusively concerned with ratings.

Inevitably, mixed-goal producers seek to change their programmes, and in practice subtly to alter the precise mix of goals. Over several annual runs of the series, these small changes can add up to a major change of direction. Some producers focus on popularity, become absorbed in audience research, commission new research on presenters and content, and refine the mix in the direction of improving the ratings. Other producers deliberately refine the mix in line with quite different career-goals. One producer, whose past career and future ambitions lay in current affairs, said that while he continued to make multi-item programmes and to carry some very popular items, he also wanted to include

> the kind of journalism that would not look out of place in *Panorama* or *World in Action*; I try to include in each series four or five stories of 18 or 20 minutes each.

Some producers seek to send a message to baronial executives at the top of the system. This also involves the usual practice of trying to secure press attention; these producers make the usual observation that much press coverage of television goes to documentary and current affairs. Thus a mixed producer will be proud of even a few press pieces on the recent series run. Some mixed producers exert considerable efforts to achieve press coverage. A producer who had recruited some press journalists (without TV experience) into his production team said that one reason was to use the journalists' personal contacts in order to achieve newspaper coverage for the programmes.

INNOVATION AS 'YOUTH' PROGRAMMING

Given that the major factual areas such as documentary and news have their established traditions and lengthy history, it is hardly surprising that the British TV industry tends to look towards mixed factual areas for programming innovations. Here we consider the example of 'youth' programming in general and the particular case of *Network 7*, a 'youth' programme produced by London Weekend Television (LWT) for Channel Four in 1987–9.

Network 7 represented both an advance and a retreat. It was an advance in programming not only aimed at, but produced by, young adults. It also pioneered new ways of organizing a production team – a mixture of exciting youth opportunity and the exploitation of youth at the height of the Thatcher–Lawson boom. *Network 7* mixed current affairs with current popular music and other entertainment; it put green-haired 24-year-olds on to national television. It was also, in 1987, in the forefront of casualizing programme production work at LWT and encouraging independent production competition.

The rise of youth programming is associated with the decline of original children's programming, which had long been part of the public-service project. The main forerunner of *Network 7* was *The Tube*, a youth/music show produced by Tyne Tees Television and transmitted by Channel Four during its first five years (1982–7). *Network 7* was described by Jeremy Isaacs, chief executive of Channel Four, as

> a post-modern pioneer of youth journalism, all fast, flash graphics and shortening attention spans. I thought it rather fine, live from its studio base of a disused warehouse on Canary Wharf.[3]

Network 7 attracted enormous press attention as the latest example of youthful fashion and style. The style drew heavily not only on *The Clothes Show* (which began one year earlier on BBC) but on American music-videos and films, and on British TV commercials. *Network 7* only ran for two seasons. One of its producers, Janet Street-Porter, left LWT and *Network 7* as early as January 1988 for the BBC, where she started up a sizeable youth programming empire.

Network 7 derived from the change-over in incumbents in the 'Commissioning Editor, Youth Programmes' job at Channel Four. The first such commissioning editor had been the patron of *The Tube* during his and its five-year span. It was a former researcher from *The Tube*, John Cummins, who became Channel Four's second Youth Commissioning Editor and was persuaded to hand over more than half of his youth programmes budget to LWT, *Network 7* and an independent production company. Another change in the youth commissioning editor role found the third incumbent, Stephen Garrett, cancelling *Network 7* and spreading his budget around a wider range of programmes; *The Word* was his youth flagship but he retained money for a wider range of programming from the very cheap (*Remote Control* and *Star Test*) to expensive drama (*Teenage Health Freak*). A fourth commissioning editor for youth at Channel Four, Bill Hilary, was appointed in 1992.

Network 7 drew upon several strands of London life and television. One of its LWT creators, Jane Hewland, had been a leader in LWT programmes aimed at blacks and Asians; another creator, Janet Street-Porter, had been involved in numerous LWT regional arts (*South of Watford*) and regional current-affairs programmes. *Network 7* featured many short items which could most easily be based on the London music scene and other London youth happenings. As for any London-based programme, it was far cheaper to focus on London than to send film-crews around other British cities.

Probably more genuine innovations (for British television) were some of the production team's working practices in *Network 7*. The programme depended on rapid pace and short items. It claimed to be current affairs for young people who would not view conventional current affairs. The producers had difficulty in recruiting presenters to front their compilation of numerous short items. This led Hewland and Street-Porter to convert their researchers into reporters who presented their own short stories on screen. This arrangement saved money, increased producer control, and put enormous pressure on some very inexperienced people in their early twenties. *Network 7* worked its young production staff hard. Several said that they had been exploited, but also received an accelerated training – 'three years' worth of production experience in six months'.

Those who had worked on *Network 7* in 1987–9 were two years later to be found in the BBC and in their own independent production companies; some of these and other youth producers were already in charge of continuing series and still in their late twenties. Youth programming had thus provided an additional fast career-track. These young producers also tended to describe themselves as 'workaholics':

The real down-side is that you have to give your life to it; we work full-time and don't know what weekends are.

The *Network 7* team worked extremely long hours because there were many stories to cover and hours to fill. There were a lot of young Indians all chasing after stories and experience, presided over by three Chiefs (Hewland, Street-Porter and Keith Macmillan). Many older producers (at LWT and later at the BBC) undoubtedly regarded these youth programme personnel as gimmicky, inexperienced and lightweight.

The *Network 7* producers seem to have developed a programme ideology which sprang from the production circumstances, rather than vice versa. The programme orthodoxy stressed that it was researchers who knew the facts, and who should thus operate as researcher-reporters presenting the facts to camera; since they were researcher-reporters, speaking their own words, no autocues were allowed – the young researcher-reporters would establish their expertise by talking (not reading) to camera.

Network 7 came from LWT whose (John Birt's) house orthodoxy stressed the centrality of the written-down word, before, during and after filming. *Network 7* preached the exact opposite of the Birt orthodoxy that current affairs should be long and serious. However, John Birt had himself been an advocate of alternative styles in non-flagship minority (ethnic and other) programming. Moreover, the *Network 7* producers, despite their flashy clothes and emphasis on the visual, conformed to other LWT orthodoxies. The junior programme staff were taught the key importance of budgets and money; *Network 7* practice did require a written account of what was to be filmed; and another early orthodoxy of youth programming concerned the law – the importance of involving the lawyers at an early stage of any legally delicate topic.

Several of the young producers and presenters were women.

Andrea Wonfor was already the director of programmes at Tyne Tees during the reign of *The Tube* (1982–7) and she went on to one of the top jobs at Channel Four; Jane Hewland was an experienced producer before *Network 7* began, and became a top programming executive at LWT, before going independent. Janet Street-Porter moved across to the BBC.

The youth-programme movement by 1992 was to be found mainly in the BBC and in independent production companies. The definition of youth now seemed to have extended from children to teenage, to young adult, to simply 'young at heart'. A key problem was that young adults actually prefer much the same programmes as everyone else. Some 'youth' programming was more effective at repelling older age-groups than in attracting young adults.

Some producers claimed that youth programming was more importantly a chance to innovate, to engage in research and development, to explore the potential of the medium, and to combine new forms of video-graphics with old formats like the rock-music show and current affairs. From 1988 onwards the BBC became the main focus for, and home of, youth programming. Within the BBC the new entity, set up by Janet Street-Porter, steadily expanded: it still produced youth programmes such as *Reportage* and the *Rough Guides*, but it also purchased foreign programmes; and it introduced new programmes across virtually the entire programme range, except comedy. Youth was no longer the hot exciting new type of mixed-goal factual programming; youth programming was now established as one such category within the many possible categories of factual programming.

VOLATILITY, AUTONOMY AND INSECURITY

Compared with other factual producers, those in the mixed-goal fields were both more autonomous and more insecure. The workaholic habits developed by the producers of youth programming were generally present across these mixed-goal fields. A young series producer says:

> You get to know the meaning of the word 'pressure' . . . It lives with you, it's always there . . . in the office with ten people who need to talk to you, each one wanting advice on an important decision; you're working 12 to 14 hours a day – I haven't had a day off for seven weeks – and I don't thrive on pressure, I hate it.

An older producer who was in charge of 26 multi-item hours per year, plus additional programmes, was clearly anxious about the goals and genre-mix of his programme; he was unhappy with the scheduling and the attitude of his executive producer. In addition to running a complex programme on a modest budget, he was himself directing a number of films and described this as 'leading from the front'. He was keeping his producer-director credentials up to date in case he was removed from producing the programme, which indeed happened soon after our interview.

Compared with more securely anchored programme formats, these mixed programmes are volatile along several dimensions. There is volatility as to the goal-mix – the combination of popularity and prestige, or the precise edinfotainment combination; there is volatility and uncertainty as to the genre-mix – the combination of, say, pop music and current affairs, or of consumer information and consumer fantasy; linked to these, there is volatility in the membership of the production team. Presiding over these several kinds of volatility there is the series editor. This producer in charge of such a series is asked to be the juggler-in-chief, handling the multiple uncertainties, the multiple odd combinations, the common mismatches of programme resources and goals with the facts of scheduling and audience.

BBC2 especially has a number of well-established mixed-genre programmes. Over one hundred such series run each year on the four conventional channels; most of these series have very limited life-expectations. There is a massive turnover of new programmes and a massive churning also in the programme production teams. This obviously makes for production-team insecurity. These producers say that, when staffing a new programme or filling gaps in an existing team, they typically look at hundreds of applications, but usually end up choosing people with whom they have worked previously. With so much uncertainty and so much volatility, producers prefer to rely on associates whose performance and personalities are known quantities. In this way the producer becomes a juggler not just of goals, genres and budgets, but with individuals' work and career prospects. Producers also largely determine what most individual team-members are paid.

Some types of mixed programming are so constructed as to open a very wide range of possibilities. 'Youth' programming can cover almost any subject-area in almost any style, so long as it appeals to the 'young at heart'. Adult- or continuing-education programming can cover anything from gardening and cooking to heavy industry and running a business so long as it has an educational/informative flavour. Ethnic and minority programming also has many possibilities. The same is true of daytime programming; daytime producers offer a deliberate mix of enlightenment and entertainment. One daytime producer said that during a week he could cover South African politics and the crisis in Russia, as well as baldness, abortion and nursery education. These producers claim that viewers welcome an element of seriousness which can relieve the guilt of daytime viewing.

Producers in the wide-ranging factual-programming units see themselves as mixing current affairs with entertainment, or spicing public affairs with individual cases, studio debates and audience participation. Some claim that they work amicably with current-affairs colleagues; others say that current-affairs producers resent the fact that youth or daytime or adult education programming is presenting social and political issues in more effective and audience-friendly ways. Whether mixed-goal programming competes with, or complements, current affairs, the wide freedom of the mixed-goal producers in subject-choice is unambiguously put on display.

Often at the launch of a new programme there is much departmental discussion as to the programme's content. One producer described this as 'not so much a programme brief, more just a hotchpotch of suggestions, possible names and promising themes'. The one specific requirement to emerge from this departmental 'culture of consensus' was that the new programme should do no worse than its immediate predecessor of last year:

> My boss kept saying 'make sure we do as well as that', but funnily enough, once we got going, nobody mentioned it again, because our programme took on an identity of its own; now we've been re-commissioned for a second run and nobody particularly did it on the basis of finding out whether our ratings were better or worse than the previous programme.

As its production team assembles, the mixed-goal programme may well be seen to have an unusually steep hierarchy within the team. The attempt to stretch a lowish budget across a demanding production plan may have led to an inexperienced production team. Mixed-goal programmes, because they involve factual material and use the multi-item magazine format, are heavily dependent on research; the team personnel will be weighted with young and inexperienced researchers who are hoping to advance to reporting or directing. For subject expertise the mixed-goal programme may depend on print journalists, including editors of trade publications. Such heavyweight outside experts often, however, are only available to the programme on a consultancy basis (perhaps mainly on the telephone). The producer may recruit one or two celebrity presenters, who fit the programme in between other obligations on certain days of the week. Often the producer must rely heavily on two or three fully experienced people: perhaps a unit manager who runs the finances, and one older 'retired' producer now working as a jobbing producer-director. In such common circumstances as these, the series producer is at the top end of a steep hierarchy, carrying what he or she sees as an excess of power and responsibility.

In addition to this present series, the senior producer may well be planning or producing several other one-off or special programmes. The exceptional volatility of these mixed-programming areas drives departmental heads and independent company managers to develop new projects with which to entice commissioning barons and channel controllers. Sometimes these special offerings are quite separate from the series, including programmes which are being produced on a speculative basis. In other cases, the series producer is required by the executive producer to hand over some of his budget for such special new projects; another variation finds the series producer required to make, say, three programmes to a higher production standard, involving more filming and a bigger share of the total series budget, which may then be offered up the system as a separate mini-series, and which – if rejected for this purpose – can be re-integrated back into the continuing series.

As mixed producers talk about such latter tactical moves – and the resulting difficulties such as yet more work on less budget – they also complain about the indecisions and whims (as they see it) of the channel controllers. From these mixed producers' viewpoint the channel commissioning hierarchy appears to have a short attention span. Occasionally, directions and fresh guidelines come down from on high; but mostly the mixed producer operates with little direction from above.

Asked about the best and worst aspects of their work, these mixed-goal producers express unusually strong emotions in both directions. They relish the 'amazing' and 'extraordinary' freedom, which means 'I can do almost anything'; but both 30-year-old and 50-year-old mixed producers also lead over-worked lives of quiet desperation, fearing that their current series may be their last.

Part II

Fiction and entertainment

Introduction

Two non-factual categories of programming account for the great bulk of the Top Forty rated programmes each week on British television.

Table 6.1 Weekly Top 40 rated programmes, 1991 (%)

Type	Channel BBC1 and 2	ITV	TOTAL
Drama/fiction	21.3	35.0	56.3
Light entertainment	11.2	16.6	27.8
SUBTOTAL	32.5	51.6	84.1
Factual	8.6	7.3	15.9
TOTAL	41.1	58.9	100
Number			2,080

Source: William Phillips (1992) 'Look who's gawking: TV since 1990', Admap, June, pp.11–15.

Table 6.1 shows that 84 per cent of these most highly viewed programmes in 1991 belonged to either drama/fiction (from soaps to movies) or light entertainment (which includes comedy, quiz/game shows and 'people' shows).

The enormous popularity of drama/fiction is also clear from Table 6.2. 'Soap episodes' (mainly British, but also Australian) are much the most popular category. Soaps, fictional series and situation comedies account for 59.4% of weekly Top 40 programmes. Some of the very popular news bulletins were helped to these high positions by being scheduled adjacent to super-popular entertainment. Game shows account for twice as many popular programmes as films and

Table 6.2 Selected programme categories in weekly Top 40 ratings,
1991 (%)

Genre	BBC1/2	ITV	TOTAL
Soap episodes	17.0	18.6	35.6
Series episodes	2.2	10.9	13.0
Situation comedy	7.0	3.8	10.8
News bulletins	5.2	4.6	9.9
Game shows	2.0	7.7	9.7
'Other factual'	2.9	2.1	5.0
Films, TV movies	1.9	2.5	4.4
Sport	0.5	0.6	1.1

Source: William Phillips (1992) 'Look who's gawking: TV since 1990', *Admap*,
June, pp.11–15.

TV movies; this latter is the only category in which Hollywood
imports constitute a large fraction of the total category.

Given that ITV is the conventional channel which most seeks high
audiences, it is not surprising to see again (Table 6.3) that ITV
carries more fiction and entertainment than do the other three
channels.

Fictional and entertainment programming is also, on average,
much more expensive to make. In particular, drama, but also
comedy, is expensive to make because it requires expensive talent,
large casts of performers, large numbers of technical specialists, and

Table 6.3 Non-factual programming hours, 1991 (%)

Type	BBC1	BBC2	ITV	Channel Four
Drama, series, films	25	24	35.5	26
Entertainment including comedy and game shows	10	4	17.6	14.5
Children's	13	3	7.3	8.8
Total Non-Factual	48	31	60.4	49.3
Factual and continuity	52	69	39.6	50.7
TOTAL	100	100	100	100

Source: BBC and ITC.

heavy expenditure on design, sets and outside filming. The data in Table 1.2 show that if the average cost per hour of all BBC programmes is rated as 100, then drama averages 534 and light entertainment averages 179; but acquired programmes (mainly acquired from Hollywood and Australia), at 42, cost less than half the overall programme average.

IMPORTS AND BRITISH VIRTUE

The latter figures pose an acute dilemma for British television. Hollywood and Australian drama/fiction can be imported for under 10 per cent of the cost per hour of British-made drama/fiction. As in other European countries, the home-made products are significantly more popular overall than the imports, but not ten times as popular.

This is a dilemma that pre-dates television. During John Reith's 1922–38 rule at the BBC, entertainment was regarded as a highly delicate and sensitive area. BBC radio was dominated by various kinds of serious and popular music: in 1937 three entertainment categories (variety and vaudeville, revue and musical comedy, and light drama) together accounted for only 7.3 per cent of total BBC radio output.[1]

Entertainment was held back for several reasons apart from the initial definition of radio as primarily a music medium. One reason was that British popular music and entertainment was seen as too vulgar, too 'adult' and too working-class. Popular radio entertainment was also seen as associated with Hollywood entertainment and advertising-supported radio as provided by Radio Luxembourg and other commercial radio stations in France.

During the 1939–45 war the BBC, under new leadership, relaxed some of its inhibitions against entertainment. The same kind of moral disapproval, however, operated during and after the 1955 introduction of advertising-financed television to Britain. ITV, especially in its early years, was vulgar, did appeal directly to working-class taste, and did rely heavily on imports. ITV imported US crime series, westerns and situation comedies, as well as acquiring the British rights to many US game shows; it also showed plenty of Hollywood feature films.

ITV's regulators, especially from 1962 to 1992, confined it to quotas of such morally suspect types of programming as US-imported series and British-made game shows. The BBC operated its own similar, but slightly more serious, rules. The Broadcasting Act of 1990 relaxed some of these rules, but still keeps some of them in place and still sees the news and other factual programmes as the core of the schedule. Around 1990 the British broadcasting establishment's moral disapproval of unregulated entertainment had not disappeared; indeed, it was reinforced by the presence of satellite television in general and Rupert Murdoch's Sky television channels in particular. The same old reasons for suspicion were again present: much of the Sky programming was of US series or US-format game shows; most of it appealed aggressively to British working-class tastes; and some of it broke previous barriers such as the prohibition against 'adult' material before 9 p.m.

British TV regulators, legislators and channel controllers have long had a kind of Gresham's Law of Entertainment as one of their main anxieties – a fear that bad entertainment will drive out good. 'Good' has tended to be equated with British-made, a formulation to which the trade unions for many years gave their muscular support. If British is best, however, British is certainly also more expensive. Thus better moral value, higher cost, better artistic value and better industrial value have coalesced together; cheapness has tended to be equated with lesser virtue.

Consequently, a fog of moral values hangs over the fiction and entertainment areas. Across the various genres, the quiz/game show has a lowly position because it is seen as a US formula and cheap in most respects. 'People' shows, such as chat shows and people/surprise shows, are also seen as cheap imported formulae. On the other hand, both drama/fiction and comedy are seen as occupying higher positions on several moral dimensions. British TV dramas are seen as truly British, as artistically superior, as dealing in non-factual forms with real issues and real concerns; British drama and comedy series are both expensive and prestigious.

This moral hierarchy, which operates between genres, also operates within each genre. There is a more-deserving (and more-expensive) and less-deserving (and cheap) dimension within each field. Within drama/fiction the multi-episode soap ranks bottom and single plays or TV films rank top in both prestige and cost. Similar rankings are recognized between better and worse comedy; between more demanding or difficult or simple and cheaper game shows. There is also a hierarchy between the top chat show and the lower depth of chat shows.

PRODUCTION SYSTEMS, PRODUCERS AND OTHERS

These fiction and entertainment genres of programming have gone further, than has British factual programming, towards the publisher model. Television fiction programming has long been more free-lance than most British television; and much drama is contracted out to either a freelance producer or an independent production company. The picture is more varied in the other genres.

Each of these genres has its own variants of the standard TV division of labour. The producer's own job-definition and tasks vary between genres. In studio-based game shows, for example, the studio director controls the multiple in-studio cameras and camera-operators. But in comedy there is quite a long tradition of the producer-director. In drama the separation between the producer and director roles is sharpest; since drama involves a lot of money, people and logistics, the task of directing the actors and filming the scenes keeps a director extremely busy; in a single drama the director may dominate. Most drama is, however, in series and here a single series producer usually employs several directors.

British television tends to honour the sole writer, or the comedy writing partnership, and allows the writer's creative instinct to play a very big part in the comedy enterprise. Writers are clearly also crucial in drama; but the number of writers varies greatly with the number of episodes, although soaps are the only British entertain-ment area fully to have accepted the large team of writers.

Research, more than writing, is of central importance to both game shows and people shows. This 'research' differs from that found in, say, current affairs. These entertainment researchers are looking for contestants and participants and for questions. Larger shows employ sizeable teams of such researchers.

The more expensive forms of drama, comedy and studio entertain-ment are expensive mainly because of the large technical crews, the design and related specialists and the acting and other talent. In some cases there is a dominant star and the producer and the star may effectively control the show between them.

More common, however, is the show that is led by its script. This is true of most drama and comedy. In this case the script-editor part of the producer's role is crucial.

Chapter 6

Drama/fiction

Fiction is the most expensive type of British-made programming; it is also the most glamorous in show-business terms. British-made TV fiction also stakes artistic claims in terms of quality writing, acting and production.

The various terms used to describe British TV fiction reflect national circumstances. The traditional term is 'drama', because the early TV drama of 1936–9 consisted mainly of stage-plays transported to the studio. The terms 'play' or 'single play' have traditionally also been used to distinguish one-offs from series. The term 'film' has been used recently both to indicate the use of film (not videotape) and location (not studio) filming; 'film' also reflects the pious hope that somehow TV films could fill the empty space where the British movie industry once was.

Television fiction may be a low-budget form of feature-film making; but it is an expensive form of television for two reasons. First, TV fiction/drama is expensive anyway because it uses so many people over such long spans of time. Second, much TV fiction/drama deliberately seeks high 'production values' because it is competing head-on – in the same language – with imports of both Hollywood movies and TV series.

British TV drama seeks to score higher ratings than imported US series and films; it seeks to be more entertaining, by appealing more directly to the emotions of the domestic British audience. It also seeks to achieve higher artistic levels, to be of higher quality. It is these combined goals of entertainment and quality that are so demanding and so expensive. This may be achieved by a more lavish use of resources than equivalent types of output achieved in Hollywood. Where an outdoor-location-made Hollywood action 1-hour

series episode would film for seven days, the British equivalent
might film for eleven days.

Drama accounts for 39 per cent of all location 'filming' (and
taping) in the BBC; this is lavish indeed, since drama only accounts
for 4 per cent of TV hours produced by the BBC. Drama is also much
the biggest user of the BBC's 'design and scenic' services (45 per
cent of the total). *GBH*, a 10-hour drama series which cost Channel
Four six million pounds in 1991, involved 125 speaking parts and in
total employed nearly 200 people. If one includes technical teams
and the acting team, the typical drama producer employs around 100
people at the height of the production sequence. 'On location'
usually means shuttling between several different locations, and the
full production team on the road between these locations is a caravan
of 30 or 40 vehicles, including vehicles devoted to camera, to props
and to catering. Car parking and traffic are often major problems.

LOW HOURS AND OTHER CONSEQUENCES OF
HIGH-COST DRAMA

British TV drama operates on a basis of fairly high costs and a
relatively small annual volume of output. Of the over-500 hours of
TV each week on the four main national channels only some 20
hours per week is British-made drama – less than 1 hour per channel,
per evening. Those 20 hours per week include many early-evening
soap-operas such as *Coronation Street* and *Eastenders*.

None even of these soaps, in fact, fills more than 90 minutes of
television per week. British drama mainly takes the short-series
form. This is true of 'serials' – short series of perhaps 6 or 8 hours
with a continuing story often based on a novel. It is also true,
however, of 'series' that continue from one year to the next; few
British drama series make more than 15 hours per year, and some
successful series produce much less – say, 25 hours spread over
three years. This prevalent short-series approach is justified with
several linked arguments. The more carefully made, it is said, the
greater will be the entertainment impact; long preparation and
generous filming will protect quality. Drama is normally scheduled
at desirable times such as 9 p.m. or 9.30 p.m. and obviously such
high-audience time-slots are in short supply.

British TV drama places enormous stress on the writing; and some
writers are better known in the industry, and more celebrated in the
heavier newspapers, than are their actors. This conception of the

writer derives from the live-theatre tradition. It is widely agreed that the producer's most crucial function is to find good writers and to work with writers on developing and sustaining projects:

> Without a good script, there's no film; if you go ahead with a weak script, you're always propping it up.

Along with the creativity of the writer, and the low total output of non-soap drama, goes a pattern of lengthy preparation of the scripts.

However, it is not only the producers, directors and writers, but also the actors, who favour a mini-series pattern of relatively few hours of output per year. A British actor or actress will often in a single year work in television, in the live theatre and appear in commercials. Leading actors may alternate between London live theatre, or feature films, and parts in TV plays, either one-offs or short serials. Celebrity actors often make additional stipulations to fit in with other obligations, such as insisting on certain specific weeks for filming or not being available for subsequent publicity appearances.

With a few exceptions (such as Scottish Television) the bulk of TV series and serials are based in London, including those made by non-London ITV companies. Most of the historic roots of British TV drama are in London: the theatre, BBC radio, and the British film industry. Most of the actors and technicians live in London; this means that many series and serials can film on the streets of London without the massive hotel and related travel costs of much location filming. One consequence is that certain suburban areas within a few miles of the BBC's TV headquarters in west London are heavily used by film-crews. The connection with the London theatre fits with the rhythms of television in other ways. For example, outdoor filming is concentrated in the months between March and October when it is usually possible to film without the additional expense of artificial lighting. This also happens to fit well with the propensity of stage-plays to aim for pre-Christmas openings. Both light and theatre fit with the tendency to schedule new drama series (the March starters) in the autumn, with a second wave in the New Year (which perhaps filmed from June to October).

FORMATS, PRODUCTION SYSTEMS, PRESTIGE

Television drama in the 1950s was transmitted live and it was common practice to transfer a live stage-play to the live TV studio in front of multiple studio cameras. Although some of the older producers we talked to had worked in live TV drama, the majority had acquired all their experience with recorded drama. In the 1960s drama was first rehearsed and then recorded on to videotape using a multi-camera studio; in the early days of videotape, editing was virtually impossible. Today, soap drama uses the same procedure but there is also some editing and tidying-up.

In the 1970s British TV-drama series such as *The Sweeney* (Euston Films) pursued a more authentic style on the London streets. Many other programmes, including comedy dramas, have taken to the streets and the outdoors. A common 1980s practice with a successful comedy, such as *Minder* (Thames Television), was to have, say, 10 days of location filming and 2 days in the studio per each 1-hour episode.

Until the mid-1980s, most British TV drama was made within the BBC or the ITV companies, using a complete in-house 'factory' service of studios, camera-crews, technicians and design people. Into this permanently staffed factory setting came the freelance actors who performed in the particular productions. Along with this troupe of freelance actors came freelance writers; many of the drama directors and some of the producers were also freelance, with one foot in the theatre and/or in films.

This pattern of (strongly unionized) staff technicians and outside freelance artists was established in the 1950s and 1960s when much TV-drama output consisted of 'single plays', one-off dramas often collected into an anthology series with a regular and well-publicized slot in the weekly schedule. In 1969–70 the ITV network alone made 152 single dramas; but series were steadily taking over. In 1979–80 ITV was down to only 50 single dramas a year, and by 1990 ITV was doing no single dramas. In 1992–3 the BBC was still doing about 20 single dramas per year.

By 1990 most ITV drama, and increasingly also BBC drama, was being farmed outside to freelance producers. As the BBC followed the lead of Channel Four and ITV, a freelance-producer pattern became the predominant, but not sole, pattern. This 'freelance producer' might be a partner in an independent production company, or a completely free-floating individual, or a producer sitting inside the BBC (or an ITV company) but employed on a freelance basis.

Increasingly after 1990 the only in-house drama producers still working on a full-time staff basis were heads of drama departments in ITV companies or section heads in BBC drama, plus a few other very senior producers and script editors. Most producers of specific series are either freelances or part of an independent production company. Television drama, which always had a strong element of freelance employment, has largely reverted to the completely free-lance pattern of the commercial theatre. These arrangements, however, as with much else, differ considerably between different drama formats, and in particular do not apply to soap drama.

Table 6.4 indicates how the single drama contrasts with the soap. The single drama is high in prestige, high in cost and usually low in audience. Single drama consequently is something like twenty times as expensive per viewer as the soap. This Table greatly simplifies a highly complex reality and ignores the basic point that scheduling strongly influences audience size; the main purpose of the Table is to show that there are massive differences in cost per audience-hour and that high cost goes with high prestige and low cost with low prestige.

The single drama takes its most prestigious and costly-per-viewer form in Channel Four's 'Films' and BBC's *Screen Two* offering. These single dramas often use established actors and some have cinema runs before appearing on television; other single dramas involve new writers and/or new directors. These single dramas also have an international flavour – including co-production finance – but the overall thrust is toward British authenticity. In the early 1990s the heads of drama at both the BBC (Mark Shivas) and Channel Four (David Aukin) were directly involved in commissioning single dramas.

Most drama serials attract a somewhat higher audience; the serial's typical 3–8 episodes give both the audience and the publicity machines something bigger to get hold of. Like the one-off drama, the short serial gets favourable scheduling; it also gets a budget that allows relatively generous filming, spread over several months. The larger scale allows for some economies, making the serial a more economical choice for prestige drama investment. This form poses major challenges to all the leading participants; the leading actors have massive and exhausting roles; the (usually) lone director faces some six months of high-octane filming, followed by a huge film-editing task.

The third main type is the continuing series, which, if successful, run a number of years. Even so, many successful British continuing series run for a few years and then stop, while still high in the audience ratings. *Upstairs, Downstairs* (London Weekend Tele-vision, LWT) in its 5-year run (1970–5) averaged fifteen 50-minute

Table 6.4 British TV drama: prestige correlates with cost per audience-hour

Format	Audience size	Prestige	Episodes per year	Typical transmission time	Minutes used per day of filming	1992–3 cost per hour (£000)	Cost per audience hour (p)
Soap	Large	Low	104 or 156	Before 8.30 p.m.	15	100–150	1
Continuing series	Large–medium	Medium	6–15	8 p.m. or after	5	300–800	5–10
Serials (short-series)	Medium	High	3–8	9 p.m. or after	3–5	500–700	10–15
Single drama	Small	High	1	9 p.m. or after	3–4	400–800	15–25

episodes per year and then stopped; twenty years later 15 episodes a year was still regarded as a maximum by most producers of continuing series.

The reorganization of ITV in the years around 1990 led to growth in the budgets put into continuing series; increasingly outspending the BBC, ITV in general (and LWT in particular) stressed its dedication to 'quality-popular' drama in continuing-series form. Much of this quality-popular material featured detective stories, but reflected an effort to reduce the Hollywoodesque and violence-on-the-streets overtones of earlier police series. Series such as *Inspector Morse* (Central Television), *The Ruth Rendell Mysteries* (TVS), *Taggart* (Scottish) and *Poirot* (LWT) epitomized the popular-quality-series notion. The ITV network planners, in considering how to attack the BBC's mid-evening schedule, also decided to make some 2-hour episodes for the 8–10-p.m. slot. All these series were made with much love and care and with large budgets. The same was true of *London's Burning* (LWT) which involved exceptionally heavy use of fires and special effects. BBC1 faced many difficulties in competing with these well-made costly series. The BBC's *Casualty* – a hospital story using a permanent set – established new levels of medical authenticity at a lower budget than the ITV high-profile series.

Another development of recent years has been comedy drama. Breaking away from the studio-based 'sit com' (see Chapter 7), the comedy drama runs for 50 minutes and is made on film and on location. *Minder* (starting in 1979) was important in this drama development.

All these trends involve quite modest changes. In Britain the re-sale, repeat, market has been fairly weak and British television has not followed the Hollywood urge to accumulate 100 episodes in order to hit gold in the syndication market. Quite successful British series make perhaps 30 episodes over a 3-year run and then cease production.

Three years has been a common length because the leading actors in a new drama series usually sign a 3-year contract; as they initially sign they are typically in a relatively weak position and pleased to have the work. If after three years the series is modestly successful, the actors (and their agents) are in a much stronger position; they are now better known, probably have other offers and are prepared to flex their muscles by demanding sizeable pay increases. Quite often the BBC or the ITV company sees the prospect of the series costs rising faster than either audience-size or potential prestige would justify. The series is then cancelled.

Experienced series producers have invariably worked on a number of series. One such producer had been the series producer on seventeen separate series including several big successes. Because even successful series may not have very long runs, and because British television releases a flock of new drama series every year, the launching of new series is a major, even the major, task of the drama-series producer. If the series does last beyond three years, a new set of problems present themselves. A key task is to retain the loyalty of any star players and, equally important, the writer or writers. If the format, production system and leading talent are all fairly success-fully in place, the producer – after, say, four years' experience with the series – may be moved, perhaps to launch yet another new series. Meanwhile another producer will be drafted in to continue with the successful series format.

SOAP SERIES

The fourth and final type of drama, the soap, derives its name from US 1930s radio drama. British TV soap differs from US TV's five-times-a-week daytime soap and from the *Dallas* 23-episodes-a-year 'soap' series. British soaps are a compromise between the low episode numbers of most weekly series and the potential 260 episodes-per-year weekday series. British television has established a tradition of soaps which run either two or three times a week, either 104 or 156 episodes a year. One successful ITV soap, *Crossroads*, did for a period have four episodes a week, but the regulators (the Independent Broadcasting Authority) made it return to three times a week in 1979.

British soaps are distinctive also in appearing in early evening, before the 'adult' threshold at 9 p.m. They are thus defined as 'family viewing'. Their extraordinary grip on the audience can be regarded in many ways. Their popularity has probably been increased by the policy of both BBC Governors and ITV/Channel Four regulators that the number of soaps should be restricted.

As Table 6.4 shows, the soap is at the bottom end of the drama-prestige scale; however, because all drama is high-prestige, the soap itself – and perhaps even more the successful soap producer – is well respected in British television overall. Successful soaps, of course, achieve large, or very large, audiences at a remarkably low cost per audience-hour, and at a surprisingly low total cost per year. The successful soap achieves this happy financial result with a specialized production system designed for a continuous through-put of drama.

When the BBC launched its new Spanish-based soap, *Eldorado*, in 1992 there was much press comment on the cost of ten million pounds; but this figure included the capital cost of constructing a set with permanent buildings in the south of Spain and the cost of making the first 156 half-hour episodes. This roughly matched the low £100,000-per-hour figure shown in Table 6.4.

The number of people involved in a soap production is similar to that involved in the other types of drama production – perhaps 120 people. However, these people are employed around the year, and actors typically sign a 2-year contract. Soaps are on the screen 52 weeks per year, and they stop production only for very brief periods, such as one week at Christmas. Consequently, a soap like *Eastenders* which is on the screen for one hour per week has also to make one hour of material each week. The actors are kept extremely busy, day after day and week after week, learning lines, rehearsing, and taping large slabs of material.

The producer is in charge of a streamlined production system, in which scheduling and deadlines require a rigid discipline. The soap producer presides not just over a small production factory, but over a sizeable script-writing team. Soaps obviously have a ravenous appetite for scripts. In 1991–2 the twice-weekly soaps each had about twelve full-time writers, while the thrice-weekly *Coronation Street* had seventeen writers. There is the longer-term function of plots, story-lines and sub-plot strands running through several episodes; soap producers typically have story-line writers who prepare outlines for batches of eight or nine scripts. Then there are other writers who individually write the detailed dialogue and the complete script for one of those previously agreed scripts.

The soap producer has to oversee much else besides the scripts; but the scripts are not only the words the actors will speak; the scripts are also the advance plan – the working blueprint – for the whole enterprise. The script involves plot details, camera and scenery requirements, outdoor-location filming; the scripts also temporarily omit actors who will be on holiday. Amongst the highly systematic and bureaucratic procedures of soap production, the script conference has a central place. This script conference meets every three or four weeks and considers a 3 × 3 or 4 × 2 batch of scripts. The producer presides over this meeting, which lasts up to two full days. These script outlines will be on the screen in perhaps four months; in between there is a much bigger sequence of other scripts being written, being finalized, in production, in post-production, about to be aired and subject to publicity:

> On any one day, I've calculated, I've got 60 scripts in different stages of transition on my desk.

In this industrial system the soap producer typically employs about four directors, to whom completed scripts are handed. In any week there will be one director at work with the actors recording a batch of two or three episodes; two directors may be in pre-production preparing their production weeks, and another director will be in post-production, editing together the studio and outdoor-location material into the final product.

Soaps achieve some of their biggest economies by repeated use of the same sets. In the 1980s major changes occurred in this respect. Phil Redmond, the creator of the Channel Four soap *Brookside*, in 1982 introduced the major innovation of making his soap in a group of real houses; he also abolished the traditional 'common-space' soap device of the pub or shop where characters can easily meet – *Brookside* focused almost entirely on the families within the separate houses. Redmond's real houses revealed the weakness of the skimpy three-wall sets (often moved in and out of the studio each week) of the other soaps. Eventually, all the other soaps moved towards a new pattern of semi-permanent sets within new space dedicated solely to the soap. Under this 'warehouse' concept the soap has a set with more rugged and much more real rooms and spaces in which to operate. *Emmerdale* (Yorkshire Television), in fact, moved into an old mill-building in Leeds, and the genuine-police-station look of *The Bill* (Thames) was achieved inside a real office building. This warehouse concept also allows more space for both actors and cameras and provides, for example, real windows with views.

The soaps – in line with the continuing thrust towards 'quality' in all British drama – also in the late 1980s added more location filming. An obvious example was the heavy use by *Emmerdale* of farm locations and beautiful Yorkshire countryside. *Coronation Street*, similarly, leaves its Granada Television warehouse and goes out and about in Manchester. Consequently each soap operates on a mix of days inside and days outside.

Permutations in the production system are important decisions for the overall TV organization. Because of their massive audiences and their 104- or 156-times-a-year frequency, each soap occupies an important position in the overall company's output. *Coronation Street* is Granada's most celebrated programme. *Eastenders* is also an important part of the BBC's ratings strategy and a significant ingredient of the BBC's overall image; the BBC was not happy with a mere soap, but consistently tried to upgrade quality in *Eastenders* and its focus on difficult and delicate contemporary social problems. Consequently, when the producer of such a programme wants to tinker with the script and production formulae he is also tinkering with a prominent piece of the corporate structure. Soap producers thus tend to get involved in internal corporate negotiations in a way that most producers do not. In this, and other respects, the soap producer is more like an executive producer in his (or her) own right.

Well-established soap producers are few in number but highly respected within television. They tend to move or to be head-hunted, from one soap to another. The soap producer who achieves or retains a high audience plus some quality, and who keeps a complex, production on time and on budget, has skills admired by senior management.

Soaps are the type of drama most deliberately geared towards large audiences. The soap producer can easily observe the ratings consequences of, for example, killing off an old character and introducing a new younger character. Soap producers also regularly commission research on the audience's perception of specific characters. These producers tend to be much more attuned to audience research than most.

The soap producer also has one other type of experience of interest upstairs – experience of dealing with the press. The producers themselves tend to say that there is not much to be done about the obsessional interest of the London tabloids in the real lives of soap actors. From the producer's viewpoint there is one still more uncomfortable type of press interest – in the future plot-developments. There is not much that can be done to stop leaks, when over a hundred people have copies of the scripts several weeks in advance of transmission, and when tabloid-press interest is so avid. This being so, the soap producer is clearly tempted to engage in some deft selective leaks about future plot-developments.

PRODUCER'S TEAM AND PRODUCTION SEQUENCE

The radically different types of drama production require differing production teams and differing rhythms of work; drama productions also vary so much as to require very different styles of producer.

Anthology series of single dramas cast the overall producers into two key roles: finding and supervising scripts and scriptwriters; and finding and supervising the director of each single drama.

The serial of typically 3–8 episodes is usually written by a single writer and directed by one director. This serial will typically cost several million pounds, and choosing the script is clearly crucial. Serials are often based on novels; if the novel is already popular (and the novelist has a personal following) this may boost the audience-ratings. There is a tendency to prefer a finished book to script outlines:

> With the right novel you get original material (which it's quite difficult to find), you get good parts for women, you find de-veloped characters that people will accept, you get their romantic lives, their sexual lives, quite realistic things.

An independent producer can immediately offer the commissioning executive what looks like a substantial package – a popular pub-lished book with serial potential, plus the names of the director and the main actors or actresses, and the name of the writer who will convert the novel into episode scripts.

The serial of, say, 6 hours' screen-time takes many months to complete all the main production phases. First and longest will be the writing phase; the drama executive, having agreed short outlines, then commissions the producer and writer to generate the six 1-hour scripts; it may take one year or longer for the scripts to be written and agreed. (In the majority of cases the project itself is not commissioned but is rejected somewhere in this script phase.)

Second, there comes the warming-up phase. The producer now has the budget agreed and starts to build the producer's team, which, in addition to the writer will now include the director, plus a unit manager or accountant. Another important producer team-member is the location manager who selects the filming sites and begins to make the required complex arrangements. Now the leaders of other teams come on board: the design team of the people responsible for art, sets and costumes; the technical team of the camera, lighting, sound and related personnel. By this time the director (and producer) will have cast the main acting parts and, with a casting director, will be casting lesser parts.

Third comes the production phase, which in a biggish-budget serial will consist of location filming; 6 episodes may mean 65 days, or up to 3 months of filming. During this phase the director takes the lead but the producer has to oversee many individuals and many details. In the fourth stage, of post-production, the team shrinks back to a handful of people: the producer, the director, an editor, an assistant editor and just one or two others.

The continuing series of, say, 15 episodes a year is in some respects merely the 6-episodes serial on a larger scale; but the rhythm is considerably different. While this year's episodes are still out on location in the production phase, the producer will be negotiating about next year's series, and – if the go-ahead is given – will already be commissioning scripts for next year. The greater pace and volume of work makes it quite impossible for one director to direct 15 episodes per year. The continuing-series producer typically employs several writers and several directors. Often the producer will be relying especially on one writer whose previous scripts were especially good; this writer might do five scripts, with the remaining scripts written by perhaps three other writers. There is usually, but not always, a separate (senior) script editor. The producer might employ four directors, each directing about four 1-hour episodes; each of these directors will have a small team such as a continuity person, a first assistant and a 'gofer'.

A continuing series may employ its actors for up to 8 months of the year; all these 8 months will be taken up with rehearsing and filming. In the common case of a series which relies heavily on outside-location filming this is typically done between spring and autumn, perhaps March to October. A 15-week 1-hour series might be shooting for 165 lengthy days. The aim is to be able to use an average 5 minutes from each day's filming, and this obviously involves a large post-production phase. Towards the end of the location-filming stage, perhaps in September, the series producer will still be consulting with one director and writer over the last one or two episodes-in-preparation, but will also be dealing with another director who is currently filming and a third director who is editing an early episode. The producer in October will also be worrying about the need to push forward the scripts for the early episodes of the new series, due to start filming in March.

Different producers have different strengths and weaknesses

which influence their style of work and the teams they select. The producer obviously chooses a director to fit the requirements of the project in hand; some directors are studio specialists, while most prefer to film outside on location. All drama producers oversee a huge range of detail and separate individuals. Some producers seem to focus primarily on the direction and see themselves as supervising the director's filming and editing performance; other producers seek to drive the series through the scripts and the selection and supervising of the writers.

The producer of continuing series sees the role as that of the architect or the conductor of the series. Not only does he (or she) choose all or most of the players, but the producer – especially of a new series – takes the lead in a range of other strategic decisions. Centrally important is the general technical and filming strategy – will the series use all-film, or all-tape, or a mix of the two? Will the main location filming involve big hotel and overnight costs or will it be done close to the base studio? And so on. In some series crucial decisions must be taken on the overall visual style – and this especially affects period-pieces such as *Poirot* and *The House of Eliott*. The latter series is unusual not only in being set in the 1920s but in dealing with a fashion house; the series producer (Jeremy Gwilt) decided to make his London-based story in Bristol and at other nearby locations, a decision that profoundly affected all aspects of the production. The continuing-series producer also emphasizes the need to maintain the look, style, pace and sound of the production across the work of different individual writers and directors.

All drama producers emphasize the centrality of the budget and remain acutely aware of the cost-implications of delays and disputes. Some producers, however, seem happy to leave the financial management almost entirely to the unit manager or accountant; others have a more active, even entrepreneurial, involvement. Drama producers emphasize the great importance of diplomacy and respect for the traditional interests of the numerous crafts and professions involved. In particular, a director who can be trusted to stick to the script and the schedule is usually allowed to dominate the filming phase. Nevertheless, most producers regularly visit the production site – locations as well as studio – and practice 'management by walking about'. Some producers say they do not want actors or crew to regard a visit by the producer as a special occasion; the producer is frequently around to sort out problems and to see at first hand how the production is going. Another daily task is to look at the last batch of film 'rushes' or the day's tape; this is often done quite late at night, with another 8-a.m. start in prospect the following day.

These demanding conditions and long hours are yet another reason why producers choose carefully their key personnel. Drama especially deals with human emotions, and the production of drama may require even higher emotional commitment than do other TV genres. This has also a positive side. A producer who has survived long months of production on an amicable basis with a director or a production manager may have established a very warm personal relationship; these relationships undoubtedly contribute greatly to the sense of personal fulfilment and creative satisfaction that a drama producer experiences.

ORIGINS

The variety of career origins of the drama producer parallels a similar variety in the origins of TV drama itself. The London theatre was a major influence in the early days and continues to be so today, especially because both theatre and television draw on the same reservoir of acting talent; there is a strong element of repertory-theatre working practices transported into television. The playwright tradition is strong, as is the emphasis on the novel. Many TV writers also write novels.

Radio is another important influence, since many TV writers and actors once worked in the BBC's large output of radio drama; some of the historical influences in British soaps derive from radio soaps. The film industry of the mid-century was also enormously influential, not least because around 1955–6 large numbers of film technicians (and their union practices) jumped ship from the sinking British film industry and boarded the ITV companies. Also important have been other areas of British television. 'Drama' shades off into several other areas – comedy, children's drama and documentary, especially in the case of documentary-drama (docudrama), which has been an active genre since the earliest days of British television.

The origins of the TV-drama producers themselves do not precisely match this variety of influences, but predictably their career origins are quite varied. 'The play's the thing' is a strong common theme; a large majority of these producers had either worked in the theatre as actors or been involved in TV writing. It is acting in the theatre, not in television, that is the main career theme. The second commonest background was in TV writing; while the third pattern is entry via one of the technical skills such as film editing.

At least half of these producers had early in their careers also shown some signs of management skills, as a young repertory-theatre director, as a script editor, or in one of the craft/facilities areas. These latter areas may be especially relevant to success as an independent producer in drama. Most, but not all, of these producers had previously worked as a TV-drama director. Some continued to work occasionally as a director or to operate as a producer-director. The combined weight of acting, writing and directing experience accurately reflects the predominantly artistic orientations of these producers. Before they had to handle multi-million-pound budgets, most of these producers had served an extended apprenticeship with many long weeks of directing actors and managing scripts, scenery, performances and rehearsals. Like the actor-managers of British theatrical tradition, these people had been artists first and only subsequently became producer-managers. All are confidently literate, but some are distinctly hesitant on numeracy.

The repertory-theatre model seems relevant in another way. As these drama producers discuss their previous careers they tend to be very vague on dates; but they are extremely specific about which executive producer gave them what job in the past, and also about which directors and actors they themselves employed and cast into key roles. Often several of their own key career-moves in the past were job offers from the same individual senior producer. As these producers themselves became more established and successful, they have established their own loose equivalents of repertory-theatre teams in the form of TV-series teams.

EXECUTIVE PRODUCERS AS TV-DRAMA PUBLISHERS

The drama/fiction genre has been ahead of other British TV genres in moving towards the publisher model. By the early 1990s the ITV companies had followed Channel Four's lead in contracting out drama; while the BBC was still making much drama in house, it was increasingly moving in the publisher direction, with even in-house producers encouraged to adopt an increasingly entrepreneurial style.

About a dozen senior drama executives in practice spend British television's entire drama budget of over £300 million (in 1992–3). Even within this group of a dozen, power is now focused on just one or two ITV central commissioners and one or two BBC executives;

the BBC 'Head of Series' spends about one-quarter of the total British TV-drama budget.

Two drama executives control Channel Four's drama expenditure. Apart from its thrice-weekly soap, *Brookside*, the channel focuses on single drama/films and two or three major serials each year. Its total output of original non-soap drama is only about one hour per week. The channel has focused on trying to make a few successful one-offs and at least one acclaimed serial each year such as *A Very British Coup*, *Traffik* and *The Manageress*. However, attempting to make innovative series on such a low total budget poses acute dilemmas. Its 1991 success *GBH* with its 7 lengthy episodes received much acclaim, but also spent half the serials budget for the year.

BBC2 has a somewhat similar policy to Channel Four and relevant drama producers of these two channels claim that no other general (non-premium) TV channels in the world have an equivalent investment in avant-garde pieces produced to such high artistic levels. The BBC, in addition to its more demanding serials and its single-drama anthology series (on both BBC channels), has some other 'non-commercial' output, such as a commitment to employing new writers and directors on various mini-drama formats.

The bulk of BBC output and nearly all ITV drama output has turned, however, towards either soaps or popular series and serials. Greg Dyke of LWT has promoted the concept of 'popular-quality' drama, and both the BBC and ITV are in practice committed to much the same thing. ITV began spending more money on popular drama before the ITC re-franchising of 1991 and the BBC also sharply raised its drama spend from 1991–2 onwards.

Increasingly, the pattern is of a dozen or so executive producers in the main networks who act as commissioning editors, and pay sums of the order of £600,000 (or about one million dollars) per hour. There is, then, a second tier of drama producers who actually produce the series, serials, soaps and one-offs. Some of these producers are still listed on the in-house rosta of the BBC but they are mostly freelances of one kind or another. Increasingly, the independent producer is the predominant type of drama producer.

This independent drama producer performs two key functions. Most obviously, this producer actually makes the drama; the producer comes to be effectively the employer of those one hundred or so individuals who create the show. Second, the independent drama producer is a packager who puts together drama packages – an independent production company with a track-record, a property such as a book, a writer, a director and perhaps two leading actors. In some cases the producer also offers co-production finance – a US cable deal, Australian network interest, or a deal with an eastern European network which will facilitate cheaper location filming. The dozen or so key commissioning executive producers are well-known people within television and in the drama and theatre worlds. Typically, they have impressive track-records and were in the past producers of series whose reputations have lived on. They know each other well; their career paths have crossed at one of a few key places such as Euston Films (the Thames subsidiary) or at BBC Birmingham (which for many years has produced the work of young TV writers and directors). Most of these men (and a few women) entered TV drama in the 1960s or 1970s. While their attitude is not one of simple nostalgia, they do tend to regret today's greatly reduced opportunities for innovation and for risk-taking with untried people and concepts. They regret the decline of the single drama; while expressing some pride in their currently successful continuing series, several of them would clearly prefer to terminate a successful series and spend the money on something risky and new:

We've tried awfully hard but haven't been able to save the single play, because everybody who does my job would rather have single plays – that's where the new series ideas come from – but the Director of Programmes finds it risky, and the Director of Advertising Sales hates them; they'd rather have an on-going success.

There is a kind of sadness that in this job only four years ago if you said 'I'm going to make this' you knew you could get it made; so there's a lot of sadness in turning down an awful lot of good stuff . . . things that you'd love to see made.

Of the various kinds of difficult drama which do still get made, one is the docudrama. In this area the drama executives vie with factual producers who are more attuned to the kind of research involved. British docudramas of recent years have tended to focus on real-life political – often international political – dramas which involve elements of mystery, skullduggery and violence. The Falklands War and events in recent Irish and middle-east history have been popular topics. Along with the international themes there is often co-production involvement; producers also say that the dramatic depiction of living people leads to scripts being lawyered and 'legalled' through many versions. Although docudrama presents legal risks, its basis in recent history makes it instantly recognizable to a significant fraction of the audience; this is not a case of something completely new and different.

Serials, especially, have become a new pinnacle of artistic achievement in TV fiction. The most highly acclaimed writers in early British television mainly focused on single dramas. Some of these, such as Dennis Potter, began with single dramas before writing their classic serials. Some later writers, such as Alan Bleasdale (*The Monocled Mutineer, Boys From the Blackstuff* and *GBH*), have focused on the serial.

One of the main tasks for drama executive producers these days it to place bets on new series. The initial stage of this is to commission any number between one and all of the scripts. At any one time the executive producer will be talking to, and commissioning scripts from, a sizeable number of writers:

Most of my time is rejecting stuff . . . You spend your whole time reading stuff that's interesting but you can't buy it; a problem is having to tell people bad news and keeping others strung along without any news, good or bad.

Several executive producers said that they read a large selection of newish novels, both middle-brow and high-brow. One said that he always visualized the scenes in the novel. All this skimming can be quite pleasant and is one excuse drama producers give for only watching one episode of many new TV dramas. The difficult decision is whether to go beyond the script commission. One executive producer said: 'I have to make the right choice 55 per cent of the time.'

Chapter 7

The comedy enigma

Comedy is, after drama, the second most popular genre in British television. The schedules of ITV and BBC1 tend to place comedy after the early evening soaps and before 9 p.m. Comedy is also the second most expensive programming to produce. The situation comedy, especially, is comparable in several ways to studio-based drama. It is usually recorded in a multi-camera studio with an audience and only minor post-production editing. Within British TV comedy there is a strong sense of an established tradition of live performance. In the early days of BBC radio most available types of live comedy were considered too vulgar to be broadcast. Until 1938 BBC radio comedy was confined to brief comedy items within variety and vaudeville formats. Around the time of John Reith's departure in 1938, the BBC was cautiously beginning to take on board two types of comic vulgarity, namely British working-class humour and US imports. British broadcast comedy has experienced several waves of comedy imports. The first wave of Hollywood imports in 1938–42 (Bob Hope, Jack Benny) stimulated Britain's first wave of popular and zany broadcast humour, such as *Much Binding in the Marsh* and *ITMA*. Another wave of comedy imports involved *I Love Lucy* and other examples of early Hollywood TV comedy. A third wave occurred in the 1980s when Channel Four cheaply boosted its ratings with such super-popular US series as *The Cosby Show*, *Cheers* and *Roseanne*.

Compared with the Hollywood assault in the drama/fiction field, the comedy imports were always less popular and less strong competition. Nevertheless, these imports from both radio and TV Hollywood were one cause of British TV comedy emphasizing its Britishness. Television comedy did this by leaning heavily on British radio humour and on current live-performance humour. This live humour has come from the London Palladium, from Christmas pantomime, and summer seaside-theatre shows; it has also come from working-class clubs and pubs; and it has come in recent years from more up-market London comedy venues.

British TV comedy has been extremely varied but it has mostly avoided – or not succeeded with – suburban-family formats. The big successes of British comedy have focused on the oddball and zany, and on working-class loners, misfits and bigots. The archetypal British TV comedy was *Steptoe and Son*, about the embattled relationship between a rag-and-bone-man and his eccentric and exasperating old father. Like many subsequent successful series, *Steptoe and Son* had a meagre total output (about 5 episodes a year over a 9-year run); and it depended on outstanding performances. *Steptoe and Son* also helped to consolidate a tradition of authored comedy; its writers, Ray Galton and Alan Simpson, were honoured in television as the comedy's true celebrities.

This tradition of authored comedy raised obvious questions about the role of the producer. Some other oddities of this tradition were discussed in 1966 by Frank Muir, the BBC's then boss of comedy:

> In this country all our comedy is written by about twenty-four gentlemen. No ladies. Only a handful of these gentlemen write full time for television . . . Comedy writers – wittingly or un – put a lot of themselves into their work – this means, of course, that their yearly output is much smaller than that of a writer whose work is ninety per cent technique . . . The working life of a comedy writer writing situation comedy should be reckoned as about twelve to fifteen years . . . Also you can't get rich writing television comedy . . . Once you have become highly successful, which can happen quickly, your income can be more or less static unless you move into films or the theatre.[1]

Some of this has changed – women have proved that they can write TV comedy. However, a key paradox remains in place: British television still sees comedy writers as central; it still honours writers, but it still leaves them feeling inadequately paid and looking elsewhere for additional work.

Most comedy actors also have one foot in the TV studio and the other foot on the boards of the live-theatre stage. Some writer-comedians try out their material on live audiences before using it on television. Short TV series allow popular comedians to perform in TV comedy while also appearing in live shows. A common comedy practice is to rehearse on weekdays and to record in the studio on Sunday, thus allowing actors to appear in London live theatre at the same time. Comedy producers say that even the best-known stage actors want to play non-continuing or cameo roles in successful comedies ('Do keep me in mind, darling, when you're casting'). Most comedies run for about 6 or 13 episodes per year. However, the writer or writers of a successful comedy are allowed to stick at 6 per year; some successful British comedies only reach their one hundredth episode after 16 or 17 years. The prevailing attitude was explained by the producer of one 1990s success:

If you've got an absolute gem, you shouldn't flog it to death. Leave the audience wanting more.

The same producer agreed with the widespread view that the best British comedy comes from the writer's personal vision and personal experience. There is a strongly-held belief that comedy should be more than a 'formula'. The comedy should grow and develop in ways that appeal to the writer. This, then, becomes a counter-formula; it is a comedy system that honours not only the writer, but the writer's idiosyncrasies and oddball, zany or eccentric humour.

'MAINSTREAM' AND 'ALTERNATIVE' TV COMEDY

Mainstream TV comedy incorporated the impact of US situation comedies, but was anchored to predominantly British working-class comic traditions. A comedy such as *Till Death Us Do Part*, when it began in 1964, was considered daring in its screen portrayal of a working class bigot, it was only adapted into the US *All In The Family* seven years later. However, the series (or the Alf Garnett character), which ran on into the 1990s, had long since entered the mainstream. *Last of the Summer Wine* (starting in 1974) was another eccentric but mainstream series. In these, as in many other mainstream cases, the writers (Johnny Speight and Roy Clarke) were widely acclaimed. These and other comedies appeared on the main channels (BBC1 and ITV) and attracted large audiences; by the 1980s they were considered by the schedulers as safe material suitable for family viewing before 9 p.m. Mainstream comedies also received much press attention, especially in the tabloid newspapers.

'Alternative' comedy is inevitably difficult to define, not least because it tends, after an interval, to join the mainstream. There was one big burst in the 1960s that included *That Was The Week That*

Was (1963), the birth of BBC2 (1964) and *Monty Python's Flying Circus* (1969). A fresh burst of alternative comedy occurred in the early 1980s, especially on Channel Four (from 1982 on) and BBC2. Most of this alternative comedy did not aim for mass audiences. Many of the leading participants came from Cambridge University or, by the 1980s, from Cambridge or Manchester University. These people lacked the typical mainstream comedian's lengthy apprenticeship in front of live audiences. The alternative-comedy people were London-based; many had worked in BBC Radio, not on large-audience programmes in the 1940s manner, but on the all-talk, and fairly up-market, BBC Radio 4. They also worked in London comedy venues and fringe theatres, as well as in West End commercial theatre.

A key difference from mainstream TV comedy was that the alternative comedians typically wrote their own material. They did not simply seek mass-market success; unlike the mainstream, they received extensive coverage from the more serious TV writers in the more serious newspapers. They adopted deliberately non-commercial approaches; for example, the strong vein of political satire was not geared to massive ratings success. Indeed, several alternative shows deliberately included an element of topical references to recent events; *Spitting Image*, *The New Statesman* and *Drop the Dead Donkey*, by including topical political references, were reducing the long-term, repeat-asset, value of their output. (The producers of all three of these shows did not, in fact, own the repeat rights to the shows, because all three were made by independent producers. This perhaps added to alternative comedy an additional dimension not present in the mainstream. Much of the less well-known independent programming was made for Channel Four in the expectation that not many episodes in total would be bought.)

Alongside these two broad categories of comedy, British television also found itself with two parallel categories of comedy producer. The mainstream-comedy producers in the early 1990s were typically in their forties; they had worked for twenty years or so in the BBC or in one of the large ITV companies where they had, or had only recently given up, staff status. The typical mainstream producer had been to drama school and/or had worked in the theatre, before entering television and working up via a career-ladder of assistant stage manager, stage manager and director, to producer. During these twenty years the mainstream producer had worked, in various capacities, on a long succession of both successful and

unsuccessful comedies and, perhaps, variety shows as well. Most of
these comedy producers had worked in the BBC and were enthusiastic admirers of its wonderful back-up facilities and the BBC
tradition in TV comedy. Among the mainstream producers a favourite
newspaper was the *Daily Mail*.

Alternative-comedy producers in the early 1990s were younger,
and were much less likely to have followed a lengthy TV career
route. They tended to have moved from university into BBC radio
comedy, where they had obtained script-writing experience. Some
had then jumped across directly from radio producer to TV comedy
producer. Their more maverick careers were also likely to have
included spells as a freelance producer or in running an independent
production company. The alternative-comedy producers' favourite
daily was *The Independent*.

Some producers expressed sharp criticisms across the mainstream/
alternative divide. These strongly expressed opinions broadly paralleled public exchanges between certain performers and critics. Some
alternative comedians saw British TV comedy as mindless, male-
chauvinist and reactionary; the response was that alternative TV
comedians were pretentious, male-feminist, left-wing and untalented.
This dispute was clearly not only based on inter-personal malice but
was also about fundamental interests; some producers saw the
conflict as a battle to control the jobs and patronage right across
British TV comedy.

In this mainstream/alternative struggle the boundaries are continually shifting. Most, if not all producers, admire some people on
the other side. Meanwhile, not only are elements of the alternative
always merging into the mainstream, but some comedians and comic
styles, only recently regarded as too embarrassing to be still included
in the mainstream, are soon dusted down and proclaimed to be
classics. Benny Hill (who wrote his own scripts), after his dismissal
by Thames Television apparently for being outdated and sexist, did
not have to wait long to be praised (by Anthony Burgess in 1990) as
'one of the great artists of our age' and a genius of the 'Comedy of
sexual regret'. The BBC's *Omnibus* arts programme also devoted an
hour to Benny Hill in 1991, a year before his death.

BBC VS. THE REST

The British style of TV comedy was primarily developed by the
BBC and has continued to favour the BBC. The BBC has long relied

on comedy to a greater extent than has ITV. As Table 6.2 shows, situation comedies in 1991 were ITV's fifth most popular genre, while on the BBC channels comedy was surpassed in popularity only by the soaps.

The prevailing slow unfolding of comedy series, as well as the centrality of the writer, have favoured the BBC which has always tended to take a longer-term and more literary view of television. The simple fact of the commercial break has posed ITV comedy writers and producers with two awkward segments of just 12 minutes each; most comedy writers seem to prefer the BBC's standard situation-comedy format of 28 continuous minutes.

Given the range and complexity of broadcast comedy – and its need for old mainstream favourites as well as radical new alternatives – the BBC has an advantage over ITV's single commercial network which schedules comedy in mid-evening and thus can only handle shows with high ratings. The BBC has continued to use radio as a training-ground for writers, performers and producers. Moreover, with two TV networks, the BBC has been able to switch new radio talent to BBC2 before a final move to the show-business big-time of BBC1. Of course, it seldom works quite that smoothly, but the BBC has a much wider range of possibilities than does ITV. The ITV cartel arrangements previous to 1993 in practice carved up the limited comedy time between the larger ITV companies; consequently, each of those ITV companies aimed to have just one or two big comedy successes rather than to develop a comedy factory to rival the BBC.

Within its 'light-entertainment' group, the BBC has indeed developed a comedy factory. The BBC sees comedy shows and comedy talent as needing to be nurtured. New BBC comedy is normally repeated within twelve months (which adds to the earnings of performers and writers); in recent times the BBC has repeated the previous year's output immediately before a new run of fresh programmes. The audience is also encouraged to associate certain regular mid-evening time-slots with BBC comedy.

The sheer quantity of the BBC's comedy production is the most obvious evidence of its comedy commitment. Each year the BBC1 channel runs about 25 separate situation comedies of which about 6 are completely new series.[2] The BBC comedy approach is not dissimilar from that of a large magazine or book publisher, film studio or record company; in a risky and highly unpredictable business it is difficult to spot winners, so each year you try a range of new things in the hope that one or two will be winners. In practice, of course, a sizeable group are neither obvious winners nor certain failures and here the 'nurturing' approach is applied – give the writers two full years to produce a 'big' batch of 13 programmes; try a new producer; kill off half the supporting characters; and so on.

The BBC not only is the biggest user of comedy and employer of comedy talent, but also offers prestige and respectability. This may enable it to get away with paying less; but the BBC can often offer comedians more work – perhaps two series a year, rather than only one on ITV.

The BBC's ability to offer prestige and security to a larger number of comedy performers and writers stands out against the legendary insecurity of show business, comedy and comedians. The familiar stereotype of the famous comedian as an insecure or tragic figure seems in some cases even to understate the reality. Both Benny Hill and Ken Dodd, despite being 'uninterested in money', were reported to have lived alone in houses cluttered with huge quantities of bundled cash.

There has been a standard comedy progression – of writers, performers and producers – from BBC radio, to BBC television, to ITV, and then back to BBC television. This does not mean that the BBC's comedy factory has always been an all-winning, all-smiling show. BBC comedy has also been the focus of bitter criticism and fierce resentment; since the BBC's comedy effort is, in effect, the national comedy theatre, this is predictable and inevitable. The inadequacies and limitations of both ITV and BBC comedy efforts were underlined by the alternative-comedy successes of Channel Four in the 1980s.

The scale and broad success of the BBC comedy output has posed problems for the BBC's high command. It would be unwise to challenge head on the autonomy of the executives in charge of comedy, because those executives had and have the expertise, contacts and personal relationships with the established figures in British comedy. Senior BBC executives have, however, become adept at bypassing the comedy group; a number of BBC comedy shows are commissioned and controlled through other BBC departments in London and outside.

Despite the BBC's dominance, ITV as well as Channel Four have had comedy successes. During the 1980s Central Television and Yorkshire Television were responsible for two highly original comedies – *Spitting Image* and *The New Statesman*. Both took political caricature to extremes not previously seen on British television. Both were popular with the young educated audiences beloved by advertisers; both required too much interest in politics to allow mainstream super-popularity. Both were expensive to make – especially *Spitting Image* whose original notion of presenting public figures as puppet-caricatures used many writers of separate sketches and required a small army of puppet artists, puppet-operators and voice-over artists. Both shows were unique and virtually impossible to copy. *Spitting Image* seemed to go far beyond the normal restraints of good taste and the libel law; it depended in part on the assumption that no politician – however grossly abused – would be so unwise as to try to sue a puppet. Both these shows were exceptions to the rules; they conformed only to the general rule that the British comedy system welcomed the zany, the unique, the eccentric and the lovingly written.

THE COMEDY PRODUCER'S PRIVATE WORLD

The comedy producers share certain basic perceptions of their work. All, for example, honour and respect the writer and the script; at the core of comedy are funny lines, funny characters, funny situations – and these all come out of the writer's head. All comedy producers see comedy as much more than simply feeding a ratings machine with jokes. Most comedy producers have only a very lukewarm interest in audience-research data; the producer of one successful series said that he had seen no audience research for two years. These producers also are unhappy with the status of comedy in television; they see British television as controlled by people from the factual-programming areas whose low opinion of comedy is summed up by the archaic term 'light entertainment'.

Interpersonal chemistry is seen as especially salient in comedy. It is not only a matter of whether you like the writer or actor; it is also a matter of whether you think the person is funny. 'It's what makes me laugh' is the producer's definition of comedy. This laughability test operates through several sets of interpersonal relationships, but two are crucial. First, does the writer's script make the producer laugh? Second, when the executive producer, or head of comedy, receives the pilot script from the producer, does it induce laughter? The same awkward question hangs over actor auditions, rehearsals and outside filming: does he, she or it make the producer laugh?

The laughter test overlays the unfolding of the production

sequence. First, and most crucial, is the writer. Within a continuing comedy series, the writer may already have been at work for several months. With a new series, or a new writer, it may be a matter of sending, or personally delivering, a single script. Sometimes the producer is relatively new to a successful series, which the writer has already scripted for some years; in this case the producer will usually accept what the writer has written and if, for example, the actors want to make even a small change, the writer will be consulted by telephone. In other cases it is the producer who is the old hand and the writer who is taking over, or writing additional episodes; here the producer's initial response may be followed by some hours of detailed discussion.

Interpersonal relationships with the leading performers are inevitably important, not least because the comedy producer tends to be a producer-director. Being the producer-director to a performer you find unfunny is difficult:

> He did his own old-fashioned jokes and I didn't get on with him; we didn't see eye-to-eye and he didn't make me laugh one jot; I thought 'This is a nightmare, absolute complete drudgery, going into rehearsals . . . This is a talentless little shit and I can't do anything with him!'

Probably more common is the case of the producer who wants a particular performer for the part and sets out to ensnare his or her quarry:

> Both the writer and I wanted him, but he thought he was too young for it, he was adamant about it for several weeks . . . eventually I persuaded him.

> First, I got her to agree to one and then to six; after that she agreed to sign on for another run and another – but she would have refused if she'd realized at the start what I was up to.

Another testing task for the producer-director is casting the non-continuing parts. Some situation comedies have several fresh parts for each episode; each one of these parts may involve ten brief auditions in the producer's office with the actor 'reading' the lines, and chatting about his or her recent parts, while the producer anxiously wonders.

When the production team, the acting team and the design team are all in place, the opening day – usually devoted to the actors reading the script out loud – is a big moment for the producer. Even with a short run, perhaps one million pounds rides upon the success of the newly assembled group:

> All your judgement is on the line at that moment, you've got a room full of people . . . I know they're all shit-scared and they're thinking 'At least the producer is confident' – so I must act confident – everybody's nerves are in tatters at the first read-through, and mine too, but they're not supposed to know that.

All the outdoor filming (taping) may be done together in between one and several weeks; there are the usual problems of weather, transport and logistics. Next the production returns to the studio for a succession of weeks; each week is spent rehearsing the actors, then come the camera rehearsals and finally, on the fifth or sixth evening, the show is taped in front of a studio audience. This recording is another anxious time for the producer; it is also difficult for actors confronted with an audience of 300 people, plus the probing attentions of mobile studio cameras. A common practice is to use one 'slave' camera which looks only at the star. On the day following the recording the producer-director focuses on the relatively modest amount of editing involved in this type of studio-recorded production. Next day the weekly sequence begins again.

British television has operated on a tradition of a 30-minute comedy taking more than one week to tape, including the exterior filming which is inserted into the studio recording. Around 1990 there were pressures to make economies. In some comedy-sketch shows, for example, only 5 studio weeks would now be used to make enough sketches for 6 shows.

The comedy producer might make a total of 15 shows in one year. This might total between 17 and 22 weeks of combined outside filming and studio recording; for each of these weeks the producer would have spent at least another week on preliminary planning, including script supervision and casting non-continuing parts. In the remaining few non-holiday weeks of the year the producer might be working on a pilot for a new show, producing a one-off comedy special, and working on scripts submitted by independent producers.

As with producers in other genres, comedy producers give a strong impression of facing accelerating deadlines, and working a succession of 6- and 7-day weeks for many weeks each year. As with other producers, they are also potentates, in their case in the hard world of big-time comedy; many show-business people wait anxiously for their smiles or their phone-calls. However, like some other producers, they are not greatly honoured in their own industry. They know that they are regarded as show business or light entertainment. As with many other producers, some of these comedy producers aspire to drama; there is in their case an obvious avenue – namely comedy drama which shades off into situation comedy. Meanwhile they watch the wide range of TV comedy, both for competition and for potential casting. Some of them also search for talent in London comedy clubs and fringe theatres. They continue to work hard at monitoring the serious business, and private world, of comedy.

THE COMEDY DIVISION OF LABOUR AND POWER

In early mainstream TV comedy the jobs of producer, director, writer and star performer were four completely separate roles. By 1970, however, the producer-director was a common combination performed by one person. In alternative comedy, from the 1960s, the writer-performer also became a familiar figure on the comedy scene.

In the early system of four separate roles, the writer was extremely important. The writer, in turn, still needed the star; and most (but not all) comedians were impotent without a suitably sympathetic and skilled writer. It was a team effort. One defining characteristic of 'alternative' comedy was that the writer-performer became a prevailing pattern. Initially the producer or producer-director might continue to be the sole leader, as he or she shaped and refined the offerings of a team of writer-performers. However, as the writer-performers became more experienced and better-known, the importance of the producer-director role might be reduced:

> One of the best things . . . is the joy of seeing these now-well-known artists, and thinking I was responsible for putting them on television in the first place . . . even if I can't work with them now because of pressures of work or because of disagreements . . . the creative differences one might have with them as they get more famous.

Although the latter kind of conflict only occurs in a minority of cases, it illustrates nevertheless a wider truth – namely that he who controls the script and the scriptwriter will effectively control the production.

The writer-performer is only one of several possible 'hyphenate' combinations which may exercise control over the script. Another type of hyphenate combines the roles of producer and script editor. This combination seems to be common in independent production companies which make comedies, not least because it may be writer-producers who are especially drawn to running their own companies:

> The production originates with me, it gets cooked with me, and I sell it to the broadcaster. I think everything depends on the originating writer; he brings the script to me and I read it through. Then we sit down and discuss. He and I work on it together. I don't get involved in direction or episode casting. But I do visit the production, including the initial read-through. After the studio recording I go through the tape with the director and we agree the main editing decisions. Because I don't direct, I've got the time to plan ahead and actually get that first stage right, which is the script; so most of my time is spent across this table with writers, half a day at a time, fixing scripts.
>
> (Humphrey Barclay)

There was some tendency for independent producers of comedy to become aligned especially with particular channels. Hat Trick produced a range of comedy output, mainly for Channel Four. Alomo, another writer-dominated comedy producer, was the first independent to achieve an 'output deal' to supply the BBC with several new comedies. Alomo was also highly committed to the adoption of the team-writing approach, long the standard in Hollywood TV comedy. There is some speculation that British television will move towards the Hollywood approach; successful series will be commissioned for 23 or 25 episodes each year, the show would stay in production for 8 or 9 months and the scripts would be written by a team of several writers perhaps under a senior producer/story editor with an executive producer above him.

This may well happen but in the 1980s British comedy production actually moved further away from such a system. The arrival and success of substantial numbers of writer-performers was the reverse of a team of writers turning out scripts in large numbers. The successful writer-performers want not only to write their own smallish numbers of episodes, but also to be free to work outside television for substantial slices of the year.

British TV comedy is an inward-looking system, in which expenditure largely goes into 'quality' production, adequate rehearsal time, good design and a strong technical crew. British comedy lacks outside financial participation; the success of some comedy exports (such as *Monty Python* and *The Benny Hill Show*) probably depended heavily on their zany Britishness. The system is geared to British taste, and driven by a combination of popularity and prestige.

The system honours writers and gives them considerable freedom and autonomy; successful writers are allowed to author their own series at rates as low as 6 half-hours per year over many years. Performers also receive some honour, but only a few are paid even British-style superstar rates. Consequently the performers use television to establish their mass popularity; but they obtain much of their earnings in live performances, in advertising, in TV quiz-game shows. Many writers and performers look towards the London theatre and non-comedy drama, while a fair proportion have spent some time in Hollywood.

This comedy system has been self-perpetuating. Power in some respects has fragmented, not least with the arrival of Channel Four and independent production. The BBC remains the exception; the continuing comedy strength of the BBC – in terms of audience ratings, quantity of output and prestige – perpetuates the existing system.

About sixty writers dominate the provision of comedy scripts and shape the character of British TV comedy; but one comedy producer can and does produce, direct and script-edit the comedy output of about three established writers. About twenty comedy producers are situated at the core of this serious business of making the British public laugh.

Chapter 8

'Light entertainment'

This chapter deals with quiz or game shows, people or surprise shows and chat shows; these three, together with comedy and traditional 'variety', have been lumped together by British television as 'light entertainment'.* The ITV companies carefully demarcate 'entertainment' from such areas as drama, sport and news. The BBC continues with the label of not just entertainment but 'light entertainment'; this latter archaic and oddly lopsided term (there is no 'heavy' entertainment) accurately reflects traditional BBC misgivings about mere entertainment. Some of the misgivings are traditional to public-service broadcasting; but some specifically BBC misgivings concern justifying the licence fee by avoiding 'commercialism'.

The Pilkington Committee of 1962, which called for the third channel to go to the BBC, expressed some of its doubts as follows:

> television has created some forms of programme which particularly lend themselves to triviality, which lend themselves to the exploitation of artificial situations or of 'personalities' but have practically no subject matter or body of their own. Some quiz-shows and panel games obviously come into this category.[1]

Producers of entertainment programmes are well aware that the system does not honour their efforts, although it does rely upon them to achieve strong ratings. Asked about the goals of their output, all these producers mention ratings and also stress ratings performance against the competition: 'my task is to win the time-slot.'

* This chapter is jointly authored by Jeremy Tunstall and Mark Dunford.

There are several overlapping elements behind the prevailing attitude of disapproval, or only conditional approval, which the TV industry shares with the British policy establishment. One element is the notion that these programmes invade people's privacy and depend upon undesirable appeals to lower human instincts – the gossip instinct, voyeuristic inspection of one's fellow humans, simple greed, the appeal of the practical joke or of laughing at other people's embarrassment. Another industry belief is that such programmes depend upon a formula, which is endlessly repeated. A related criticism sees these programmes as not only formulaic, but also easy to produce; there is believed to be little creative challenge to the producer, who typically joins a programme which is already a ratings success and which only needs the formula to be repeated. Such programmes are also dismissed as star vehicles; the programme is seen as focusing on a single entertainment personality exuding some easy *bonhomie* while the producer plays a subordinate role. Last, but not least, there is the criticism that nearly all these shows are based on US formats or genres.

These points are nowhere written down or codified; they constitute no more than a cluster of attitudes. Each of these points is at least disputable. Take the last point – the US origins. Certainly, the game or quiz show concept comes from US broadcasting. The people or surprise show is based on early US TV offerings such as *Candid Camera*; the British *This Is Your Life* is based on another ancient US formula; so also with *Blind Date*. The same is true of the video-clip compilations, the chat show and the soap opera.

However, just as today's US blueberry croissant is less than 100 per cent French, there is considerable room for dispute as to how American these shows still are. Several of these formulae derive from traditional children's games, or such equally ancient concepts as the practical joke. In their broadcast forms they were imported from the USA several decades ago and have been heavily Anglicized. Aware of such ambiguities, some producers have tended to emphasize the 100 per cent truly British character of these programmes. When they make the USA–UK journey, these formats do tend to undergo a character change; these shows are also peopled with, and presented by, very British entertainment figures. An additional possible criticism, then, is that these shows – despite, or because of, their US origins – are produced along lines of exaggerated Britishness, with British provincial accents and local references over-emphasized to the point of falsity. There is indeed a distinctly dated flavour to the light-entertainment area of British television: not only do these programming areas derive in part from such traditions as the Music Hall, but there is a powerful tendency – in, for example, game shows – towards Victorian revivalism.

Apart from music, the early BBC provided remarkably little entertainment in either its radio or its first TV efforts. Television entertainment had its major British growth with the appearance of ITV in 1955. Some members of the first generation of young TV-entertainment producers had careers which stretched into the 1980s and 1990s.

Well into the second world war, the BBC – having allowed in some situation comedy – was still treating the potential invasion of the quiz or game show with extreme caution. *The Brains Trust*, a radio game which the BBC introduced in 1941, encouraged public participation; the three regular brains included two professors (a biologist and a philosopher) and a retired naval officer who proffered robust wartime opinions in response to questions sent in by members of the public. The initial weekly programme budget was £105; soon each recording session was producing two programmes. A more genuine variety format was pioneered by *Have a Go*, starring Wilfred Pickles who visited local towns to record the locals on their own turf answering easy questions for small prizes.

Ten years later, in 1951, BBC television bought the format of a new (1950) US show, *What's My Line?*, a game that required panel-members to guess the off-beat occupation of a member of the public; Gilbert Harding – highly British, highly eccentric and famously ill-tempered – became Britain's first TV celebrity.

The arrival in 1955 of ITV ushered in a new wave of US game shows neatly sanitized for British consumption. *Double Your Money*, *Take Your Pick*, *People Are Funny* and *Beat the Clock* were massively popular adaptations of successful US formats. Ever since 1955 ITV has relied on quiz games more than the BBC. The BBC continued to be happier with highbrow quizzes such as *Mastermind* (1972). A long list of US programmes – *Call My Bluff*, *Twenty One*, *Wheel of Fortune*, *The Price Is Right* – appeared under the same name in Britain; many other US shows appeared under different names – *University Challenge*, *Criss Cross Quiz*, *Blankety Blank*. In recent years Britain has also imported from, and exported to, other European countries such as Holland, Italy and Germany.

CHEAP SHOW, EXPENSIVE STAR

The initial attraction of game shows to ITV was the combination of popularity with low production cost. The same financially attractive combination was to be found in those other imports, the chat show and the people show. In all these cases the participants or guests provided their services free or at nominal cost; whether 'members of the public' or minor celebrities, they did not require rehearsals before answering the questions. The game show, especially, allowed for the production of several programmes in a single day.

The viewing public see the guests and participants usually performing in front of a studio audience. They also see each week (or each day) the familiar 'host' personality, who quickly becomes the vital key ingredient of a successful show. Because game, chat or people shows are broadly comedy-entertainments most (but not all) hosts are comedians; British entertainment producers also acknowledge the expertise of professional comedians in handling live audiences and managing participants with a flow of 'impromptu' humour. If the show achieves ratings popularity, the host (via an agent) is in a strong position to acquire large pay increases. The producers of a successful show can easily afford this. Another financially benign aspect is that – since these shows tend towards a large quantity of output – the host may not have to be paid huge amounts per hour in order to earn big amounts per year.

In the case of some lower-output entertainment series, the star may do two separate shows for the same network. A common combination is a comedy show which requires a heavy input of original scripting (and thus 'eats material') plus another show, such as a game show or a chat show, which in effect generates its own material. Some agents and managers discourage their comedian clients from thus moving beyond comedy; but the comedians themselves and the TV networks seem to like the two-series arrangement.

Producers of these entertainment shows typically find themselves producing a high-profile and highly paid entertainment star. There are other production factors common to most of these shows. They are mainly studio-based shows, either transmitted live or recorded 'as live' with only minor editing. Most of these shows also involve a studio audience, which enables the host to exercise theose live-audience skills.

These programmes, especially at London Weekend Television (LWT) and other ITV companies, also tend to be heavy users of research, a point which runs against their traditional reputation as cheap shows. There is research on guests and participants, research on the questions to be asked (and the correct answers) and in some cases research on the studio audience as well.

GAME SHOWS

Quiz or game shows vary from very simple general knowledge to very difficult specialized knowledge; some shows go out in daytime to small audiences, while others achieve high ratings in early-evening slots; some quizzes are simple word games requiring only a very small production team, while others are part cheap game show and part expensive variety show.

The regulators in both the BBC and ITV have strictly rationed the hours allowed to this suspect form of TV. ITV devotes a far greater amount of time to popular entertainment than the other channels. Typically, these programmes are shown either in prime time or in the less profitable daytime slots, where economies of scale can be exploited. The BBC operates under more severe self-imposed constraints on hours transmitted, the size of prizes awarded and the 'level' of the game.

Game shows are widely dismissed as very simple programmes for the working class or a means of occupying bored housewives. However, audience research indicates that, even with the inevitable variations within the genre, game shows have a very similar profile to the TV audience overall. British viewers each watch about 90 minutes of these programmes in an average week.

There are three broad scheduling categories. First, there are the daytime shows, which are cheap shows commonly stripped across five days per week; these use light material – such as the popular-music orientation of *Keynotes* – and are aimed at retired people and women at home with small children. Second come the afternoon shows scheduled between 4 p.m. and 6 p.m.; these shows, seeking to include older children in the audience, focus on word games and general knowledge. Last come the evening shows, which are more varied, and more expensive; they usually have some distinctive theme and a high-profile host.

There is a big cost contrast between the simple daytime shows and the more elaborate evening shows. The daytime shows typically use simple questions (such as word puzzles); the contestants are few in number and may be recruited from people who apply; the studio set is simple and the show is limited to on-screen performers. A simple show of this kind requires only a small crew, studio and studio audience. The host, although important, is not a big star name. Some such shows recruit their contestants from the world of minor celebrity. In, say, a 3-week burst of production, the studio set can be left in place and perhaps over 60 shows may be recorded.

At the other extreme, a big evening show will spend much more money on several or most of the quiz-game items. The questions, clues, problems or challenges may be more elaborate and may include film clips, which involve copyright payment, film searching and editing. The contestants will be selected through elaborate research and sifting – the producer often wants a particular type of contestant with enough interest and personality to ensure a successful TV programme, and 'contestant researchers' visit a number of non-London locations. These contestants require travel and hotel expenses. The evening game show may have a panel of experts who tend to be actors, journalists or sports stars. The evening show may also use professional musicians and dancers, who may be hired for days of rehearsal per each show performed. These bigger shows have audiences of up to 500 people, which requires a large studio. Such shows are technically quite complex and typically use a large number of studio cameras and a large overall crew. Some evening shows do outside filming; *Blind Date* camera-crews travel to Europe with their dating couples; *The Krypton Factor* films contestants on an assault course; and *Through the Keyhole* probes around the homes of two mystery celebrities. Finally, the big shows use big stars who command big salaries.

In the case of a daytime quiz, the channel can commission, say, 120 shows at a time. Re-commissioning can then be left quite late. Within only a few weeks of the go-ahead, a daytime show can have the next batches of contestants in place, ready to churn out another 30 programmes a week. With high-rating evening shows, however, the network may want to increase the number of programmes, but the producer and the star may say that 16 or 20 a year is the maximum possible. Each programme may take a week to produce; typically, the big star has a second show and genuinely has no spare time available. Some production teams work on a yearly cycle, making two different series for the same host each year.

Since game shows are not only highly popular, but also fairly scarce in the schedule, there is a strong case for spending more money in this supposedly cheap field. Thus, mainly at the weekend, high-profile shows are pushed into the early-evening schedule in an attempt to attract audiences to the more prestigious programmes scheduled later in the evening.

The limited amount of air-time also means that the evening quiz series typically run for relatively short seasons of between 12 and 20 programmes; then one show stops, often to be followed by a similar show in the same time-slot. On the commercial TV network this has been connected with the usual compromises between companies. For the BBC a successful game show becomes both an embarrassment and a necessity. This problem is manifested in the more commercial aspects, such as prize-giving; the BBC has always restricted the value of its prizes below the levels allowed by ITV's regulators.

On Channel Four there is the usual preference for innovation and change. The full list of evening game shows reveals a remarkable diversity – from helicopter-assisted treasure hunts, to simple cross-word puzzles and the extraordinary demands of improvisation on *Whose Line Is It Anyway?*

The budgets of most quizzes tend historically to creep upwards. Producers not only upgrade the apparent difficulty of the questions, but also argue for somewhat larger budgets. Some of the apparently cheaper shows are not so cheap as they may look. *Blockbusters* has, indeed, been stripped across weekday early evenings in England and recruits its teenage contestants from schools; however, it recruits teenagers from all around Britain and this is not so cheap, since it involves researchers travelling to the schools to interview possible participants and entails travel, hotel and chaperone costs for the contestants. *Blockbusters'* serious questions reflect a Reithian mix of education, information and entertainment. Other daytime shows such as *Countdown* also draw on public-service principles.

Producer and team

On a big evening series putting out 20 programmes per year, the production team might number up to fifteen people for most of the year; a studio-based quiz that makes several programmes during each studio day obviously stays in production for relatively few weeks, or even days, of production each year. In addition, for each show there would be a team of craft people employed directly in the studio on recording and rehearsal days.

The producer's core team usually consists of researchers, the director, a production assistant and secretarial support. A prime-time show will employ a larger number of research staff and perhaps two senior researchers or assistant producers. A feature of a high-profile series is the amount of research devoted to each programme. A major people show can require up to seven research staff employed throughout the year. The researcher's role involves regular contact with members of the public as guests, participants or contestants. The job requires tact and diplomacy. An evening quiz programme will usually employ a contestant researcher, who, clipboard and questionnaire in hand, will scour the country evaluating potential players. In contrast, a less-well-resourced daytime show will recruit contestants by vetting written applications.

Some shows only require the involvement of the producer and team for four months per year. Commonly, the producer actually works on two shows, sometimes producing one, while directing another. One show might be in production from late August to Christmas, with a second show in February–May. In such cases, at least some of the team will work on both shows. After the second show finishes in May, the producer's attention will switch again to the other show. The most strategic considerations are the budget, the likely time-slot, the format and the host. Budgets on ITV are strongly influenced by the ITV tariff, which might be £15,000 for an afternoon half-hour and several times as much for an evening slot.

The host and the format are the guts of the quiz show. All producers agree that the host is crucial; the show depends on his (or her) personality, popularity with the audience and skills with the contestants. The quiz show is commonly recorded in one long take and subsequently edited to fit the scheduled time-slot. Throughout the recording the host is in effective control:

> He is what gives the show its particular flavour; without him it would be unthinkable, it would be a totally different programme.

In the case of a new show or a new host, the producer's job is to marry the two together. For a new show the British rights will usually have been bought from a US or European quiz-format seller, or it may have been developed in conjunction with an independent production company. There may be one or more pilot programmes with audience research to match. The producer will not, however, adopt the format in its entirety. The show may need to be longer ('so we added the bonus round') or it might seem too simple ('British contestants have a broader general knowledge'). Ingredients may be added or subtracted to match the host's strengths, such as an opportunity for spontaneous zany humour or a liking for hyperactive movement across the studio.

It continues to be a key producer task to keep the marriage of host and format in good working order. 'Tweaking the format' happens mainly between seasons; but the producer is continually enthusing the host and in some cases restraining the host from making excessively sexist or racist jokes. Two other strategic issues are the set and the prizes. Available budget and the host obviously influence the decision on the set. Prizes are an area where regulatory disapproval is prominent. The Independent Television Commission has greatly relaxed the old Independent Broadcasting Authority (IBA) rules; the IBA thinking was to fix an absolute maximum prize limit at the price of a small new car. BBC producers feel still more constrained, because the BBC is even more keen to restrict perceived greed, commercialism and sponsorship. British producers argue that they do not wish to see the excesses of US quiz-show prizes and the free promotion of sponsors; however, they typically favoured some relaxation of the current restrictions on prizes.

With the overall strategy in place, the producer will focus on contestants and/or celebrity guests. Bigger shows may have several contestant researchers who each tend to favour people they themselves have interviewed; the producer must decide. Many producers feel a need to attract as wide a range of contestants as possible. Popular entertainment is one of the few places where ordinary people, rather than TV professionals, are on screen. Producers regard it as their role to ensure that the plurality of the TV audience is represented. One anxiety is to avoid contestants who have already appeared on other shows, especially the bigger-audience shows.

If the show uses 'celebrity' guests, the producer must decide which category to pursue. There may be very specific requirements, such as (in *Through the Keyhole*) being willing to let a camera-crew into your home and then to show the results on television. More commonly celebrity guests are required to add to the humour and entertainment of the show, and the producer is acutely aware that the ability to talk amusingly on television for 90 seconds is not a universal skill. As the celebrity research generates lists of names, the producer begins telephoning agents, both to spread the word and to discover availability.

The usual publicity dilemmas are perhaps exacerbated for quiz-show producers. These shows are thought by newspaper TV reviewers to be fairly dull, repetitive, bland and cautious. On the other hand, quiz-show hosts include some of the best-known – and highest-paid – names in British show business. Producers complain that their host is really a very decent person, the show truly is good clean fun, and consequently the tabloid newspapers are prone to be exceptionally negative, since they constantly look for scandal and gossip.

Editing is another significant function for the producer. British quizzes are mostly recorded 'as live' but at greater length than is required. This allows the editing-out of any major mistakes, including contestants who completely dry up or otherwise make complete fools of themselves. The producers typically insist that apart from the editing-out of small sections, and some consequent necessary fiddling with the sound, they do not add cosmetic sound and they never add canned laughter. Few shows would want or need to add applause or laughter because the studio audience typically includes enthusiastic fans of the programme; some shows also encourage (or discourage) relatives and friends of contestants. The studio audience is often given considerable emphasis; it adds to the semi-participatory character of the quiz/game show. For the production team, and perhaps for the host in particular, the studio audience contributes powerfully to the overall experience. Although the producer sees research reports, he (or she) is often uncertain about the popularity of a particular segment, joke or performer. The producer gets feedback on this from the contestants and celebrity guests; one producer said that he always noted the response of videotape editors – if they crowded round to watch a sequence, that was a positive sign. The producer has the response of the host who likes big live audiences and is an experienced judge of audience reactions. The producer also has his own observation of the audience as the show is recorded, and again during editing. Ratings are the goal of the successful variety-show producer. Although advertisers and consultants are interested in profiles, the producer is usually confident that a large-enough rating will ensure the future commissioning of the programme. A series that fails to attract sufficient ratings is either quickly dropped or shunted into the low-prestige daytime schedule where economies of scale can be more fully exploited.

PEOPLE/SURPRISE SHOWS

The people or surprise shows depend on enabling the viewers to watch a human encounter, which has been contrived but is genuinely surprising to the persons seen on the screen. *Beadle's About* is the *Candid Camera*-type of surprise; a hidden camera reveals a practical joke, sometimes of alarming complexity and cost. *Surprise Surprise* depends upon re-uniting people with their long-lost loved ones. *Blind Date* presents girl-meets-boy as a lucky-dip spectator sport; the camera-crew then accompany the couple on a short holiday. *This Is Your Life* depends upon sentimental recollections heaped upon a celebrity at a surprise gathering of relatives and friends.

Three of these four shows are LWT products and people shows are mainly found on ITV. Since they tend to be long-running shows, there is a strong element of year-round production-team commitment to a formula that has been refined and polished.

All these shows can be dismissed as dependent on a trick, a gimmick or a small deception. This element of trick or surprise does not, however, mean that the programmes are easy to make. Indeed, all these shows involve a heavy element of research into choosing and finding out about the people involved. *Beadle's About* requires careful research on the subjects of the practical jokes; this involves discussing with the subject's family his or her likely reaction, as well as researching the physical practicalities of flooding the house or blowing up the garage, and casting the subject as the unwitting star of someone else's comedy drama. *Surprise Surprise* requires careful research to find appropriate relatives, who both wish to be re-united and will not have an on-screen heart attack. *Blind Date* involves research on the 'contestants' and their suitability for this very public dating-ritual. For *This Is Your Life* relatives and friends must be elaborately consulted so as to discover, not only family revelations, but also family skeletons to be avoided.

Each of these programmes has some of the complexity of a specialized military operation behind enemy lines. *Beadle's About* has the problems of the hidden camera, an unfamiliar location and professional actors playing passing citizens; the programme uses an elaborate sequence of location planning, scripting, rehearsals and briefings for each of its 60 short films per year. *Surprise Surprise* grapples with such intricate details as long-lost relatives anywhere from Australia to Zimbabwe. *Blind Date* has elaborate procedures intended to avoid boring young viewers or shocking their parents or grandparents. *This Is Your Life* has the delicate task of matching the 'pick-up' of the victim with an appropriate venue for the 'studio' phase.

These are complex and difficult programmes to make; but the professional skills of the producers are not adequately recognized, because people or surprise programmes are regarded in the industry as the lightest of light entertainment.

CHAT SHOWS

The talk or chat show established itself in 1970s British television with such hosts as Michael Parkinson. The chat show was another US formula for cheap programming; the guests generated the show's material and, in return for the publicity, were paid little or nothing. The only significant costs were the host, a small production team and a simple studio operation. As with other US formats that it imported, British television altered the US chat formula. The British chat show was of less-than-daily frequency but it was pushed into a higher-audience time-slot, such as early evening.

Perhaps the high (or extreme) point of British-style chat was *Wogan*; hosted by Terry Wogan, this show ran for seven years (1985–92), three times a week, 156 shows a year. *Wogan* was placed on BBC1 at 7.00 p.m., surrounded by super-popular early-evening soaps. In *Wogan*'s later years Channel Four ran *Tonight with Jonathan Ross* about 90 times a year. However, the most highly rated chat show, *Aspel and Company*, ran only some 15 times a year. Several other chat shows had similarly short runs.

A three-times-a-week chat show is supported by a production team of about twenty people. The biggest single category consists of researchers, who specialize partly by subject-matter (books, music, Hollywood) and are also split into groups which work one week on the current week's shows and one week in preparation.

None of these shows carries high prestige in the TV industry. They are regarded as bland: in order to attract a strong supply of guests, the host will give the guests an easy ride; and the guests – through contact with the researchers – know this in advance. Many guests are plugging their latest film, book, record or programme. There is often an odd mix of guests, reflecting a desperate attempt to widen appeal. One chat producer described the show as 'bubble-gum television', but another said 'the trick is not to become solely a plug show'.

The producers are, indeed, faced with a central dilemma: to attract audiences in millions, the guests must have some pulling-power. In terms of probable pulling-power there are several levels. Some total unknowns are invited – actors playing their first big part, apprentice book authors, and new musical groups – but such unknowns must be used sparingly. The already-fairly-well-known include established

TV performers, sports stars, authors, musicians and politicians; but most of these people are already frequently on television and in the press; moreover, they also are likely to be plugging their latest creations and achievements.

The guests most wanted by the chat producer are those super-famous people who have seldom or never been interviewed on British television. Most famous British actors, musicians, politicians, sportspersons and members of the royal family have already been frequently interviewed. The biggest supply of recognizable celebrities, seldom or never interviewed on British television, is located in Hollywood. Consequently these producers are very interested in major US stars, and chat-show researchers spend much time on the telephone to Los Angeles. However, this celebrity supply has its own dilemmas. Hollywood stars arrive in London in substantial numbers, but they are usually on a publicity tour; the star wants to be on all the shows, while the chat-show producers want the star exclusively, or at least want to be before the competing shows. Different members of the star's entourage have different ideas as to the desirability of a London chat-show appearance. Especially if the star is on a publicity tour, the personal publicist will be in favour, while the agent can see that no serious money will be earned.

Money is a dilemma for the producer. The general policy is to pay semi-nominal appearance rates – such as £200 – or a little more if a preliminary interview with a researcher is required. (Producers say that at least half the press cuttings about entertainment stars are untrue; therefore a preliminary interview with a researcher is desirable.) Producers do, however, make exceptions. Each show is keen to have some big stars in order to maintain its image and its audience. Occasionally this leads to flying a star over from Los Angeles to stay in a London hotel and/or paying a few thousand pounds. However, none of this ensures that the chat show gets a massive audience. In fact, the British attempt to push chat shows high up the ratings has met with rather limited success. Moreover, despite the music (which can be expensive), the young stars and the trawling of items like the Edinburgh Festival Fringe, the chat-show audience remains similar to the particular channel's overall audience profile.

Another oddity is that most Hollywood stars are not especially popular, although the occasional mega-star does push up the ratings. The show's host is a much bigger star to the British audience than is the average fading Hollywood star. Moreover, the centrality of the host poses its problems. In terms of audience, the more the host attracts sizeable numbers, the more the same individual also repels or bores sizeable numbers as well.

The frequent chat show has obviously worked out an efficient system for handling its large through-put of guests. Earlier in the day the host is briefed by the relevant researcher, the producer-director of the week and the series producer. The guests are chauffeured in, accompanied by an average of two other persons each; the studio audience is given a few warming-up jokes and the chat show commences.

The chat-show production team engages in many negotiations with many potential guests. The bigger catches and their entourages are often subjected to a lengthy version of what one producer called 'the seduction process'. Record and film companies sometimes offer a big star if the producer is also willing to invite an unknown with a new project. In order to attract the attention of US stars and agents, the producer may visit Los Angeles once or twice a year.

The chat-show host is obviously in an especially dominant position. Chat-show producers genuinely do admire the skills of their host. Each host is encouraged to play to his or her own strengths and preferences. Barry Humphries in *The Dame Edna Experience* is admired by producers for a style that involves insulting and putting down the star guests; the guests, however, are fully warned in advance (with videos of previous shows) and apparently welcome the chance to play a somewhat-subordinate cameo role in this unique chat show.

In practice, the successful chat show depends upon an amicable partnership between the host and the series producer. The producer-and-host team have between them a huge degree of autonomy; they really do have a blank sheet of paper in choosing their guests. However, they are in entertainment and they must live by the ratings.

PRODUCER CAREERS

As in other fields, the previous careers of these producers were quite varied; but there was a marked lack of elite and precocious career elements. None of these producers had been chosen as a special BBC trainee; none of them had been placed in charge of a major programme at an unusually early age. Also lacking here was the pattern common in drama of the producer who had moved quickly from acting into theatre direction.

Only a minority of these entertainment producers are graduates. Others have been to art school or are determined self-educators, and

entertainment producers overall are not much less 'intellectual' than
are most other producers. These producers do tend to regard themselves as combining unusually good understanding of popular taste
with strong general skills in television and management.

Some only got into television on the basis of substantial experience elsewhere. Others infiltrated from commercially orientated
media into the business or administrative side of television. The
most common entry-gate was a craft skill (such as assistant floor
manager, sound, videotape editor, design). The second entry-gate
was the making of TV commercials or other promotional work.
Third, some had entered via radio or a regional TV centre.

Most older producers came to specialize in light entertainment
through accident. They typically have substantial experience of
studio direction. Often they have directed a wide range of in-studio
programmes – children's, regional news and current affairs, as well
as light entertainment. As producers, these people regard themselves
as highly experienced; some continue to direct as well as producing.
Overall this group are unusually strong on the craft areas and
generally are multi-skilled.

The close relationship between entertainment or variety programming and the general public is often cited as the most satisfying
or enjoyable aspect of the producer's job. That the programme is
enjoyed by several million people is 'a staggering thing to realize',
said one producer. These producers know that they are in a low-
prestige field, but they have still achieved their ambition to make a
career in popular television. They are in show business on a national
level.

Among the older producers there is also a marked element of
frustration and dissatisfaction, a sense of having reached a career
plateau or cul-de-sac. The possibility of combining the producer role
with directing another type of programme was quoted as an advantage. The desire to move beyond popular entertainment into a
higher-prestige type of TV production was expressed as a specific
unfulfilled ambition:

> I mean, I'd love to do drama, but it's very very difficult . . .
> because you're seen as a success in a certain area . . . and people
> only advance in a very narrow cul-de-sac.

> If I took quiz programmes seriously as my career . . . but I don't;
> my filing cabinet is full of plays and documentaries that I've
> written or would rather like to make one day.

Entertainment producers collectively take a very negative view of the hierarchy inside their own organizations; they regard it as designed to benefit the more prestigious areas of programme-making. They are especially hostile to bureaucracy in general and accountants are described as 'wankers in suits' and as followers of a new religion.

TV is the most fun you can have with your clothes on, and they pay you money as well, it's a life-style, it's not really a job, if you are committed and totally immersed and I love all of it . . . the people, the artists, the audience; and suddenly we are accountable to men in suits and it was never meant to be about that.

This hostility towards 'bureaucracy' derives from the producers' belief that they are the ones who have been protecting their employers' financial and public-service interests by producing programmes of above-average popularity at below-average cost.

Part III

Producers and organizations

Chapter 9

The independent takeover

Independent productions and programme imports accounted for over one-half of all British networked television by the early 1990s. Did this mean, then that by 1993 vertical in-house factory production was already defeated and that British television had fallen to an 'independent takeover'? Representatives of the independent companies would certainly point to many qualifications and complexities to such an assertion: regional output, repeats, the fact that some contracting-out is by Channel Four to ITV companies, that there is a difference between hours and expenditure, and so on.

In retrospect, the near-total control of domestic British TV production within the network factories lasted only for the twenty-year period of 1960–80. In its early difficult years (1955–60) ITV contracted out much of its entertainment programming. The 1961 completion of the BBC Television Centre in west London symbolized the in-house era. The arrival of Channel Four in 1982 marked another phase, with the new channel making everything outside, while the established three networks still made all domestic programming in-house. It was the 1986 Peacock Committee Report that first suggested a big extension of independent production to other networks. This was taken up by the Thatcher Government and in August 1987 an Independent Broadcasting Authority/ITV agreement was made to contract out increasing proportions of ITV output to independent companies. A similar undertaking was later made by the BBC.

In 1980 the independent-production sector in London was focused on commercials, feature films and promotional films; there was almost no independent production for television. By 1990 some one thousand companies claimed to be independent TV producers. In the year 1991 Channel Four made programme payments to 668 separate independent production companies.

Independent production has split producers into two groups – if not sheep and goats, then buyers and sellers. Producers increasingly are either patrons or clients. The independent producer is a supplicant, seeking to become the client of a patron; the patrons are the producers who still work in the networks and still act as gatekeepers to the airwaves.

The massive growth in independent production is largely the result of Thatcher Government and Conservative Party policy during the 1980s. However, both Channel Four and the independent production industry were compromises negotiated between TV producers, who wanted more autonomy, and politicians who wanted more competition. Both have resulted.

This somewhat paradoxical combination is increasingly echoed throughout British television in general and within independent production in particular. Independent production is, in business terms, fiercely competitive; in place of the previous domination by two vertical giants, there is tooth-and-claw competition between a thousand small businesses. Alongside this small-business competitive economy goes a high degree of insecurity. Channel Four from 1982 established a practice of spreading its patronage widely and of changing both the patrons (its commissioning editors) and the clients (independent producers) at frequent intervals. Independent producers thus not only had to compete hard for that elusive series commission; while making the commissioned series, they also had to continue running hard and competing for new business. Independent producers found themselves in the same situation as actors, frequently auditioning for work in an overcrowded job market.

Although the business competition was fierce, this was very far from being a total triumph for commercial values over producer autonomy. Alongside business competition went continuing producer autonomy; Channel Four from 1982 onwards represented perhaps one large stride towards commercialism, but it also represented another large stride towards renewed producer autonomy. Its commissioning editors shunned efforts to maximize the audience; instead, they focused on their legal obligations in the directions of 'distinctive', 'innovative' and 'minority' programming. Many independent producers found themselves in highly autonomous control of highly innovative (or eccentric) programme projects.

While sending plenty of chill competitive winds through the system, the independent production innovations also strengthened some existing producer-led tendencies of British television. The new

independents were themselves overwhelmingly producers (not advertising people, accountants or engineers); the Channel Four commissioning editors were, in practice, executive producers who
farmed their work outside. Established producers in the BBC and
ITV found themselves still making programmes in-house, but also
wielding commissioning (or executive-producer) powers in relation
to outside independents.

CHANNEL FOUR: IDIOSYNCRATIC PATRON

'Commissioning Editor' was a new term introduced to British
television by Channel Four. Below the top management level were
some fifteen commissioning editors, each with a budget of, say, ten
million pounds to spend on perhaps 200 hours of programming per
year. The commissioning editors knew they were only due to stay for
a few years and typically they divided their money between numerous
single programmes, several short series and one or two major series
intended to earn prestige for the channel and the commissioning
editor.

A commissioning editor during the 1980s stayed at Channel Four
typically for about five years, and this often included moving
between two different commissioning jobs. The commissioning
editors saw themselves as having only a brief tour of duty in which
to make their reputations. Given television's long lead-time and the
additional year or two required for a series to acquire a following, it
was hardly surprising that the newly appointed commissioning
editor typically closed down most of his or her predecessor's
programmes – including, perhaps especially, the successes. Within
two years in the job the new commissioning editor would have a
largely new line-up of programmes on the channel. This pattern was,
and is, widely recognized by independent producers who, for instance, say that they are 'waiting out' a particular commissioning
editor's term of office. It is widely believed also that Channel Four
commissioning editors assemble a team of their own previous
colleagues and associates:

> If you look carefully at who he's commissioned, you'll find that
> they tend to be old friends, and people from where he worked
> previously.

Commissioning editors tend to acknowledge that, while taking a risk
on innovative programming, they also seek some security by giving

the commission to someone whose work they already know at first hand.

Commissioning editors see themselves as patrons of producer talent ('my independents', 'my programmes'). These editors see themselves as 'enabling', protecting and allowing their chosen producers to get on with the job. They see themselves as using their patronage to support serious, innovative and non-commercial programming:

> There are very few broadcasters anywhere in the world who would do the kind of television which we do here at Channel Four.

Channel Four's commissioning editors tend to favour a number of factors which fit into the channel's legal remit but also fit with maintaining, or increasing, the commissioner's power and patronage. There is little interest in using big, established, expensive (and powerful) star performers; better to be original and to gain prestige by discovering new, cheaper (and weak) unknown performers. Commissioning editors normally want to agree the main presenter or on-screen personality in a new series; typically, they seem less keen on the conventionally handsome establishment look, but prefer 'alternative' faces, reading-glasses, protruding ears, small speech-defects, and non-standard accents. Commissioning editors also seem reluctant to enter co-production arrangements, especially as junior partners; instead, they emphasize innovation:

> For a programme to come alive on my desk it really mustn't remind me of any existing programme; if it does, then I'm instantly much less likely to be drawn to it.

This emphasis on innovation was present in the legislation that founded Channel Four and in the policy of its first chief executive, Jeremy Isaacs. Although he had begun in TV current affairs, Isaacs had moved towards major documentary series; he also had very wide interests in drama, film, music and the arts generally. He saw Channel Four in terms of expensive creativity subsidized by cheap entertainment:

> Three broad areas deserved early appointments: fiction, news and current affairs, and education – the IBA required educative material to constitute 15 per cent of our output. In the beginning I attached no similar importance to entertainment; everyone agreed that the channel was to offer a more serious mix in its programmes

than did ITV. Again, whatever brave face I put on it, money would be tight; there would not easily be ample funds for every programme category. I would buy in entertaining programmes cheap, as there was nothing to stop my doing, and save my pennies for the fare that would make the channel's reputation.[1]

In his new team of commissioning editors, Jeremy Isaacs deliberately included several who had no previous TV experience. Unusually for a British TV channel, none of the senior appointees was a hardened TV (or radio) journalist. The usual political neutrality constraints were deliberately weakened; Isaacs acknowledges that much of Channel Four's factual output in the early years leant to the political left.

While Isaacs in the early days did get involved with many programmes and producers, Channel Four evolved (under both Isaacs and his successor Michael Grade) into a broadly two-tier structure. At the top were the controlling forces focusing on financial tidiness, scheduling and outside negotiations with politicians and regulators. At the second level was the team of fifteen or so commissioning editors (and their assistants) making the specific patronage and programming decisions.

In some respects Channel Four was merely a later model of BBC2. Both channels aimed at obtaining only a 10 per cent share of the total audience. While Channel Four accepted most of BBC2's minority, complementary and innovative, programming goals, it also took them somewhat further. A common Channel Four belief – quoted by commissioning editors and independent producers alike – was in the concept of a 'Channel Four audience' which was younger and better-educated than the audience at large. This was, in fact, a myth: the Channel Four audience-profile is very similar to the UK TV audience-profile overall (although it is younger and more up-market than the ITV audience).

Channel Four was, however, distinctive in the very sharp differentiation between the expensive programmes that would 'make the channel's reputation' and the cheaply acquired entertainment. In practice, Channel Four developed three levels of programming: first, there was the high-prestige material, taking up about 15 per cent of air-time. This included the expensive fiction offerings, which in the early days were conceived of as films to be released in cinemas and on Channel Four. Subsequently a few prestige fiction serials (of a few hours) were added; both types of expensive drama

generated one or two prestige successes each year, but delivered
rather modest audiences overall. Another prestige offering was the
50-minute news programme, which was made by Independent
Television News (ITN).

Among Channel Four's own commissions the soap opera *Brookside* and five-times-a-week game shows such as *Fifteen to One* and
Countdown were the continuing ratings leaders. The only other big
entertainment successes were a large batch of imported US comedies
(such as *The Cosby Show*).

Neither high-prestige nor low-prestige categories made much
impact on most of the people who worked at Channel Four. The
channel's own drama/fiction output existed in a separate small world
of its own, constituting in effect a low-budget film company. The
Channel Four long news was made at ITN by TV-news professionals. Similarly with the low-cost entertainment: the US shows
were purchased by one person; the quiz shows involved little
commissioning effort; other low-cost, high-volume programming
was farmed out to ITV companies, such as London Weekend
Television's horse racing. *Brookside*, based in Liverpool, was too
long-running to require much direction and too successful to be
cancelled.

The great bulk of attention, time and personnel in Channel Four's
commissioning effort went into the remaining programmes which
include its – mainly small-audience – comedies; but the majority
belong to the areas of documentary, current affairs, adult education
and a large slice of edinfotainment or mixed-goal programming.
Many, many Channel Four factual programmes have run for two,
three or four short seasons of 4, 6, 8 or 10 programmes, only to be
cancelled. Throughout the 1980s most had small budgets and even
smaller audiences. It was only after 1990 that Channel Four at last
began to develop a collection of factual programmes with audiences
of over two million (4 per cent of the UK public).

While a very few individuals at Channel Four commissioned a
small amount of expensive drama and a large amount of cheap
entertainment, the bulk of the commissioning effort dealt with, and
handed out, several hundred commissions each year to small British
independent producers. Much of this money went out in very small
amounts for just one, two, or three programmes in an anthology
series; in 1991 Channel Four paid each of 470 separate independents
total sums of less than £100,000 – averaging, probably, about two
hours of Channel Four air-time in a year. Most of the commissions

will have been for factual, fairly serious, fairly ambitious programming which achieved low audiences of around one million (2
per cent of the UK public). Thus most of the channel's commissioning
and most of its independent clients were still in the early 1990s
working away at quite high-minded, low-audience, television of a
freelance, minute-scale, cottage-industry kind.

GOING INDEPENDENT: SMALL BUSINESS CULTURE SHOCK

The thirty-six independent producers we interviewed worked in
thirty-one different companies. Nearly all had previously been
employed as producers in BBC television or for one of the ITV
majors; but one-sixth had come direct from commercial film and
video-related areas. The median age of these independent producers
was about 40; but several were over the age of 50, while some were
aged around 30. Some had gone independent after experience only of
producing single programmes; but one-third had held senior positions in the BBC and/or ITV and had been in charge of sizeable teams,
major programmes or whole departments.

Only a small fraction claimed to have gone independent primarily
in order to make money. The great majority had seen going independent in terms of increased opportunity in choosing programme areas
as well as freedom in programme production. In some cases the
motivation had been to escape from what looked like a blocked
career; a related motive was to get away from being tied to one very
specific type of programme in the network schedule:

> Here I'm no longer time-slot-led, but rather led by my own ideas.
> You can make one-off programmes for different strands, but in my
> head these make sense as my own series.

Some had gone independent only after being given the 'golden
handshake' treatment; they had used the redundancy lump-sum on
dismissal to invest in setting up a company. Others had left with a
'sweetheart deal' – the producer of an existing programme was
allowed to take the programme with him into his new independent
company.

Most current independent producers had experienced more early
problems than they had anticipated. Some had considerable difficulty obtaining any commissions; we only spoke to independents
who had programmes on the air, but probably a high proportion of all

independent-company launches are a total, or near-total, failure.

The producers to whom we spoke, who overall are atypically successful, nevertheless reported what amounted to culture shock. Previously part of a nationally prestigious large organization, the newly independent producer was now sitting in a small and modest office with a partner, a half-time secretary, no work, no team and no back-up services. These independents did not severely miss the studio and technical facilities, which can be acquired from specialist companies eager for the business. They did miss, however, the very high standard of the camera personnel and other specialists. Most of all they complained about the lack of numerous editorial-support services. Inside the BBC, the producer who wants a particular still picture or a particular piece of music or film only has to pick up the telephone, and 'it'll be there on your desk in the morning'. The BBC and ITV companies have general copyright agreements which streamline obtaining permission; these large organizations have professional experts on just about everything, who are easily available for advice and help on the hundreds of small editorial problems that programme-making generates.

Some independents clearly also felt isolated from their professional colleagues; no longer were there people down the corridor working in the same department and with experience of similar problems. A big organization, furthermore, acts as a continuing filter of new talent and potential team-members. A producer, selecting directors for episodes in a new series, has all the department's personnel (both regular and freelance) potentially available. For an independent producer, picking young directors becomes more hazardous:

> There's a major problem because when you've got a commission, the people who commissioned you want to know who's going to be making it; they may not want to take a gamble and they say 'Who is this young guy?'. So you get a situation where the people who like the idea and are prepared to put up the money, would be terribly happy if you were going to make it yourself; but if you say 'I can't actually take a year out to do this because I've got half-a-dozen other projects which I'm producing', then they may get nervous.

Independents tend to report the best thing about their work as being free to choose their own priorities, to create their own ideas and programmes. The worst feature is the administrative and commercial

load of running a small business without adequate back-up: the small
independent has to worry about the rent, the furniture, the computer,
signing the cheques, the law, the numerous programme proposals,
and the part-time employees – on top of the usual endless list of
details involved in actually making programmes, and the paperwork
that needs to be completed after the programme is finished. Asked
about their occupational self-image, many independents are unsure
whether to describe themselves as business executives and managers
or as TV producers and programme-makers.

An especially negative aspect of the independent producer's work
is bidding for, and negotiating about, programme commissions. In
some cases the bidding takes on movie 'cattle-call' proportions with
over one hundred preliminary submissions; these completely open
invitations appear to derive from the inexperience of some commissioning editors. Often there is a final short-list of three or four.
Another complaint is of inadequate time to prepare a good bid;
successful bidders also say that the process can leave inadequate
time between the success of the bid and the scheduling of the first
programme. The general wear-and-tear is also seen as a waste of
time and creative energy:

> I have no uncertainty about my own abilities, but it's [an] enormous
> leap of faith to persuade other people that a particular programme
> idea is a good one, selling it and getting it on the air, or getting it
> re-commissioned, and I spend an enormous amount of nervous
> energy on something that's worth nothing.

> The down-side is dealing particularly with middle management at
> places like the BBC, and going into endless negotiations about
> some tiny point in the contract, or trying to persuade them . . . that
> they are paying for it, fine, but they shouldn't have 100 per cent of
> it, because it's our sweat and blood and creativity.

Most independent producers are worried about both the quantity and
the quality of the press coverage they receive. The networks which
commission the independents claim to handle the publicity, but the
independents typically see the network's publicity performances as
inadequate. Most independent commissions are for short series with
modest ratings potential. Consequently the larger independents
spend additional money on their own publicity; they employ a public-
relations agency. Here, as elsewhere, press publicity is important to
the producer in several ways:

Press preview coverage is very important, in terms of boosting the ratings, for the morale of the team, and also for Channel Four's perception, because they like to read about their shows in the papers; nice mentions in the review pages are also very important, especially if it's in *The Independent* or *The Guardian* which frankly are the only ones that Channel Four people ever read.

A few independents either have prominent programmes, or have a company image that attracts press attention. One chief executive regretted having recently been involved in several high-profile newspaper interviews:

> It's good for business, but it scares me because it incites resentment on the part of your peer-group, and it also makes negotiations difficult because they all think we must be millionaires, which we're not; it's very much a double-edged thing.

Their press relations are yet another area of ambiguity and uncertainty. The network does not, however, seek to interfere; in press relations, as in so much else, independent producers are both highly autonomous and highly insecure.

MEDIUM-SIZED INDEPENDENTS

Below the largest 15 or so companies, the next 35 independent producers can be described as Britain's medium-sized independents. In 1991 these companies all had between 10 and 100 hours of television on the four terrestrial channels (and a few had long time-spans of cheaper satellite or cable output). These medium independents had turnovers in 1991 of between one and five million pounds.[2] They are well aware of the strong trends towards a small number of large fish and a very large number of small fish. The medium independents know that they must grow quite fast even to maintain their existing placings in the industry league-tables of hours and financial turnover. They also emphasize that, despite perhaps two or three million pounds in annual cash-flow, their profit-margin is very low: 'We're not creating anything which we can leave to our children.'

Most of these medium independents have a current output of on-going series, plus several one-offs and specials; they also list a number of projects at the development and bidding stages. However, these companies typically rely on just one or two projects, which may have a low chance of long-term survival. One company had a four-million-pound turnover in the previous year, but had just lost the one programme commission which accounted for well over half that amount.

Medium independents typically have between one and three founders and a very small staff of assistants, secretaries and an accountant. For a specific series commission the company then hires a freelance producer and a production team for perhaps 15 or 20 weeks. The total number of people employed by the company during the year may be twenty times the size of the core continuing staff. There is a strong temptation to exploit vulnerable people – for instance, employing a freelance producer for less than his or her previous rate. The independents also say that some of their competitors exploit students and other novices by employing them at nominal – or even nil – rates of pay.

Medium independents typically obtain most of their work from just one of the four channels; in practice, this may depend on the patronage of just one executive producer, or one commissioning editor. This may also involve a friendly relationship with the head of the channel in question. It is important, these independents say, to know what the channel gatekeepers want, rather than to offer ideas on a purely speculative basis. These medium-sized independents tend to be quite optimistic, despite seeing the future as extremely uncertain and insecure. Most would welcome steady, rather than spectacular, growth; typically, they emphasize the importance of maintaining creative quality, both to please themselves and to maintain a quality reputation.

Despite these steady-growth ambitions, most of these medium-sized independents find themselves locked into an often obsessive and emotional involvement in running the company and making programmes. They also evince a strong sense not only of personal rewards but of personal punishment:

> The best thing is the job; it's an incredible job to have and to work with the people I work with; the worst thing is not being able ever to get away from it; I find it very hard not to think about it.

> The worst thing is the lack of power. I've got no power over money, air-time, slots, anything; independents are hideously patronized, and I'm lumped together with beginners . . . who could not run a budget.

> Independent production is an incredibly precarious and stressful

business; you go in and you put an idea on the table, and it's hard not to take it personally if they don't like it; it's very hard not to end up hating a person simply because they don't agree with you.

There is considerable variation within this group of medium-sized independents, but most seem to fall into one of the following categories.

The young insurgent company

The young insurgent company might involve three youngish partners (two men, one woman). The young partners typically worked for a few years in the BBC or ITV; they then went independent and their first success was an innovative Channel Four series, which gave an 'alternative' approach to current-affairs, comedy or arts programming. Since then the company has had several other short series, but there is still a strong air of insecurity; the ambition is to obtain a stronger footing with the BBC or ITV. After an opening year or two during which the company was run in a highly chaotic manner, one of the founders has emerged as the effective chief executive. Another founder may specialize in developing new projects.

The established-name company

The established-name company is often named after its founder, an industry celebrity with a respected track-record; he or she has been in charge of a department or a large programme team in the past. The established name saw running this company as an escape from being an executive producer or department head in the BBC or ITV. He or she tends to emphasize a combination of artistic and business goals:

I specialize in coming up with talking-point oddity series – less profit, more fun.

What I enjoy most doing is these big one-offs, but when you get a steady runner as well then that keeps the money flowing.

The established-name independent is friendly with at least one of the top network barons – they probably worked as colleagues some years ago. This kind of producer is highly regarded also by direct competitors: they talk of consistently high-quality output, an original vision and also a safe pair of hands. Even these established names express anxiety about the future ('How much longer will I stay in fashion?'); but their approach is less frenetic than that of the young insurgents. The established name is explicit about preserving autonomy as well as quality. Some of these names continue as producer-directors or script editor-producers, because of the creative satisfaction involved; one or two cannot resist the temptation to write the book of the series (which in simple entrepreneurial terms must literally be a waste of time). The established-name individual is often in business with a partner who may carry the main adminis- trative load, or even the main producer load if the individual name chooses to focus on writing and/or directing.

The partnership of established names

A few independents involve several well-established producers. This can lead to rapid growth, with each partner (or his personal company) attracting one or more sizeable commissions to the central company. Despite its undoubted strengths, this type of partnership can prove quite volatile. If the company specializes in one field, such as current affairs or drama, the individual partners inevitably will not all be equally successful. If the company involves partners, each of whom specializes in a different field, that partnership may also prove quite hard to hold together. One partner tends to become chief executive, while the other established names may come and go (to set up their own personal companies).

The talent-based independent

This company is a partnership between a star (of acting, comedy or talk shows) and an experienced producer. Obviously such a company will depend quite heavily on the star's success and durability; such companies may seek to go beyond dependence on a single per- former. This type of independent is likely to become increasingly important in the future, as the performing talent demands a bigger slice of both the production power and the money.

THE LARGE INDEPENDENT

The widely predicted emergence of ten or fifteen dominant indepen- dent producers had already broadly occurred by 1991; these com- panies each did over five million pounds' worth, and/or over 100 hours per year, of production for terrestrial channels. A few also made quantities of satellite programming such as Action Time's five-times-a-week *Love at First Sight* on Sky One.

In addition to Action Time there were other game-show specialists (such as the British subsidiary of the Australian Reg Grundy company); sports specialists – such as Cheerleader and Grand Slam – also made big numbers of hours; by contrast, Zenith, Cinema Verity and Carnival specialized in high-cost drama. The biggest comedy specialist was SelecTV; the biggest light-entertainment specialist was Mentorn Films; while Broadcast Communications was the biggest news and current-affairs specialist.

Several of the largest independents had a substantial element of management decentralization. Zenith Productions had three companies: Zenith South, specializing in expensive drama; Zenith North, based in Newcastle; and Action Time, which was the British leader in game shows (their production, co-production and format licensing). SelecTV owned two subsidiaries – Alomo and Witzend – both specializing in situation comedies and comedy drama; this company was also a leader in the introduction of team comedy writing in Britain and in various independent business practices. Another decentralized company was Broadcast Communications which, while specializing in current affairs and documentaries, developed and bought several smaller independent companies located in separate London offices.

'We want to create an asset-base of rights': this statement by one executive was typical of large independents but would have been atypical of a medium or small independent. Large independents spoke easily about finance and business; they were numerate and they took a well-informed interest in research data. They believed themselves, compared with smaller independents, to have better access to the programming barons and a more informed conception of what the networks wanted:

> We don't work in a vacuum, we're marketing-oriented, so we cultivate contacts with them . . . we have regular meetings with them; we talk to them on the phone frequently; we think of ourselves as specialist suppliers to a large company, just as in any other business.

Clearly the channel controllers also have an interest in cultivating a close relationship with what they regard as the biggest and best independents. For example, of Channel Four's 25 highest-rating entertainment commissions in 1990, about one-half (13) came from just four independents (Hat Trick, Channel X, Chatsworth and Mersey).[3]

REVERSE TAKEOVER?

The expansion of independent production after 1982, plus the 1990 Broadcasting Act and the 1991 Independent Television Commission franchise decisions, all ensure that the publisher system is playing an increasingly central role in British television. The independent production companies will also be major domestic suppliers to the expanding satellite channels.

The 'independent takeover' of British television will, it might seem, be ever more heavily underlined. However, just as Channel Four was an ambiguous innovation (part commercial, part public service), so also independent production involves its several ambiguities and paradoxes. In particular, the relationship between the networks and the independent companies remains unclear.

One marked trend has been for some individual large and medium-sized independents to become closely associated with one particular channel. Indeed, in the early 1990s the larger independents increasingly developed continuing business relationships with the broadcast channels. SelecTV made an 'output deal' to supply the BBC with new comedies for the three years 1991–3. This kind of deal went a step further in the franchise decisions of 1991; Carlton Television – the new London weekday contractor – took an ITV lead in placing total programming reliance on independents. In some cases independents acquired a minority-ownership interest in the ITV company; and in other cases the ITV company became a minority owner of the independent.

These deals between networks and independents were inevitably a cause for anxiety among the vast majority of smaller independents. These deals could be seen as the large independents 'changing sides' and aligning themselves with network partners. Second, these 'output deals' threatened to escalate further the growth of some already-large independents. A third related development could be seen by smaller independents as yet another major threat; until 1990 all four terrestrial TV channels had insisted upon acquiring all subsequent rights to any programming commissioned from independents. However, some large independent producers such as SelecTV began to insist that they must retain some hold over the rights to subsequent showings. One type of deal involved the independent retaining the foreign-sales rights, while the commissioning network would acquire the domestic UK rights for a limited number of years. The details of such deals remain swathed in secrecy, but this looked like the beginnings of 'deficit financing': if the network does not obtain the full rights, it will not pay the full cost; 'deficit financing' requires an independent to fill the financial gap either by issuing more shares, or through bank debt. This development, then, can be seen as pushing independent producers into a bigger and more dangerous financial league, on top of all the other uncertainties.

Loose alliances between independents and particular channels already exist and are based on several kinds of common interests, bargains and negotiations. The networks and some large independents are partners in the sense of cross-ownership; in some cases they share rights in popular programming; in other cases they make 'output deals'. Since both networks and independents specialize, this also encourages loose partnerships: an independent which makes quality popular drama has its best market in ITV; a current-affairs or documentary independent may look mainly to the BBC, and so on.

PRODUCER-DRIVEN INDEPENDENTS

In a TV industry that increasingly operates on a 'publisher' basis, there is a clear division between buyers and sellers; in this situation the buyers (the networks) are the patrons and the sellers (independent producers) are the supplicants. How exactly this relationship – and the British TV industry – will evolve, depends at least in part on future lobbying, legislation and regulation.

However, a remarkable feature of the emergence of independent production in the first decade after 1982 was the degree to which both producer-buyers (commissioning editors) and producer-sellers (independents) were devoted to a producer-driven style of television and were mainly interested not in making money, but in making programmes.

Chapter 10

Women producers

Both the men producers and the (thirty-seven) women producers (and senior executives) we interviewed were agreed that there had been a significant change during the 1980s in the employment of women as TV producers. By 1991 women occupied three of the top eight programme posts at the BBC and Channel Four. By 1993 there were four women on the thirteen-person BBC Board of Management. At some point soon after the year 2000 a majority of senior producers in British television may be women; and women may occupy one-half of the top positions in the BBC by 2000. On the other hand, there have been other advances of women, followed by retreats, in the history of British broadcasting: the 1930s, 1950s and 1970s saw reductions in the number of senior women compared with the previous decades.

British broadcasting history has largely defined the TV producer's job as a male role. Several different occupational traditions fed into the definition of the producer's job as not a 9-to-5 activity; it was more than just a job and it required 100 per cent (and therefore male) dedication and commitment. The civil-service-mandarin tradition of the early BBC and the craft film unions of the early ITV tradition alike left little room for women. The military tradition – which remained strong in the BBC personnel department well into the TV era – also had strong male overtones. An invasion of women, whose commitment might be less than 100 per cent, would be undesirable.

Yet other broadcasting traditions incorporated male assumptions. One was the notion of the fast-track or elite career; a small number of people (in practice, male graduates largely from Oxford and Cambridge) had been recruited through a special entry-gate for elite careers. This elite-career model fitted civil-service tradition, paralleled military tradition and was not out of key with the traditions of stage or show business. All these recognized the need to select future top civil servants, generals, or theatrical actor-managers and impresarios.

The concept of selected young 'leaders of men' entering through a special entry-gate excluded women. These elite entrants then typically worked in several different areas. There was no prescribed career or speed of promotion and the BBC operated a much-praised 'attachment' system, which allowed individuals to be transferred to another department for a limited period; the individual might stay or might return to the original department. A flexible set of career arrangements, which were designed to reflect the complexities of a cultural bureaucracy, probably had the unintended result of retarding women's promotion.

To get yourself promoted you had to apply, and to apply you needed a positive view of yourself and an optimistic view of your career prospects. Ambitious male producers undoubtedly applied for promotion in order to stake a claim this time, in the hope of getting a promotion next time. You then had to be interviewed competitively by a board of your (male) seniors; you had to impress them with your ability to manage sizeable teams of cameramen, engineers, directors, actors and journalists. For three decades after 1945 few women completed this male-built obstacle course. Instead, most women in British television remained in secretarial work and in other lowly positions, such as production assistant – quite often assisting men who were not only younger, and less experienced, but also less competent than themselves.

PRODUCER AS MALE ROLE: THE HISTORICAL BACKGROUND

A landmark study called *Women in Top Jobs*, published in 1971 for Political and Economic Planning (PEP),[1] showed that women occupied a lower proportion of top jobs in the BBC than they had forty years earlier. It was not until 1974, after more than fifty years of BBC radio, that the BBC appointed its first woman radio national news reporter. The then head of BBC TV news told the present writer in 1968 that the time was not yet ripe for women to present the TV news; he quoted a colleague (Ian Trethowan, later BBC Director-General) as saying 'To read the TV news, you need a pair of balls.'

Formally the BBC had always believed in equal opportunity and had, for example, always paid men and women equally for the same work. In its very earliest days, from 1922 onwards, there were several women in key senior positions; but in the 1930s male dominance asserted itself. Then in the second world war many women were promoted during the BBC's huge wartime expansion. This forward march of women was, however, again followed by a retreat after the war. The big TV expansion of the 1950s also saw women pushed aside. A few women moved in to high positions in television in the 1960s, but the great majority of new TV producers were thrusting young men. Film-industry craft unionism took over the main technical areas in ITV and helped to confirm the established BBC tradition of male dominance.

The 1971 PEP study documents the position that obtained in 1968–70. Women were doing best in radio, where they occupied 33 per cent of producers' jobs; 15 per cent of national TV producers were women, but these women producers were mainly in women's and children's programming areas. The study documents difficulties faced by women at entry, in career and promotion, and in terms of exercising authority. In particular, women were blocked from entering through technical gates such as the camera traineeship and through the fast-track elite entry-gate; in the years 1954–69 only 7 per cent of BBC general trainees were women. Another medium-fast-track entry-gate into radio allowed in 50 per cent women; but most women (including graduates) had to enter as secretaries. Women were also promoted more slowly than men. Women who were promoted (outside a few preserves such as children's television) faced major problems in asserting their authority as producers. The PEP study reports the unwillingness of male technicians to accept the authority of a young woman director or producer. Women were thought unsuitable for hard news reporting on television and also unsuitable as producers of entertainment output. Women producers who confidently asserted their authority were regarded as shrill, unladylike and over-emotional. Only just over one-third of the senior BBC women had children.

Returning to the BBC ten years later, the same researchers found that the situation of women at the top of the BBC around 1980 was much the same as in 1970 and in 1930. At the basic producer grade and the two grades above, women had only advanced from 5.7 per cent of senior BBC women in 1969 to 6.7 per cent in 1978. Most women producers still became stuck at the basic 'producer' grade, and still did not become senior producers in editorial charge of programmes, let alone executive producers or departmental heads.

Indeed, in terms of Top Jobs, the researchers pointed out that their previous forecast had proved correct; during the 1970s the proportion of women at the most senior levels of the BBC had slightly declined. The women who had achieved rapid promotion in the second world war had now retired and been replaced by men.

During the 1970s decade the male organizational culture at the senior levels of the BBC seems to have changed very little. A few departments – especially in the documentary and arts areas – were willing to promote women; other areas – such as sports and light entertainment – remained determinedly male. The male culture of the BBC itself depressed women's ambitions. They were slower to recognize that promotion was possible, slower to apply for promotion and much slower to get promoted.[2]

The 1981 PEP study did report a massive change in recruitment of women into the BBC, and these recruitment changes were one major factor in the sea-change of the 1980s in both the BBC and ITV. By 1979 the BBC had four graduate-trainee entrance schemes and in that year 43 per cent of the successful candidates were female (sixty-four young women graduates entered through the BBC's expanded elite entry-gate in that year).

The Equal Opportunity principle was included in the 1990 Broadcasting Act. During the 1980s equal opportunities had gradually become increasingly real for women (if not for ethnic minorities). Channel Four, as a new-style public-service channel, from the outset employed substantial proportions of women in senior positions; two of the three initial senior commissioning editors were women. At this time both the BBC and ITV also introduced breakfast programming and expanded their daytime coverage; many of the new producer jobs were filled by women. Gradually during the 1980s equal opportunities and the need to have more women in senior positions became part of British TV orthodoxy. The woman producer became incorporated into the public-service-broadcasting project. During the 1980s this goal was only fully achieved at the lower producer levels; in 1989 while 51 per cent of BBC 'assistant producers' were women, only 25 per cent of senior TV producers were women. At the 'producer' level women were 35 per cent.

Television work has remained very heavily segmented by gender. In addition to secretarial work, and other junior positions such as production assistant, another group of jobs – including vision mixer, wardrobe and make-up – are heavily female. The researcher role (at the bottom of the producer hierarchy) became predominantly female

in the 1980s. Another big batch of jobs are predominantly male –
camera, sound, lighting, engineering and post-production, including
both tape and film editing, as well as senior management.

The thirty-seven women producers whom we interviewed were
aged between their late twenties and their mid-fifties. They fell into
three roughly equal groups in terms of their entry into television: one-
third entered through an elite graduate entry-gate such as the BBC
news trainee scheme; one-third entered television via radio, print
journalism or market research; the other one-third entered through
one of a wide variety of TV jobs – such as film editor, actress,
facilities management, TV presenter, TV news-desk assistant or
production assistant.

Both men and women producers in the early 1990s tended to agree
that there were more good female than male candidates applying for
work as, or promotion to, producer. While broadly agreeing that
women producers were at least as good as men, some senior male
producers still chose some rather ambiguous arguments:

> If you think of things which women are classically good at, such as
> looking after a home or cooking – 'I've got these five things on the
> stove and they've all got to come to the boil at the same time' –
> well, that's a lot like TV production.

Women producers tended to use slightly different arguments:

> Women work harder; you can't generalize too much, but women
> crack on with it, while a man will be sitting having a cup of coffee
> and thinking about it.

> They're more conscientious, there's far less bull-shit, and they're
> much more straightforward; there's a strong sense of women
> having other things to do – such as families – so they work hard all
> day, and they don't sit around telling other people how they
> should be putting their stories together.

Many 1960s ideas about women in television (as reported in the PEP
1971 study) had been rejected by the early 1990s. Foreign filming
trips – once thought unsuitable for women – were accepted as part of
the woman producer's life; a dozen or more extended and exhausting
foreign visits in a year were regarded as normal by several women
producers. One described herself as being 'one of the boys'; certainly
few 1990s women producers would tolerate being described as either
a 'lady' or a 'girl' (terminology common in the 1960s). Fewer male

technicians and assistants now regard a woman producer as an exotic freak or a deliberate challenge to their manhood.

The increasing number of women producers in some areas seem to have precipitated further increases. When a particular department or genre acquires a reputation as welcoming women, it attracts more women. Those few women who in the early days of television reached senior producer levels tended to employ and encourage other younger women, who in turn did the same thing. A number of women producers found themselves employing women as at least half, or more than half, of their production team. Women senior producers often favoured a 50/50 mix of male and female producers; however, fewer able men may be keen to work for a woman programme editor, thus forcing her to employ a majority of women.

Women producers, while accepting that the 1980s brought a major change in both attitude and behaviour, recalled their own less-happy early experiences which made their promotion slower than that of male contemporaries. The woman producer of a highly successful current series had spent ten years in her first lowly job in television. Several women had, as recently as the 1980s, experienced hostile craftsmen:

> I've worked with dubbing mixers in the past . . . whose attitude was completely wrong; they didn't want to be there, they weren't happy working with women, they were incredibly rude and obstructive – that will not happen any more.

In the early 1990s the experience of women producers differed quite sharply between different genres. Amongst BBC senior production personnel (departmental executives, senior producers and producers) in 1992 women occupied about one-third of such senior posts in documentary, drama and children's programming; this includes two of the most prestigious areas in British television. However, women constituted only around 17 per cent in three other important areas – light entertainment, sport and news and current affairs.

About two-thirds of the women producers we interviewed had no children; but about half the women producers aged 38 and over were mothers, although some had a completed family of only one child and others of two. Those who were mothers had become full-fledged producers before they had become mothers. Several women producers contrasted the generous current policies in this area against the harsher organizational attitudes of the past. Some producer/ mothers who in the past had taken more than the briefest maternity leave had been severely penalized and demoted. Other women said that they had deliberately decided to pursue their careers rather than have children. One producer said that for weeks on end each year she scarcely saw her husband and that she felt such a job was not compatible with motherhood.

A number of these producers said that some producer jobs were more compatible than others with family life. They pointed out that while their job involved longish hours ('9 to 7, not 9 to 5'), it was nevertheless predictable. One woman in charge of a large team made such a point and added:

> My family is still my first priority; if the school phoned to say one of them was ill, I'd be off like a shot.

In some, but not all, fields there was a common belief – amongst both men and women producers – that some kind of 50/50 balance on the production team was desirable. This was sometimes explained in terms of the audience also being composed equally of women and men. Several programme editors, male and female, argued that members of their producer team tended to choose the topics of programmes, meaning that the gender mix of producers affected the balance and gender appeal of the programmes. One woman producer also liked to maintain a gender balance among the producers around the office:

> I've got three or four women either just about to give birth, or having just got pregnant or trying to get pregnant again so what I try to do is keep the balance, not because I think it's got to be 50/50, but I don't like the atmosphere when it gets to be too many women or too many men down the corridor; it's definitely noticeable when all the women are away filming – all the boys get a bit uppity.

WOMEN AS SENIOR PRODUCERS AND EXECUTIVES

There seems to be a tendency for the cause – and the numbers of women producers in British television – to advance rapidly for a short period, and subsequently to stay still or even to retreat somewhat. One rapid advance occurred with the recruitment of many young women (mainly graduates) from the late 1970s onwards.

Another such burst occurred with the 1982 launch of Channel Four, the growth of independent production and the huge expansion of broadcast hours. However, the proportions of women involved here can be exaggerated. Many women did indeed set up as independent producers and some, such as Verity Lambert (Cinema Verity), Jennie Barraclough (Barraclough, Carey) and Denise O'Donoghue (Hat Trick), became leading independents. However, a check on the principal names involved in 35 larger independent production companies in 1992 found that only 27 per cent were women. Within Channel Four itself the position of women can be exaggerated; the annual report for 1991 reported women as 30 per cent of middle management and 21 per cent of senior management. At the channel there are more women in senior programme jobs than in general management, accountancy, engineering and technical services.

A third big increase in the employment of women in senior positions occurred in the BBC, from the late 1980s onwards. In the 1980s BBC Governors (such as William Rees-Mogg and Jocelyn Barrow) argued for more women in senior positions, as did a wave of younger male senior executives in the Michael Checkland era (including Michael Grade, John Birt and Will Wyatt). Various reports published by the BBC and others documented the position of women.[3] In the late 1980s the BBC adopted equal opportunities as a corporate strategy and established a system of targets, monitoring and active implementation. A study of equal opportunities in 500 British companies published in 1992 found the BBC to be ahead of most large British companies and ahead also of Channel Four and some large ITV companies. The BBC's equal-opportunities policy included recruitment, monitoring, positive action, crèches, career breaks, job-shares and flexible hours.[4]

1989, which saw a big boost for women in BBC television, was also a year of substantial general growth. In 1989 many men were promoted in BBC television; it was also a year in which many senior BBC people were offered huge pay increases to go to British Satellite Broadcasting (BSB) – some producers were offered more than twice their BBC salary by BSB. Against this background, between February 1989 and February 1990 the number of women in BBC TV's Band Five (senior managers, executive producers, editors of major programmes) and above increased from 40 to 60. There was an even higher increase in Band Four (which includes producers); and a still bigger increase in Band Three (which includes assistant producers), where the numbers of women doubled from 181 to 372. Because these bands include many people not in programme production (including many seniorish people in technical areas), and because of the general large expansion and upward movement, the percentage increases for women producers were smaller. There were, however, also percentage increases in all of Bands Two to Five. By March 1991 the proportions of women in BBC television were as in Table 10.1.

Table 10.1   Women in the BBC, 1991

Employment band	Jobs included	Women (%)
Band Five	Executive producers and editors of major programmes	25
Band Four	Producers	20
Band Three	Assistant producers	30
Band Two	Researchers	38

The figures, however, also reveal some reductions in numbers of women. In particular, in the six months from September 1990 to March 1991 the proportion of women in BBC TV's Bands Two to Five actually decreased very slightly. In broader terms, the proportion of women in these four grades was overall stalled at about 32 per cent; this was against the background of an overall decline in the BBC TV work-force in the same months.

In ITV women have never done so well as in the BBC. A check on senior programming executives in the five major ITV companies shows that the proportion of women increased from 7 per cent in 1982 to 10 per cent in 1992. The only large ITV company with a significant proportion of women top executives in 1992 was Granada Television; it may not be a coincidence that Granada in recent years has paid lower average salaries than the other larger ITV companies; a league table of ITV pay in 1990–1 had Granada in eleventh place out of 15 ITV companies.

Within the all-news company, Independent Television News (ITN), of senior producers only 6 per cent were women in 1982 and 11 per cent in 1992. ITN also was a clear case of women's advance followed by some retreat. Of the top names in all areas of ITN including producers, administrators, editors and reporters – about 150 people – in 1990 women made up 20 per cent of the total, while two years later, in 1992, this had fallen to women as only 17 per cent of the total. ITN was in some financial difficulties in 1990–1 and cut back quite severely on its total numbers. It also introduced much more demanding requirements for all its journalists, which involved working longer hours and also being available on short notice during days off. These moves – typical of the general trend of British television around 1990 – were seen by many women at ITN as unintentionally discriminating against them. A number of ITN women journalists, especially those with young children, left their jobs. At the same time ITN was not recruiting any new staff, leading to a reduction in the percentage of women in middle-level and senior posts.

CONTRARY TRENDS

The overall picture is complex. In some areas, especially in the BBC, the proportion of women seems still to be increasing. In other areas, especially in ITV, the movement, if anything, is in the other direction. Moreover, despite some rhetoric about equal opportunities, the ITV system lacks an effective policy; it consequently also lacks basic data on the subject.

The women producers whom we interviewed believe that – despite much genuine male goodwill and general support – women are still regarded by the men in charge of certain specific areas as a challenge and a threat:

> I find it incredibly hard to go and have a meeting with someone who's fuelled by resentment; not only are they talking to someone who's very successful, but I also happen to be female and it sticks in their gullet.

Senior women producers report that when attending departmental meetings, they are still often the sole woman, or one of only two women, present. Phrases such as 'a meeting full of suits' recurred frequently. Some senior women producers (like some men) found meetings irritating and time-wasting, a distraction from their creative task of running a programme series. Some women were aware that their irritation with time-wasting meetings, plus their fairly forceful personal style, could easily contribute to their being stereotyped:

> I think people found me rather sort of bossy and pushy and loud, and I was genuinely quite disturbed by this, and then I thought, well . . . you know, all I'm trying to do is get the series on the air and use all of those techniques I've learnt . . . such as never letting an interviewee say no.

Even while a woman was being promoted to a senior position, such male doubts could be expressed. On one such occasion the successful female candidate, it was said, had been asked at the 'board' interview in the BBC whether picking up the children from school ('the school run') would be likely to pose difficulties.

Some large areas of television still have very few women in senior positions. This includes the whole of regional television and the whole of national news and current affairs, as well as sport and most areas of comedy and entertainment. Some female advances may also be followed by unanticipated consequences. For example, the studio-director role has been filled by substantial proportions of women; but the other director role – directing single-camera filming (or taping) on outdoor location – is more prestigious and has retained a male aura. It is possible that the 'loss' of the TV-researcher role to a preponderance of women could lead to more assistant producers being recruited via other more male (perhaps craft) career routes.

One male independent producer said that he found himself employing a high proportion of women freelance producers, who tended to be pregnant and/or mothers of small children. He was able to offer them very flexible working conditions, and they were able to offer him high-quality work at a relatively modest salary level. This situation could be seen in terms either of further female advance or of further male domination.

A larger version of this somewhat ambiguous situation may be played out across the entire British TV industry. How will the gender divide be affected by that increasingly important divide between programming made within the TV networks and programming made by freelances and independent producers? Will male executive producers and commissioning editors continue to exercise the main power and control as the secure buyers of, and decision-makers over, programming? Will the programming increasingly be made by a much less secure and much more feminized group of freelance and independent producers?

Chapter 11

Programme barons and power

British television, this book argues, is 'producer-driven' in the sense that producers of specific series are given a high degree of autonomy; within very broad guidelines the producer is allowed – indeed, encouraged – to get on with the job. However, the series producer, although given great tactical autonomy, is still strategically dependent on decisions made from above. The key decision is whether to go ahead with the series run of a certain number of programmes. More broadly there are, incorporated into this decision (made once or twice a year), three linked elements: first, there is a decision on the broad editorial direction of the series; second, a decision on the budget and the number of programmes in the series; third, there is a decision on scheduling – the day and time at which the programmes will be aired (and possibly repeated).

In any national TV system these strategic decisions will obviously be made by people at the top of a national network. However, the British mixed system (partly commercial, partly public service) seems to result in what internationally may be an unusual amount of strategic power being placed in a few hands. One or two individuals in charge of each of the four British terrestrial channels exercise much of this power; of course, these individuals are also constrained in various ways and themselves depend on colleagues, subordinates and committees of superiors. Each of these few individuals, plus a surrounding team, does exercise huge power in the British system, which traditionally sees network decisions as best taken by one executive rather than by a committee. The British system also leaves much of the operational definition of the mix of 'commercial' and 'public service' to the individual channel controller.

Most of these key programme individuals and also the chief executives of the overall organizations have had, and still do have, a programme-producer background. The four British conventional channels, looked at overall, are producer-driven in the sense that the programme-producer hierarchy stretches from the lowly programme researcher to the Director-General of the BBC, the ITV Network Director and the Chief Executive of Channel Four.

BARONS: DRIVEN BY RATINGS OR WHIMSY?

Producers are keenly aware of the strategic powers exercised over them by the network barons. Individual producers, whether they see themselves as recently having received baronial punishment or baronial reward, support the prevailing system under which decisions are taken by individual barons rather than by committees. Producers also tend to see some decisions as taken almost entirely on the basis of ratings and popularity, while other decisions can be attributed to the personal preferences or the 'whimsy' of the network baron in question.

Broadly, the ratings-orientated decisions occur on BBC1 and ITV, while the whimsical decisions prevail on BBC2 and Channel Four. There are many financial and other relevant variables involved in these commissioning and scheduling decisions; but there is, indeed, a distinct difference between the mass channels and the minority channels.

ITV has never been 100 per cent ratings-driven; the requirements of the regulators for news and other programming, plus the territorial claims within the ITV cartel, have prevented any single purpose from having absolute sway. The main thrust of ITV is, however, towards ratings. Any ITV producer whose series is high in the ratings, or is winning the audience battle in its time-slot, is likely to have the series renewed for next season. BBC1 is broadly similar to ITV, but somewhat less ratings-driven. The baronial boss of a primarily ratings-orientated network still has big choices to make, and big amounts of finance to deploy. It is the current barons of BBC2 and Channel Four who have a much wider range of choice within channels which seek smaller audiences with smaller financial resources. The only way to get a 35–45 per cent audience share is to focus heavily on high ratings and popular programming; but there is very much more leeway in achieving an 8 or 10 per cent share of the total audience. The mix of series which the current BBC2 or Channel Four baron chooses cannot be defended as the only possible, or self-evidently the wisest, choice. Consequently, some producers, whose output the minority-channel baron seems to like, tend to praise the baron's flair and wisdom; producers whose output the baron seems to dislike are more prone to refer to the baron's whimsical decisions or arbitrary use of power.

BARONIAL BACKGROUNDS

There is a stereotype of British broadcasting being run by Oxford-educated journalists. Like many stereotypes this one is neither entirely true nor untrue. Hugh Greene perhaps personified this stereotype; Oxford, *Daily Telegraph* journalist, had a good war (BBC German service) and was BBC Director-General (1960–9). Throughout the years from 1946 to 1986 most of the people who ran British television had some of these characteristics – fee-paying public school, wartime or national-service officer, Oxbridge arts graduate, TV-news or current-affairs producer; but few such people had all these characteristics and some had none. While a sizeable number were south-of-England WASPs, a significant number were Scots, Jewish, Welsh, Roman Catholic.

Over the decades since 1946 there have been numerous changes of the guard. Two such changes in the top echelons of British television occurred around 1987 and around 1992–3. Whether one is looking at the top two people directly in charge of each national TV network, or at a wider group of some fifty top people, there was a comprehensive change in the top people between 1987 and 1993.

Both before and after 1987, however, the representative top person in British television was a man who reached his elevated position at around the age of 40. This man was a humanities or social-science graduate who came up through one or more of the prominent factual programmes.

There were, however, some pre- and post-1987 differences. More of the BBC's pre-1987 barons belonged to the ex-military, slightly macho, leaders-of-men school. Huw Wheldon was the most important single baron in BBC television from 1965 to 1975; Wheldon, who attended the London School of Economics, was a pioneer BBC producer of arts programming and was also head of BBC documentaries. As a young army officer Wheldon was awarded the Military Cross in Normandy in 1944; he retained a somewhat ex-military personal style. 'Manly' was a favourite word and he liked to tell General Montgomery stories.[1] Wheldon was a compelling public speaker and undoubtedly dominated his junior barons through the force of his personality, his (cautious) opinions and his individual style. Some fifteen years after his departure from the BBC, more than one interviewee quoted Wheldon's exertion of personal magnetism as one means by which the producer's will could be made to prevail. This exuberantly extrovert style seems to have gone along with a somewhat cavalier approach to network management and scheduling.

When Michael Peacock, as BBC2 controller, launched the new channel in 1964, it was fairly clear that neither he nor anyone else in the BBC had yet decided what to do with a second channel. BBC2's initial scheduling approach involved focusing on a different genre for each night of the week. Even after its early disasters, BBC2 continued to be scheduled in a remarkably amateurish way. The BBC's barons in the 1960s and 1970s seem to have concentrated mainly on making programmes, with much less thought given to where and when the programmes would be scheduled. There was also a distinct tendency to overspend; Huw Wheldon was one of many front-office boys whose naughty over-spending habits led to chiding from clever accountants, such as Michael Checkland, and from backroom girls such as Joanna Spicer.

Michael Checkland, when he became BBC Director-General in 1987, introduced an entire new echelon of BBC barons, such as John Birt, Will Wyatt, Alan Yentob, Jonathan Powell and (in 1991) Jane Drabble. These five new young barons had some of the same characteristics as the previous echelon – all five were producers from current affairs, documentary or drama. However, Checkland's barons differed from Wheldon's in some other respects. The new barons were too young to have done military service; all five of them were TV intellectuals; Jane Drabble – as number two to the Managing Director of Television – was the most highly placed woman programme executive in BBC history. Although some of them had worked briefly in radio, these new BBC barons were TV professionals, with a greater depth of TV experience than their predecessors. They were also much more concerned with the financing and budgeting sides of television.

Channel Four was only launched in 1982 and had much in common, from the outset, with BBC2. The Channel Four version of the executive producer – the commissioning editor – was in charge. There were several gradations of commissioning editors from the junior level up to Jeremy Isaacs, the first chief executive who also acted as his own head of programmes. Isaacs was a much-admired and highly distinguished programme-maker. The early years of Channel Four, 1982–7, were in some respects closer to the patterns of the 1970s than to the late 1980s or early 1990s. Jeremy Isaacs had moved from current affairs to documentary and while in charge of programmes at Thames Television in the 1970s had brought to life many impressive series. Isaacs surrounded himself at Channel Four with a team of commissioning editors notably short of TV-production experience. The channel's opening weeks and months were chaotic, even by British standards of TV launches. Jeremy Isaacs used his superior expertise and experience, as well as the warmth of his personality, to exert an extraordinary dominance over Channel Four in its early years. He was much more interested in programme quality than in finance, management and scheduling; in the Wheldon manner, he was rescued by a small, efficient group of backroom boys (such as Justin Dukes and Paul Bonner) and by backroom girls (such as Gillian Braithwaite-Exley and Pam Masters). In 1987 Jeremy Isaacs left Channel Four and a new era of more systematic manage-ment was ushered in by Michael Grade as the new chief executive.

Channel Four has followed the BBC baronial pattern in giving the major emphasis to people with producer and producer-orientated backgrounds. It is, of course, the ITV system that, of the four conventional networks, is the exception. ITV is, however, only a partial exception. Until 1992 ITV differed from the two BBC channels and Channel Four in that there was no network chief executive. ITV appointed its first chief executive in 1992 in the person of Andrew Quinn who had a general TV-management back-ground at Granada Television. This 'general TV-management' back-ground is important at the top of the ITV system. It was these general managers – in practice, often largely involved in managing the production factory and the trade unions – and not the advertising sales managers, who shared with former programme producers most of the chief executive posts at ITV since 1970. Each of these chief executives has always had his director of programmes, who in-variably has a programme background.

ITV's fairly strong traditional emphasis on production experience in its top executives has, of course, been related to regulatory requirements and this factor was clearly present in the 1991 franchise bids. A number of senior TV personnel have news and current-affairs backgrounds, but there may since 1987 have been a switch of emphasis towards entertainment, not factual, production experience. These ITV trends were reflected in the appointment in 1992 of

ITV's first-ever Network Director; Marcus Plantin had a successful track-record as a programme producer at the BBC and at London Weekend Television (LWT); he was Director of Programmes at LWT for two years and thus effectively took the lead in scheduling ITV at the weekend. Marcus Plantin also conformed to recent ITV trends in that his background was not in TV journalism, but in comedy and entertainment.

BBC BARONS AT WORK

Ever since 1964 the BBC has had its two national channels and over the decades it has learned to run them with gradually increasing sophistication. After BBC2's opening eccentricities, an attempt was made to run these channels on a complementary basis with cross-promotion of each other's programmes. The controllers of BBC1 and BBC2 both had offices on the sixth floor at BBC Television Centre and they were supported by a single planning team.

The then controller of BBC2, Brian Wenham, described in 1982 how he had increased his channel's audience share from 8 to 12 per cent:

> BBC2 used . . . to have a heavy educational bias in the early evening, and that was followed by a heavily journalistic bias. Often general programming didn't seem to start on BBC2 until about 8 o'clock . . . One of the key things that we've done over a period of five years is to shift that around, so that BBC2 now puts on not a highly popular face, but a general programming face, from teatime onwards.[2]

Wenham also successfully used his baronial powers to spread large quantities of (newly popular) snooker across his channel. Sport still gives BBC2 some of its highest audiences, not least when major sporting events switch back and forth between the two BBC channels. BBC2 also does well with established edinfotainment and consumer programming. With the ratings well-bolstered in such ways, the BBC2 controller is faced with less ratings anxiety than is the boss of any of the other three channels. Within the BBC system the BBC2 controller is expected to operate a schedule which complements, and contrasts with, BBC1's schedule. This tradi-tionally means that BBC2 schedules comedy and entertainment against BBC1's 9 p.m. news, and schedules drama against BBC1's sport on Wednesday evening. BBC2 is also expected to carry much education and some Westminster politics in daytime and it must carry *Newsnight* at 10.30 p.m. This also means that Auntie BBC takes care of much of the low-audience times; the main requirement on the BBC2 controller in the high-audience times is to counter-programme to BBC1's evening entertainment, drama and news. This involves mainly factual programming, spiced with some entertainment and films, in the 5.30–10.30 p.m. high-audience hours. In scheduling and commissioning this factual programming – from a wide range of separate BBC departments – the BBC2 controller has a remarkably free hand. As one programme baron said:

> You still hear in British television some very singular voices; you see the work of particular individuals.

The public also hears, to some considerable extent, the particular and singular voice of the BBC2 controller. When Brian Wenham (a former news and current-affairs producer) was BBC2 controller, the output and image of the channel reflected his scheduling strategy. After Alan Yentob took over as BBC2 controller in 1987, the channel's image (as reflected in research) shifted. Yentob had previously been head of music and arts and BBC2 duly expanded its arts coverage, both in terms of hours and to encompass new subjects such as architecture; BBC2 (partly in response to Channel Four) also targeted a young audience, new writers and new trends in the arts.

Because of its two TV channels, its large programme-making factory (and the large radio output) – as well as the normal cumbersome logistics of television – the BBC organization chart is complex; channel controllers are expected to attend, or to chair, numerous committees. This organizational complexity does not smother the channel barons' powers; on the contrary, it makes obvious sense – against this complex organizational background – to allow the channel barons to exercise their baronial powers to the full.

The BBC's chief TV baron is the Managing Director of Television to whom report the heads of all the main non-editorial areas: Resources, Production (studios and facilities), Finance, Personnel, Planning and Strategy, and Publicity. The Managing Director of Television is also the chief link between the TV service, the Board of Management and the Governors. Finally, he is the boss of the BBC1 and BBC2 channel controllers and the Deputy Managing Director (to whom the programme departments report). These wide responsi-bilities of the Managing Director of Television are consistent with much of the strategic programme decision-making being done at the BBC1 and BBC2 channel-controller level.

Each of another five key BBC programme barons is in charge of major TV expenditure. These include the heads of drama, 'light entertainment' and 'sports and events'. Also important are the heads of two combined radio/television areas: news and current affairs and regional centres (including Birmingham and Manchester). These five major areas seek largish audiences and their expensive output appears mainly on the large-audience BBC1 channel.

Somewhat lesser baronial figures are the heads of those other programme-making areas which typically are less big spenders and more of whose output appears on BBC2 than on BBC1. This includes such departments as music and arts, documentaries, education, and science features. The chief patron of these lower-audience-programming areas is the BBC2 controller, who also schedules much of the non-mass-audience output across all the programming range. With this very wide variety of departments – and literally hundreds of independent producers – to choose from, the personal preferences of the BBC2 controller can carry exceptional weight.

In the past each of the BBC's top dozen TV barons has presided over one of these highly specialized areas. Within the ITV system, however, the top dozen barons have been general managers – the chief executives in charge of the larger regional companies; each of these ITV general managers has been a chief executive in charge of a production factory, local and network programming and perhaps one thousand employees.

In the BBC system the dozen powerful specialized barons (some with their own departmental TV buildings in West London) somewhat overshadowed the small general-management staff of the Director General (located in the mainly radio-orientated corporate headquarters in central London). During the early 1990s the BBC general managers were focusing on government policy (Broadcasting Act 1990, and the November 1992 Green Paper), the phasing-in of independent production and the cutting-back of in-house factory production (the 'Producer Choice' initiative). A weakness of BBC central management was indicated by the large unnoticed overspend revealed in late 1992. After this the early-1993 appointments of an ITV general manager (Bob Phillis) as Deputy Director General and of a senior Channel Four executive (Liz Forgan) were logical moves.

CHANNEL FOUR AND ITV BARONS

Channel Four, after its early Isaacs years, has evolved what in some respects looks like a smaller version of the BBC TV organization chart. At the top of Channel Four is the Chief Executive, who himself now does no commissioning of programmes. Reporting to the Chief Executive are the heads of key areas such as finance, engineering and advertising sales, as well as 'Director of Programmes' to whom in turn report the two top specialist-programme people. Thus the channel's programme commissioning has some similarities to the BBC1/BBC2 split, except that Channel Four's split is factual programmes against arts and entertainment. Below this top level come senior commissioning editors and lesser commissioning editors. Much of the power in the Channel Four system is exercised by some fifteen commissioning editors; each commissioning editor must argue for his or her annual budget – and there is a greater requirement than in the early days to justify and defend programme plans. The organizational culture, however, favours allowing each editor considerable autonomy to pursue Channel Four's remit of innovating and being different. Commissioning editors tend to talk about 'spending my £12 million this year' – and they speak only the truth. Channel Four today is a commissioning-editor-driven channel.

ITV has always been different. Before 1980 the commissioning and scheduling of ITV was planned by a committee of the programme heads of the five largest companies. Each company contributed programmes to the network schedule according to its share of net advertising revenue, with the five majors totalling 65 per cent. As each company representative tried to sell his programmes to the others, and to hang on to the best time-slots, these meetings were famously acrimonious: 'There was rivalry between them to obtain the best time-slots for their own programmes, and mutual trust was not absolute.'[3] This ITV cartel planning system of the 1970s was remarkably rigid. It was a production-dominated approach to running the network. There was some specialization, but most of the big companies wanted to be in most of the big programming areas. One result was fragmentation into many short series. Under this system a major-company programme director knew that he had near-complete security of control over certain ITV time-slots: 'I could tell one of my producers that his series was safe for the next three years.'

Under the old ITV cartel system, scheduling was secondary to making programmes. The Programme Controllers Group only planned six months ahead; scheduling meant looking at what the companies were already making and fitting it into the schedule. The weekday and weekend quarterly schedules were drafted on single sheets of paper by the representatives of the two London companies; the draft schedule would be discussed at one long Monday meeting, some changes would be made, sheets of paper would be discarded and a final schedule would be approved.

This very-short-term, rigid and programme-driven bargaining exercise began to change in the early 1980s; it gradually evolved into a more coherent planning system. Initially, Channel Four had small audiences, but ITV still had to take it into account and a system of mutual support developed – swapping schedule information, cross-promotion and joint buying of films. Channel Four did also squeeze ITV in terms of both finance and audience. A new South-of-England company, TVS, began to flex its financial muscle – in effect, demanding to be let into the club of the major companies. After 1982, ITV's rather crude planning arrangements were challenged by the small ITV companies, and also by a new generation of programme directors, including John Birt of LWT. John Birt argued for giving primacy to the requirements of the schedule and then commissioning programmes to fit specific time-slots and target-audiences. It was not until a decade later, in 1992, that a first chief executive (Andrew Quinn) was appointed to run the ITV network. Clearly, the present ITV system is a more schedule-driven system.

As with so much else in British television, ITV's central scheduling operation is far from being a complete break with the past. All the key individuals came from the large ITV companies into the new system. The central scheduling system broadly represents a compromise between the Channel Four system of commissioning editors and the old ITV cartel dominated by a few large companies. Similarly to Channel Four, the ITV central scheduling system has a Chief Executive to whom reports a Network Director as well as heads of finance and marketing. Under the Network Director are commissioning editors in charge of major programme areas.

The new system retains important elements of the old ITV cartel. The Chief Executive of the scheduling office reports to a Broadcast Board composed of the Chief Executives of all the regional ITV companies. This new system supposedly gave more weight to both independent producers and the smaller ITV companies; but it is a system in which the independent producers remain supplicant

sellers – power resides in ITV's central scheduling system behind
which three companies (Carlton Television, LWT, Central Television) exercise increased dominance.

SCHEDULERS AT WORK

Although each network's approach to planning has its own distinctive history, several approaches are now broadly held in common.
The planning horizon stretches about two years ahead with a long
series of meetings designed to get the schedule requirements and the
supply and financing of programmes into balance. More detailed
planning is done on a quarter-of-the-year basis. Meanwhile, planning
committees meet each week to monitor the evolving process. These
weekly meetings look at the latest ratings to see how the current
output is faring; the annual-planning-cycle documents are also
considered; particular areas of output – say, drama – are looked at in
detail; these weekly meetings also look a few weeks ahead; the
schedule is only finalized to fit the deadlines of the weekly programme guides.

All the channels have 'road-blocks' in the form of evening news –
BBC1 and ITV have two each per evening – and the schedule is built
out from these road-blocks. A common policy is to give the viewers
some fixed landmarks – such as that on certain evenings 8 p.m.
means comedy; there is the counter-consideration of change –
'freshening up the schedule' – and tactical responses to what other
networks are doing. Although schedulers can and do commission
some special research, the main data are the standard Broadcasters'
Audience Research Board continuous rating data and precedent ('we
look at what they did in the same week last year'). There is always
also a lot of current news, information and gossip about the competing networks' plans ('we usually know about their main new
series and the likely times, but we may have to guess which evening
of the week'). Some schedule planners create a complete 'dummy
schedule' of what they think the opposition will be doing and then
they try to schedule against the enemy's perceived weak-spots.

There is a strong family resemblance between the planning
approaches of the different channels. Within the baron's planning
group there are typically people who have previously worked in an
opposition planning group, so they have a good insight into what's
likely to be happening. There is also general agreement that the big
planning task is to commission and to buy the best programming to

fit the needs of the schedule and the preferences of the audience
('The schedule can only be as good as the pieces which the scheduler
has to play').

Asked about the skills and qualities required to run a national TV
channel, barons and baronial staffers indicated a broad range:

'Knowledge of the present and past schedules – what did well
before, when and why'

'A pair of glasses which can see into the future – what will excite
the public 6 to 18 months ahead'

'Confidence in your own judgement in the big areas of drama and
entertainment. Sport also. And movies, which are the bread-and-
butter of everyone's schedule'

'Knowing the research and the rules of audience flow'

'Stamina – it's a bloody hard job which never stops'

'Robustness, needed to shrug off difficult times'

'Understanding of production talent, whom to support and whom
to slap down'

'Predicting the other side's moves, who's been signed up and for
which night'

'Luck, cheek, nerve, flair, personal smell – would I watch it
myself? Anecdotes, and what my children say'

'Good judgement of your own executive producers and department
heads'

Finance being the factor that turns programme plans into a schedule,
clearly channel barons spend a good deal of time on financial issues;
but what else in addition to programme plans, schedules and finance?

Choosing people is an important activity. Barons are actively
involved in choosing heads of programming areas, and typically the
baron on whose channel, or in whose area, the output mainly falls
will in practice have a veto. Another type of key person is the
performing star. Big stars – which means mostly entertainment,
comedy and acting stars – are paid sizeable sums of money. Channel
barons typically see their top stars as making an important contribu-
tion to the profile and reputation of the channel. Often the star is
offered more than one series, perhaps in order to ensure that the
star's services are acquired exclusively for a period of time.

Promotion, presentation and publicity – in some cases all three being the responsibility of a single department – are also of interest to network barons. 'Presentation' is the final gathering-together and putting on air, and on time, not only of the programmes, but of all the small items between programmes. On-air 'promotion' has developed greatly in recent years; the channel barons set the strategy by deciding which programmes will get heavy promotion. BBC1 and BBC2 together put out about 150 minutes of promotion-time per week, which means several hundred short trails and promotions, which in turn makes this area a major user of post-production and graphics. Promotion executives use terms like 'media plan' and increasingly their activities resemble some of the activities of an advertising agency:

> You may be trying to pull ABs aged 20 to 40. Then you must place trails where that audience is.

> If the programme we're worried about is at 8.30 p.m. I might decide that promoting it directly would put some people off. So I might promote the programmes at 8 p.m. and at 9 p.m. in the hope of trapping the audience that way.

Channel barons with an ITV background have one significant advantage over those who have only held senior positions in the BBC. The federal ITV system provided what amounted to a training school for schedulers, in the form of its network-planning committee. The programme bosses of the larger ITV companies in general, and of the two London companies in particular, were involved in a committee which commissioned the programming and constructed the schedule. Jeremy Isaacs took this experience with him from Thames as a key qualification for launching Channel Four; Michael Grade took similar experience from LWT to the BBC and Channel Four; John Birt and Marcus Plantin also took LWT programme-controller experience to the BBC and to ITV respectively. Yet another leading figure, Greg Dyke, gained ITV scheduling experience while programme controller at LWT.

The BBC's arrangements provide fewer such educational experiences for its future schedulers. Newly appointed BBC channel controllers have typically had their entire experience of television within a single genre and their previous job has usually been that of department head. Initially, at least, such a BBC channel controller is at a disadvantage compared with a graduate of the ITV network school.

BARONS AND COMMUNICATION

Like the book publisher or newspaper editor who lacks time to read everything he publishes, so also the TV channel baron cannot possibly watch all the 20 hours of television per day that his channel transmits. He does watch some programming but obviously it must often be restricted to the first one or two programmes in a new series. Quite often, then, he must find himself discussing the merits of programming he has not seen.

Channel barons inevitably talk frequently to their major suppliers of programming; in the past this has meant their own programme department heads a floor or two below, but the suppliers now include a wide range of independent producers. As the commissioning net spreads wider, channel barons seem increasingly to reach out themselves to certain individual producers and independents. A visit by the baron to a remote building or an out-of-London provincial studio is a mark of status much welcomed by the producer involved. Some individual producers certainly maintain a personal relationship – breakfast with this baron, lunch with the other baron, are again highly treasured. There must, however, inevitably be a strict limit to the number of times a baron can bypass a departmental head and talk direct to the hands-on producer.

The press takes up scarce baronial time in several ways. The baron spends time giving interviews to the ever-increasing numbers of journalists who now write about television. Press coverage also finds its way into committee meetings as an agenda item and a source of information. Like the general viewers, the baron is often in the position of 'didn't see it, but did read about it'.

One channel baron said that before arriving (chauffeur-driven) at work he always looked at five daily newspapers; upon reaching work he scanned the photocopied digest of that morning's press stories already prepared by the press office. As the barons sit at their desks each morning scanning the press stories about television, they know that all the other barons, regulators and board members, are doing the same thing:

> When you have a public board (such as the BBC, ITC and Channel Four all do) you have the Great and the Good on those boards; they're hyper-sensitive to the agenda of the press, and to rows, manufactured rows, stoked up by the press.

These (often short-term) 'rows' lead to barons monitoring the press closely and sometimes replying to specific points. The barons are also aware of their longer-term responsibility for the channel's reputation and image, which leads them to make press statements and to give speeches aimed at press coverage. For some of these latter efforts the barons rely on their own publicity specialists. Meanwhile, the Director of Corporate Affairs has become a key role in certain ITV companies; some incumbents of this position, such as Barry Cox at LWT and Peter Ibbotson at Carlton, have successfully combined their knowledge and experience as senior producers (of current-affairs television) with their ability as writing journalists.

Channel barons tend to deal confidently with press journalists. The channel baron appointed at the age of 40 was typically in charge of an important programme or programme area by around the age of 30 and even before that was probably talking frequently to press journalists on the telephone. John Birt took charge of LWT's *Weekend World* in 1972 when he was aged 27. That Sunday midday series had very close links with the story-starved Monday newspapers; each Sunday the edited highlights of the programme were rushed across the river to Fleet Street.

Barons, who have long used press publicity to advance their own careers and their programmes, are also sensitive to the possible dangers of publicity. This is a major reason for barons being highly secretive, not only in relation to the press but also within their own organizations. One baron said that any open criticism from him of an in-house programme could lead to exaggerated press accounts of the programme's imminent demise.

The leaky nature of the TV industry was quoted as one reason for inadequate internal communication. There is a second major reason for such inhibitions, namely that senior producers are aware of how devastating their criticisms can seem to insecure programme staffs and contracted talent.

The BBC has tried to develop a mechanism for internal discussion and evaluation of programmes. This is the weekly 'Programme Review Board', chaired by the Managing Director of Television and attended by heads of programme departments and others. Current programmes are discussed and in some cases the editors of important new series (including independent producers) are invited. Ratings data are also looked at each week. The intention is to hold an editorial discussion in which a broad range of senior programme people express their opinions. Those who attend the meetings receive copies of the minutes. Some departmental heads make the minutes available to all their producers, while others do not. In some cases an individual producer will be told of criticisms by the departmental head.

To the outsider this seems like a somewhat hit-and-miss mechanism. We see here the BBC looking for yet more middle ways through the delicate area of internal communication. An attempt is made to convey frank comments to the individual producer while trying to avoid public humiliation. An attempt is made to establish a general BBC view of quality and success, but without establishing a narrow orthodoxy. An attempt is made by barons to talk to the working producers but without undermining the authority of departmental heads.

A basic dilemma remains. Television output is largely shaped and determined at two ends of the system. The barons on high draw the guidelines and the working series producers make the programmes. Communication between these two levels is very imperfect – largely defeated by hierarchy, the sheer bulk of unique material and the scarcity of time in which to consider it. Most of what the individual producer puts on the screen the channel baron does not even see. Most of what the baron does is also remote from, and unseen by, the producer. The main message that the producer receives from the baron is a 'Yes' or a 'No' to the proposed next run of the series.

Chapter 12

Conclusions: past

Before the final chapter, which makes some predictions about the future, this chapter summarizes selected themes from the book so far.

CHANGES IN PRODUCTION SYSTEMS

The period 1986–93 saw the breaking of the traditional British duopoly of two vertically integrated production systems; it also saw a large element of casualization at all levels of the TV labour-force, including producers.

Much change came about because of Thatcher Government policy. Not all of this happened in the ways the government originally intended (as with satellite policy); some of the post-1986 changes derived from the launch of Channel Four in 1982.

From the early 1990s Britain has had three different TV industrial systems: first, the vertically integrated duopoly of the BBC and ITV which until 1982 had produced all domestic-made programming as well as transmitting it; second, there is the 'publisher' model exemplified by Channel Four, but which is increasingly prevailing also in ITV and the BBC; third, there is the packager or themed-channel model which prevails with satellite and cable.

Previously most British TV producers had substantial security of tenure; they were like civil servants. Since 1990 this is no longer so – the entire TV labour-force, which was exceptionally secure, is now insecure, because TV workers are typically employed only for series production runs, each of only a few months. In terms of job security, producers (and others in television) are now less like civil servants and more like actors.

These are big changes; the changes which occurred in British television in 1986–93 were perhaps the most profound set of changes since those triggered by the launch of the advertising-funded ITV in 1955.

PRIVATE WORLDS

British TV producers operate within private genre-specific worlds.

Much of this book has been devoted to looking at seven different types of TV output through the eyes of the producers who produce these seven different genres. Are these subdivisions amongst TV producers any greater than those in other professional, artistic or media occupations? That is a larger question than this study is capable of answering. However, this study began in harness with, or as part of a combined operation with, a study about newspaper executives.

There are some distinct similarities in the ways in which newspaper executives and TV producers are subdivided. Both producers and newspaper executives are subdivided by subject-matter, such as sport and news. Both occupational categories work against severe deadlines; both appeal to the general public; both try to balance 'popular' with less-popular material; there is a distinction between 'mass' (channels and newspapers) and minority or more-serious. Since press and television operate seven days a week against deadlines, both producers and newspaper executives work on unusual timetables which may isolate them from other people.

There are differences. A newspaper, especially near the top of the editorial department, is relatively close-knit; the foreign editor and the sports editor attend the same editorial meetings each day. Television's technology of camera-crews, studios and outside broadcasts is more cumbersome. Most television also operates on slower timetables than daily journalism; the TV producer is absorbed in a single project – a run of the series – for months in succession. The closest TV equivalent to the newspaper is the TV news operation; however, within television the news operation is but one of the private worlds. Television covers many more areas, and in some cases it does not so much cover areas as actually create them. Many TV producers' work is closer to theatre or the movies; it involves building up from the script a TV play or comedy or other entertainment.

Each genre develops into a private world; each genre has its own characteristic goals and values, costs and budgets, and type of audience appeal. Each field within television recruits somewhat different kinds of people to be producers. There is no general TV induction; induction is done largely within one of the specialized genre-specific private worlds.

These private worlds are also arranged in a rough hierarchy of prestige and moral worth. Although TV producers live in a budget-conscious world, different genres have very different levels of expenditure. Some producers know that they are seen as providers of mere entertainment or lighter material; other producers are encouraged to think that they are doing something more than mere lightweight television – they are involved in a major art-form, they are making authored documentary statements or they are responding to – as well as setting – the national political agenda.

For audiences television is notoriously time-consuming, but it is also something which can easily be switched off when the telephone rings or a meal is ready. Television is not like this for producers. It is an enormously absorbing kind of work. There may be other forms of work – including law and medicine – which are not only more traditionally established, but which are equally or more absorbing for those involved in them; but television certainly is an occupation which does make big demands on sheer animal energy. Television producers try to use their battery of cues – pictures, words, music – to appeal to, 'to grab', the emotions of audiences. In concocting these emotion-grabbing messages, the producers make a big emotional investment in their own work. Much of that emotional investment is made within the private world of a specific genre.

LESS SECURE, MORE AUTONOMOUS

During the recent years of turbulence, British TV producers have undergone a paradoxical combination of changes: they have become less secure but more autonomous.

Few British TV producers would deny that producers overall have become less secure in recent years. This study has focused on producers whose names were in the *Radio Times* attached to productions just being transmitted. Many other producers were becoming ex-producers; indeed, a number of the producers we interviewed in 1990 were already ex-producers by 1992.

How, then, can they have become more autonomous at the same time? The paradox derives from a significant shift in the nature of the producer's job. Those producers who are (still) working are being asked to do more things than was the case before 1986. First, producers have been forced to take budgeting more seriously. Second, producers (especially in fields such as documentary and drama) are increasingly expected to take part in raising finance. Third, with the increasing contracting-out of programming by the BBC and ITV, many working producers are not only producing programmes but commissioning them out to other producers.

Fourth, producers are required to make more decisions about resources and encouraged to use outside freelance camera-crews, studios or graphics specialists, instead of the BBC's or the ITV company's own in-house facilities. The BBC in 1992 launched its new effort of this kind called 'Producer Choice'; the BBC made clear that choices would rest with series producers and not with heads of output departments.

All this adds up to more work, more responsibility, more control and more autonomy – for those producers who are still producing.

A PROFESSION?

Television producers do not constitute a profession.

Television producers collectively have some similarities to the many occupations which have been professionalizing in recent decades; but TV producers have not tried very hard to do the classic things normally done by occupations which have a strong urge to professionalize.

Television producers have not tried to control entry; on the contrary, entry has become more open. Television producers have not set up a 'qualifying association' which vets qualifications, establishes standards and the like. Television producers lack 'clients' of the kind that doctors, lawyers, architects or teachers claim to serve. Although TV producers are serving the general public, their 'hands-on' work refers not to clients or patients but to cameras, scripts, editing, performers – the business of TV production, not TV consumption.

There is another simple reason why British TV producers are not likely to go much further in a professional direction. In British television the producers – more than any other occupational category – are, or become, the general managers. Apprentice producers can start as 'researcher' and eventually become chief executive. This occupation of producer is not only a lengthy career-ladder, but also fits closely with the organizational hierarchy from bottom to top.

The TV-producer role covers a very wide horizontal range in terms of genres and types of output. In recent years the producer role has become further fragmented by the introduction of two new industrial systems, each of which introduced new definitions of producer to the British scene. The publisher model introduced the 'commissioning editor' and the 'independent producer'; the satellite or cable channels give weight to the acquisition and packaging of large flows of pre-existing production.

Some associations and organizations of a 'professional' kind do exist. There is the Royal Television Society which holds conferences and awards prizes. There are bodies which lobby on behalf of independent producers. Trade unions, although now weaker, still exist.

There is, however, no single body which seeks to preserve, defend and advance the interests of TV producers in Britain. The producers are too involved in their organizations – many devote their 'professional' loyalty to the BBC which they see as preserving the kind of television they believe in; indeed, many ITV and independent producers also express deep loyalty to the BBC and what it stands for.

Producers' deep involvement in their private genre-worlds is also in part both cause and effect of this lack of professional feeling or organization.

AN ELITE OCCUPATION?

Television production is not an elite occupation.

This study indicates that TV production is a well-established occupational category but the term 'elite' certainly does not fit many producers' social backgrounds. The producers interviewed in this study are not a representative sample of all TV producers. Of those interviewed about one-quarter were educated at either Oxford or Cambridge; about another quarter were at one of another small group of institutions (including two London University colleges – the London School of Economics and University College – as well as Bristol, York, East Anglia and Manchester Universities). The majority of these producers did not attend fee-paying schools; more went to grammar schools or comprehensives. In terms of their social and educational origins these producers' backgrounds are broadly middle-class and meritocratic. Despite having lived in London most of their adult lives, many of these producers speak with some trace of a British regional accent. In this respect, and in others, the producers are probably very similar to their presenters whose faces appear on the screen.

These are jobs, however, which many young people would like to do. A number of producers complained about the huge numbers of applicants that a single newspaper advertisement for a 'TV researcher' would attract. This occupation, of course, has no specific entry-qualification.

CHANGES IN QUANTITY, NOT QUALITY?

The programming output of British television has since 1980 almost certainly altered much more in quantity than in quality.

The four British terrestrial channels today put out twice as many hours per week as three channels did in 1980; not only has Channel Four arrived, but since 1980 the hours on the three other channels have expanded to fill all the daytime and much of the night. The biggest change in terms of quantity is the availability of multiple satellite channels.

'Quality' is, of course, difficult or impossible to define across the vast range and quantity of television. There clearly have, however, been some changes – the total output of Channel Four and a spate of new daytime programming. There is some evidence that since 1980 British TV programming has become less violent – or, at least, violent in less unsubtle ways.

If, however, anyone expected big changes in the production systems to make for matching changes in the programming, this does not seem to have happened. Nor is it easy to tell half-way through watching a programme whether it was made by an independent producer.

Some experienced producers, for example in drama, claim that they can quickly recognize the work of a specific director. This is, however, explained in terms of a particular individual's idiosyncratic manner of composing shots and editing them into a sequence. What is being said here is that the individual's mode of working continues over a long period of time, regardless of editorial arrangements or employing network.

Several women producers claimed that they could usually recognize whether a programme was made by a male or female producer. This, however, was said to be evident more from the subject-matter than from the style. Several women said that women producers were more likely to choose social subjects while men producers favoured political or business subjects. There are now more women producers and there are probably more factual programmes on social topics; but many other factors are at play here besides the gender of the producers.

PRODUCER AS EMPLOYER

In British television, the producer (of various kinds) has taken over some functions previously performed by management and also by trade unions; increasingly, the producer is becoming the effective employer.

'We have removed an entire tier of management' said one senior executive of an ITV company. Some of the functions previously performed by both specialist and general management are now heaped on to the producer.

The same is true of the trade unions, which until about 1986 in practice managed much of what went on in the craft areas. For example, the unions operated penally high overtime rates of pay which greatly affected the entire practice of location filming. The construction of sets, the operation of studios, the outside broadcasting of sporting events – all of these areas of work were partly managed by unions and partly managed by management. When trade-union power radically declined after 1986, these management tasks were not given back to management, which itself was slimming down radically.

The producer of a series run often has one, two or three million pounds to spend; and there are several possible strategic paths which could be followed. Do you do all the location filming first? Do you work alternate weekends? Do you start in the studio when the days are shorter in March? In the past all such decisions were heavily influenced by union rules. Now it is the producer who sits down, maybe for quite a long time, worrying away at the cheapest and most efficient use of the available time, resources and people. The producer makes a management plan, carries it out and is held responsible for it.

Increasingly, the producer is not just a general manager; the producer is also coming to be the effective employer. This latter has happened most obviously in independent production; but it is happening also within the BBC and ITV. With the short series runs so common in British television, employment is very often for a few months; it is the producer who effectively employs the production team, and increasingly also the technical crew, for those weeks or months. The producer who from 'inside' the BBC or an ITV company takes on a production team – via the personnel department – is increasingly likely to be either a freelance producer employed for that short series run, or a producer on a contract of perhaps one year.

British television is no less – probably more – producer-driven today than before 1986. The production systems have changed and the publisher system has become central; but the production culture has remained the same, in focusing on the producer as the person who holds the reins. The overall system has increasingly fragmented into smaller programme-making units. Everyone seems to agree that to the question of who should be in charge, in most cases the answer has to be the producer. If the producers are not driving the system, no other suitable occupational category – under British conditions – is available to do the job.

Chapter 13

Towards 2022

.

The year 2022 will be the one hundredth anniversary of the founding of the BBC. The BBC is a keen chronicler of its own anniversaries and, if it survives intact to that year, we can safely anticipate some fairly enthusiastic celebration.

Technology continues to advance, and well before 2022 there will surely be a wider range of higher-definition images than is available today. What will happen also depends upon the evolution of the economy in general and of consumer demand in particular.

The third great force that shapes broadcasting is politics, policy and legislation. Much of the change which takes place in the future will consist of the consequences – intended and unintended – of future government decisions. The history of British broadcasting has depended very heavily on legislation. Broadcasting legislation in Britain has favoured a step-by-step approach; not for Britain the French or Spanish sudden leap from three to six conventional TV channels.

The following points are suggestions as to what is likely to happen to British TV programming and producers without the impact of any new policies. These are likely developments still to emerge from the policy and industrial turbulence of 1986–93.

TURBULENCE

Without any additional policy changes the remainder of the 1990s promises substantial additional turbulence in British television.

The year 1993 marked the coming into effect of the new arrangements for ITV. These changes will take several years at least. The changes are likely to include company mergers; the regulatory position will be volatile because there are now two regulators – not only the Independent Television Commission (ITC) but also the Office of Fair Trading (OFT).

The core group of ITV are Carlton Television, London Weekend Television and Central Television; ITV's physical centre is the LWT white tower on the Thames South Bank. There will be continuing struggles between the dominant three companies, the other ITV companies and the independent producers. The schedule will be streamlined, with longer series runs and more emphatic showcasing of domestic entertainment and Hollywood films; game-show prizes will escalate; there will be more head-to-head competition in key evening time-slots, less edinfotainment, more factual entertainment such as reality crime, and a stronger focus on young, affluent, women viewers. There will be more aggressive buying-up of star talent.

However, ITV will continue to 'waste' much revenue on Treasury payments, on separate advertising sales operations and on regional buildings, personnel and output. Some companies will favour more expensive network entertainment and drama while the lesser survivors will want to limit network-programming expenditure. The mid-1990s may be ITV's finest phase; but by 2000 ITV may be finding it increasingly difficult to retain ratings dominance while only a sole channel competing against other major players (including the BBC) each with two or more channels.

Channel Four is in for a bumpy ride but there are two major reasons why it is virtually certain to survive. One is that Channel Four is still tied to ITV by the umbilical cord, or accord, of a financing arrangement which should stabilize Channel Four's advertising share and also gives ITV positive financial (as well as regulatory) reasons for protecting the channel's survival. Second, the channel is still an odd mix of ratings-maximizing as well as ratings-minimizing outputs; the overall mix lends itself to quite simple minor modifications in a commercial direction, such as its 1992 move from heavy breakfast news to light breakfast entertainment.

The BBC throughout the 1990s will be undergoing major changes – in particular, a massive slimming-down in total personnel and a big disposal of buildings. There will be many, very understandable, cries of despair by people who think that their devotion to the BBC, and their acceptance of its lower rates of pay, is now being ignored and discarded.

The satellite channels will obviously advance, and cable (spurred by the co-supply of telephone service) may grow faster. However, these multiple additional channels may still have less impact than some forecasts indicate. The British networks have some advantages which were denied in the 1980s to established networks in now highly cabled countries such as Belgium, Canada, the USA and the Netherlands. US programming is, overall, significantly less popular than is British-made material. The BBC and ITV can also use their own back-output to feed their own additional satellite or cable channels. Finally, BSkyB and other channels are emphasizing premium-rate subscription, a strategy for maximizing revenue rather than audience numbers.

Channel Five is another unknown. If there is enough advertising revenue it will be launched into a successful life; if there is not enough revenue it will not be a success. Either way, the message for the overall British system is that competition for TV advertising revenue will be fierce.

PUBLIC-SERVICE BROADCASTING

On the assumption that both BBC2 and Channel Four continue in approximately their present forms, then much of the present TV mix – including a large dose of 'public-service' or non-audience-maximizing material – will also continue.

Will the growth of satellite or cable multiple channels destroy British television as we know it? The answer is 'No', at least in the 1990s.

If we leave satellite and cable aside for the moment, then we need to remember that, back in 1980, not only were there three channels but these three channels operated for many fewer hours in the 24. Since 1980 there has also been some drift in a more commercial direction not only in ITV but also in BBC1 and BBC2. To over-simplify: BBC1 may have moved from 60 per cent audience maximizing in 1980 to 70 per cent by 1993; BBC2 may have moved from 40 to 50 per cent, and ITV from 70 to 80 per cent. Channel Four may have moved in the same way as BBC2.

There was a doubling of hours of British conventional TV output between 1980 and 1993. There was somewhat more than a doubling of the hours of ratings-orientated material. However, despite the 'commercial drift' of all four channels, there was also a near-doubling in the total hours of non-ratings-maximizing output. In 1992–3 the four conventional channels were putting out each week over 300 hours of ratings-orientated output, and they were also putting out some 200 hours a week of non-ratings-maximizing output. There are currently more hours of news programmes, more documentaries, more British drama, and more gardening and consumer programmes than any single individual is likely to want either to view or to video-record.

There are, of course, other ways to express this last point. However, it is broadly recognized in the TV industry that BBC2 and Channel Four are pillars of the present system. If either of these pillars were removed, then the whole system would be radically altered. For this reason, any proposal radically to alter BBC2 or Channel Four will cause a very considerable outcry. Television producers would be crying louder than most. However, the barons of ITV and the regulators at the ITC – and many others – would be predicting the collapse of the entire system.

What is much more likely is a gradual reduction in the funding available to BBC2 and Channel Four over a period of years. The channels have available some significant defensive tactics. One key point is that BBC2 and Channel Four carry large quantities of factual material which is quite cheap to make and quite attractive to audiences. Certain strands of programming may be threatened with extinction – such as ambitious fiction/drama on Channel Four; but there have never been many hours per year of this.

It seems probable, then, that current affairs, documentary and mixed-goal factual output will continue to feature in substantial quantities on the conventional channels. Scores of producers will continue to grapple with the dilemmas of edinfotainment programming; the death of current affairs will continue to be predicted, but current affairs will live on, especially on BBC2 and Channel Four, and certainly throughout the 1990s.

COMPETITIVE PRESSURES

Competitive pressures within the four conventional channels will significantly increase.

ITV, in particular, will continue to streamline its schedule, so as to obtain a succession of popular programmes. The independent sector will continue to be hyper-competitive. The following points, however, are more significant.

First, ITV especially will favour longer runs of successful series; there will be fewer runs of 6, 8 or 10 and more runs of 13 and 25. The BBC will follow, but will still retain some runs of 6 programmes.

Second, Channel Four will continue to act tough with the independents; it will enter into few, if any, 'output deals'. Most independents will remain highly insecure sellers, weak supplicants dependent on unpredictable patronage. Many smaller 'independents' may revert to calling themselves freelance producers.

Third, a small number of larger independents will establish working-relationships with particular channels; in some cases this will include 'output deals' – an agreement to take new shows over a period of years. In these cases the independent may retain some of the rights; but the more rights it retains, the less the independent will be paid and the more it will need deficit finance.

Fourth, even the most successful independent programme supplier may only maintain this success over a decade or so; typically major success will be largely dependent on a very small number of successful projects.

Fifth, some shows will be stripped across five days a week, which means making 250 programmes a year. But the two- or three-times-a-week 'soap' may prove to be a more flexible formula which gives a better British compromise between quantity and quality.

Sixth, soap-style working practices are likely to be transferred selectively, and in part, into other areas such as comedy and 'quality-popular' high-cost fiction/drama.

Seventh, as satellite/cable develops there will be more channels devoted to providing 'quality' programming on a premium subscription basis. There will be a gradual shift towards more expensive programming with a first showing on satellite/cable. In this and other ways, the gap in the industrial and working practices between the conventional and new channels will begin to narrow.

All these competitive pressures and industrial changes will continue to make for major changes in the working conditions of producers. As the average series size (in hours and episodes) increases – and there are fewer very-short series – the balance between the numbers of 'executive producers' and 'series producers' will shift. The executive producer, instead of being in charge of several short series and their series producers, will increasingly be in charge of just one big series.

The executive producer will be supported by a larger team of fairly senior producers and script editors. It will become more rare for one director or producer-director to direct all the programmes in a series. The typical series will employ not only more producers, but also more writers and more directors. The status of the individual director is likely to decline since he or she will only be directing, say, 4 programmes in a series of 26 programmes. Directors will have less say in the script–filming–editing sequence overall; some directors may cease to be involved in the post-production editing of their 'own' work.

WOMEN PRODUCERS

The proportion of producers who are women will greatly increase, especially in the BBC; in more and more genres within the BBC women will be in the majority. This advance of women producers will have a massive impact across British broadcasting and beyond.

Around 1989–90 the BBC began to take seriously equal opportunities for women (it was slower in the case of ethnic minorities). Even though there was a pause or small falling-back in the early 1990s, this policy has a big head of steam. The proportions of women producers at all levels will increase; and there will be a 'the more, the more' effect. Women tend to promote other women; some men do not want to work for women.

By 1992 the majority of the BBC's science TV programmes were produced by women. This trend will continue most strongly in documentary and edinfotainment areas. Drama will be in a middle position. Bringing up the rear will be sport, entertainment and comedy, although women will advance here also.

Not all producers, male or female, want to become executive producers. Probably a higher proportion of women producers prefer to stay in their present working-niche. Nevertheless, the proportions of women producers will increase for several reasons.

First, within the private worlds of the separate genres the promotion of even one or two women producers can have a big impact. When a success like *One Foot in the Grave* was produced by a woman, who could any longer say that women could not produce comedy?

Second, the BBC is especially attractive to women because of its vigorous equal-opportunities policy. There are large numbers of women in the BBC in the junior-producer ranks. They appear more willing than men to accept the BBC's lower rates of pay; although some women do become independent producers, they may be less inclined than men to go independent. As the independent sector continues to be so insecure and stressful, it looks increasingly a better bet for a woman – especially with children – to remain in the somewhat less insecure BBC.

Third, there may be a tendency for men to occupy BBC executive-producer jobs, employing a team of mainly women producers; but the BBC is committed to equality at all levels.

ITV can be expected to follow the BBC – as it often has – but at something of a distance. A number of men, as well as women, producers denounced the whole of ITV as 'male-chauvinist'. This was somewhat sweeping; but the ITC, although proclaiming its equal-opportunities loyalty, wasted a unique moment in the 1991 franchise round. However, the ITC will doubtless focus its attention on this issue in due course. There may also be anxiety within ITV that the BBC has an advantage in its greater proportion of women producers. The argument will be made that ITV depends on advertising aimed primarily at women consumers. This argument will eventually prove compelling, especially combined with the point that you may be able to pay women slightly less.

Increasingly in the later 1990s it will become apparent that the BBC is going to be the first major organization in Britain in which around half the senior management are women. This in turn will have consequences, not all of which can easily be predicted. One probable consequence is that still-stronger flows of well-qualified young women will be attracted to the BBC; it will be interesting to see how young men react.

This advance of women may not hugely change the programming output. BBC1 and ITV are already strongly ratings-driven and will get more so. However, the advance of women will finally remove those earlier conceptions of the TV producer as an ex-military man in charge of men.

STAR PAY

The talent in general, and stars in particular, will demand and get higher pay.

As the TV system becomes more competitive, as series have longer runs, as ratings become still more important, the on-screen talent – in successful series – becomes more powerful. Already in the early 1990s a few dozen comedians, 'hosts' and factual presenters were paid several or many times as much as the average producer. Some actors (especially in soaps) were quite lowly paid; other actors (especially ones with the prestige of major film parts behind them) were paid several times the normal rate for a lead actor.

Agents will play an increasingly important part in British tele-

vision. In some cases they will be successful in boosting the salaries
of their clients; in other cases they will be less successful, because
British television does not generate huge surpluses of cash. Nevertheless, 'the talent' overall will account for an increasing percentage of the total real cost of television; this in turn will squeeze
all other costs.

More producers will find themselves dealing with highly paid
stars. In some of the most highly paid cases the star will bring in his
or her own producer. This practice, which already exists, will,
however, not become the predominant pattern even in the entertainment areas.

PRODUCER-DRIVEN TELEVISION

British television during the 1990s will continue to be producer-
driven.

The extent to which British television has fragmented, and will
fragment, can be exaggerated. However, in so far as further fragmentation does occur in the 1990s, it will be producers who are in
charge of the fragments. In this, as in much else, the new independent producers of the 1980s were showing the way which others
would follow.

Increasingly sharp distinctions will be made between different
categories of producers. One important distinction will be between
buyers and sellers – the commissioning editor in the network who
buys and the seller, who will be an independent production company
or a freelance.

Executive Producers will be distinguished more sharply from the
working, or line, producer. Increasingly, EP could as appropriately
stand for 'Entrepreneur Producer'. The range of skills and knowledge ideally required of the senior producer will not be found in any
single human being. Some producers will focus more on the creative
side and still think of themselves as producer-directors or producer-
writers; such creative producers may need especially strong support
in finance and management. Other producers will be strongest on the
financial and deal-making side of things; the packager, or deal-
maker, or more finance-orientated producer may require stronger
support on the creative side. Producers who combine both artistic
and managerial creativity will be highly regarded and more highly
paid than today's producers. British television will throughout the
1990s continue to be producer-driven.

Will British producer-driven television survive beyond 2000?

Many of the BBC, ITV and independent producers interviewed for this study were extremely pessimistic about the future of British television. A commonly stated view was that during the 1990s quality programming would be submerged by vast quantities of re-runs and cheaply imported lowest-common-denominator US entertainment. This prediction seems unlikely to be true of the 1990s; but it could prove to be a more accurate prediction of the years after 2000.

All the British channels – and not least the satellite/cable channels – face many new pressures. Media policy in general, and TV policy in particular, was on the British national political agenda throughout the 1980s and the same will be true of the 1990s. The Brussels regulatory regime will continue to grate against the fragmented British regulatory regime (BBC, ITC, OFT). With much attention focusing on the BBC charter and the new ITV network, less attention may be given to the increased US control of Britain's wider audio-visual landscape (films and cinemas; videos and video outlets; satellite and cable channels, system operators and technology).

So long as a mix of in-house production and the publisher system continues to predominate, then the broad producer-driven style of television described in this book will prevail; but if, or when, the themed channels become the predominant, and no longer the minority, pattern, then the driving forces will be the operators of batches of themed channels and the operators of delivery systems. British producer-driven television will then be a thing of the past.

The interviews

The numbers of people interviewed were as in Table 13.1.

Table 13.1 The interviews

Producers	Numbers
Documentary producers	39
News and current affairs (national)	33
Sport	10
Other factual (including youth)	50
Drama/fiction	37
Comedy	12
Game/people shows	15
National producer total	196
Others	
Senior executives	27
Miscellaneous	4
National TV total	227
Regional producers	27
GRAND TOTAL	254

The 27 regional producers were all in news and current-affairs programming, but these interviews are not directly reported in the present book. The 'senior executives' included six of the seven top TV programme executives in the BBC and Channel Four; also included were Chief Executives of five major entities in the ITC/ITV system. The above numbers included thirty-six independent producers and thirty-seven women producers (and senior executives).

The proportion of initial contacts that led to successful interviews was as in Table 13.2.

Table 13.2   Responses

Result	Number	%
Interviewed	254	85.8
Refused	15	5.1
Neither interviewed nor refused	27	9.1
TOTAL	296	100

Fairly few producers refused to be interviewed, but many said that, while too busy at the moment, they would be happy to be interviewed a few weeks or months later. Some interviews indeed took place several months after the initial contact. Nearly all interviews took place in the producer's office during the working day.

The interview was based on a short list of standard points, some of which were modified as the study progressed. Interviews in almost all cases were recorded on audio-tape; the median length of interview was 70 minutes, which (minus questions) resulted in a typed transcript between 6,000 and 8,000 words, and a total of 6,000 typed pages.

This study is not based on a fully systematic sample. The standard procedure involved taking a single genre at a time; then the pages of current issues of the *Radio Times* were used to identify the producers of programmes within the particular genre which were currently being transmitted. In some cases this procedure was repeated at a later date. We also used current annual editions of *The Blue Book of British Broadcasting* (London: Tellex Monitors) and for independent producers the British Film Institute's annual *Film and Television Handbook*. We also watched names on the TV screen and telephoned for additional information about producer names. We approached the producers by letter, followed up by telephone-calls.

Most of the interviews were conducted between March 1990 and March 1992, with the last interviews taking place in July 1992.

Notes

1 PRODUCERS IN BRITISH TELEVISION

1 Tom Burns (1977) *The BBC: Public Institution and Private World*, London: Macmillan.
2 Carol Varlaam *et al.* (1990) *Skill Search: Television, Film and Video Industry Employment Patterns and Training Needs: The Final Report*, University of Sussex. Institute of Manpower Studies, pp. 19–20.
3 The BBC's *Producers' Guidelines* is a comprehensive publication supplied to its producers and also on general sale.

3 JOURNALIST PRODUCERS

1 Carol Varlaam *et al.* (1990) *Skill Search: Television, Film and Video Industry Employment Patterns and Training Needs: The Final Report*, University of Sussex: Institute of Manpower Studies, p. 3.
2 Malcolm Brynin (1985) *The Shaping of Factual Programming in British Television*, Leeds: Leeds University: Centre for Television Research, unpublished report, pp. 2–4.
3 An amusing account of this first phase is in Michael Leapman (1984) *Treachery? The Power Struggle at TV-am*, London: Allen & Unwin.
4 William Phillips (1992) 'Chronicle of a death foretold', *Broadcast*, 24 January, pp. 14–15.
5 Alasdair Milne (1989) *DG: The Memoirs of a British Broadcaster*, London: Coronet; Michael Leapman (1987) *The Last Days of the Beeb*, London: Coronet.
6 Michael Leapman (1991) 'Begin the story Sunday, screen it Thursday. Scoop!', *The Independent*, 23 February: this is a quote from Paul Woolwich who in 1987 left his BBC post as deputy editor of *Panorama*. He later edited the Channel Four programme *Hard News* before editing Thames Television's *This Week* in its last two years, 1991 and 1992.
7 James Saynor (1989) 'Sky witness news', *The Listener*, 20 July, pp. 28–31.

4 SPORTS: LIVE EVENTS

1 A detailed description of the OB coverage of the 1981 wedding of Prince Charles and Lady Diana Spencer is in Phil Lewis (1991) *A Right Royal Do: The Making of an Outside Broadcast*, London: BBC Television Training.
2 Jeremy Isaacs (1989) *Storm over 4*, London: Weidenfeld & Nicolson, pp. 43–4.

5 THE EDINFOTAINMENT MAELSTROM

1 Alasdair Milne, quoted in Deirdre Macdonald (1982) *Tonight* (BFI Dossier 15), London: British Film Institute, p. 18.
2 Grace Wyndham Goldie (1977) *Facing the Nation: Television and Politics 1936–76*, London: Bodley Head, pp. 212, 217.
3 Jeremy Isaacs (1989) *Storm over 4*, London: Weidenfeld & Nicolson, p. 179.

PART II: FICTION AND ENTERTAINMENT, INTRODUCTION

1 Paddy Scannell and David Cardiff (1991) *A Social History of Broadcasting*, vol. i *1922–39*, Oxford: Basil Blackwell, p. 240.

7 THE COMEDY ENIGMA

1 Frank Muir (1966) *Comedy Television*, BBC Lunch-time Lecture, pp. 12–13.
2 William Phillips (1992) 'Comedy situation is no joke', *Broadcast*, 15 May.

8 'LIGHT ENTERTAINMENT'

1 Sir Harry Pilkington (chairman) (1962) *Report of the Committee on Broadcasting, 1960*, London: HMSO, p. 34.

9 THE INDEPENDENT TAKEOVER

1 Jeremy Isaacs (1989) *Storm over 4*, London: Weidenfeld & Nicolson, p. 35.
2 Ed Shelton and Charles Brown (1992) 'Independent highlights', *Television Week*, 2–8 April, pp. 12–13.
3 William Phillips (1991) 'Time to fight the ratings battle', *Broadcast*, 14 March, p. 34.

10 WOMEN PRODUCERS

1 Michael Fogarty, A. J. Allen, Isobel Allen and Patricia Walters (1971) 'Women in the BBC', in *Women in Top Jobs*, London: Allen & Unwin for Political and Economic Planning, pp. 157–220.
2 Michael Fogarty, Isobel Allen and Patricia Walters (1981) 'Women in the BBC', in *Women in Top Jobs*, London: Heinemann for Policy Studies Institute, pp. 151–213.
3 A good summary of these early and mid-1980s documents is Jane Arthur (1989) 'Technology and gender', *Screen*, no. 30, pp. 40–59.
4 Scarlett MccGwire (1992) 'The bosses who know that women mean business', *The Independent*, 18 February.

11 PROGRAMME BARONS AND POWER

1 Paul Ferris (1990) *Sir Huge: The Life of Huw Wheldon*, London: Michael Joseph, pp. 202–3.
2 John Fisher (1982) 'Profile: Brian Wenham', *Professional Video*, March.
3 Jeremy Potter (1990) *Independent Television in Britain*, vol. iv Companies and Programmes 1968–90, London. Macmillan, pp 10–15.

Selected bibliography

Alvarado, Manuel and Buscombe, Edward (1978) *Hazell: The Making of a TV Series*, London: British Film Institute.

Alvarado, Manuel and Stewart, John (1985) *Made for Television: Euston Films Limited*, London: British Film Institute.

Annan, Lord (chairman) (1977) *Report of the Committee on the Future of Broadcasting*, London: HMSO.

Arthur, Jane (1989) 'Technology and gender', *Screen*, no. 30, pp. 40–59.

Bakewell, Joan and Garnham, Nicholas (1970) *The New Priesthood: British Television Today*, London: Allen Lane, The Penguin Press.

Barnett, Steven (1990) *Games and Sets*, London: British Film Institute.

Barwise, Patrick and Ehrenberg, Andrew (1988) *Television and its Audience*, London: Sage.

BBC Annual Report and Accounts.

BBC Broadcasting Research, *Annual Review of BBC Broadcasting Research Findings*, London: John Libbey.

BBC (1992) *Extending Choice: The BBC's Role in the New Broadcasting Age*, London: BBC.

BBC (1992) *Producer Choice*, London: BBC.

BBC, *Producers' Guidelines*, London: BBC.

Blumler, J. G., Nossiter, T. J. and Brynin, M. (1986) *Research on the Range and Quality of Broadcasting Services*, London: HMSO for the Peacock Committee on Financing the BBC.

Bolton, Roger (1990) *Death on the Rock*, London: W. H. Allen.

Bose, Mihir (1992) *Michael Grade: Screening the Image*, London: Virgin.

Brandt, George (ed.) (1981) *British Television Drama*, Cambridge: Cambridge University Press.

Briggs, Asa (1979) *Sound and Vision: History of Broadcasting in the UK*, vol. iv, Oxford: Oxford University Press.

Brunsden, Charlotte and Morley, David (1978) *Everyday Television: 'Nationwide'*, London: British Film Institute.

Brynin, Malcolm (1985) *The Shaping of Factual Programming in British Television*, Leeds: Leeds University, Centre for Television Research, unpublished report.

Buckingham, David (1987) *Public Secrets:* Eastenders *and its Audience*, London: British Film Institute.

Burns, Tom (1977) *The BBC: Public Institution and Private World*, London: Macmillan.

Cantor, Muriel G. (1971) *The Hollywood TV Producer*, New York: Basic Books.

Channel Four Television Company, Report and Accounts, London: Channel Four.

Chester, Lewis (1986) *Tooth and Claw: The Inside Story of* Spitting Image, London: Faber & Faber.

Collins, Richard, Garnham, Nicholas and Locksley, Gareth (1988) *The Economics of Television: The UK Case*, London: Sage.

Corner, John (ed.) (1991) *Popular Television in Britain: Studies in Cultural History*, London: British Film Institute.

Cox, Geoffrey (1983) *See it Happen: The Making of ITN*, London: Bodley Head.

Day-Lewis, Sean (ed.) (1989) *One Day in the Life of Television*, London: Grafton.

Department of National Heritage (1992), *The Future of the BBC: A Consultation Document*, London: HMSO.

Docherty, David, Morrison, David and Tracey, Michael (1988) *Keeping Faith? Channel Four and its Audience*, London: John Libbey.

Docherty, David (1990) *Running The Show: 21 Years of London Weekend Television*, London: Boxtree.

Dyer, Richard (1973) *Light Entertainment*, London: British Film Institute

Dyer, Richard, Geraghty, Christine *et al.* (1981) *Coronation Street*, London: British Film Institute.

Ferris, Paul (1990) *Sir Huge: The Life of Huw Wheldon*, London: Michael Joseph.

Fogarty, Michael, Allen, A. J., Allen, Isobel and Walters, Patricia (1971) 'Women in the BBC', in *Women in Top Jobs*, London: Allen & Unwin for Political and Economic Planning, pp. 157–220.

Fogarty, Michael, Allen, Isobel and Walters, Patricia (1981) 'Women in the BBC', in *Women in Top Jobs*, London: Heinemann for Policy Studies Institute, pp. 151–213.

Franklin, Bob (ed.) (1991) *Televising Democracies*, London: Routledge.

Fraser, Cathy (1990) *The Production Assistant's Survival Guide*, London: BBC Television Training.

Geraghty, Christine (1991) *Women and Soap Opera*, Cambridge: Polity Press.

Gitlin, Todd (1983) *Inside Prime Time*, New York: Pantheon.

Hobson, Dorothy (1982) Crossroads: The Drama of a Soap Opera, London: Methuen.

Hood, Stuart and O'Leary, Gareth (1989) *Questions of Broadcasting*, London: Methuen.

Independent Television Commission, Report and Accounts, London: ITC.

Isaacs, Jeremy (1989) *Storm over 4*, London: Weidenfeld & Nicolson.

Kustow, Michael (1987) *One in Four: A Year in the Life of a Channel Four Commissioning Editor*, London: Chatto & Windus.

Leapman, Michael (1984) *Treachery? The Power Struggle at TV-am*, London: Allen & Unwin.

—— (1987) *The Last Days of the Beeb*, London: Coronet.

Lewis, Phil (1991) *A Right Royal Do: The Making of an Outside Broadcast*, London: BBC Television Training.

MacCabe, Colin and Stewart, Olivia (eds) (1986) *The BBC and Public Service Broadcasting*, Manchester: Manchester University Press.

Macdonald, Deidre (1982) *Tonight* (BFI Dossier 15), London: British Film Institute.

Madge, Tim (1989) *Beyond the BBC: Broadcasters and the Public in the 1980s*, London: Macmillan.

Millington, Bob and Nelson, Robin (1986) Boys From the Blackstuff*: The Making of a TV Drama*, London: Comedia.

Milne, Alasdair (1989) *DG: Memoirs of a British Broadcaster*, London: Coronet.

Muir, Frank (1966) *Comedy in Television*, BBC Lunch-Time Lecture.

Newcombe, Horace and Alley, Robert S. (1983) *The Producer's Medium: Conversations with the Creators of American TV*, New York: Oxford University Press.

Palmer, Michael and Tunstall, Jeremy (1990) *Liberating Communications: Policymaking in France and Britain*, Oxford: Blackwell.

Parsons, Christopher (1982) *True to Nature*, Cambridge: Patrick Stephens.

Paterson, Richard (ed.) (1990) *Organising for Change*, London: British Film Institute.

Peacock, Alan (chairman) (1986) *Report of the Committee on Financing the BBC*, London: HMSO.

Pilkington, Sir Harry (chairman) (1962) *Report of the Committee on Broadcasting, 1960*, London: HMSO.

Potter, Jeremy (1990) *Independent Television in Britain*, vol. iv *Companies and Programmes, 1968–80*, London: Macmillan.

Ross Muir, Anne (1987) *A Woman's Guide to Jobs in Film and Television*, London: Pandora.

Rotha, Paul (ed.) (1956) *Television in the Making*, London: Focal Press.

Scannell, Paddy and Cardiff, David (1991) *A Social History of Broadcasting*, vol. i *1922–39*, Oxford: Basil Blackwell.

Schlesinger, Philip (1978) *Putting 'Reality' Together: BBC News*, London: Constable.

Schlesinger, Philip, Murdock, Graham and Elliott, Philip (1983) *Televising 'Terrorism'*, London: Comedia.

Self, David (1984) *Television Drama: An Introduction*, London: Macmillan.

Silverstone, Roger (1985) *Framing Science: The Making of a BBC Documentary*, London: British Film Institute.

Sutton, Shaun (1982) *The Largest Theatre in the World: Thirty Years of Television Drama*, London: BBC.

Swallow, Norman (1966) *Factual Television*, London: Focal Press.

Taylor, Don (1990) *Days of Vision. Working with David Mercer: Television Drama Then and Now*, London: Methuen.

Thompson, Robert J. (1990) *Adventures on Prime Time: The Television Programs of Stephen J. Cannell*, New York: Praeger.

Tracey, Michael (1977) *The Production of Political Television*, London: Routledge & Kegan Paul.

—— (1983) *In the Culture of the Eye: Ten Years of* Weekend World, London: Hutchinson.

Tulloch, John (1990) *Television Drama*, London: Routledge.

Tunstall, Jeremy (1971) *Journalists at Work*, London: Constable.

—— (1983) *The Media in Britain*, London: Constable.

—— (1986) *Communications Deregulation*, Oxford: Basil Blackwell.

Tunstall, Jeremy and Palmer, Michael (1991) *Media Moguls*, London: Routledge.

Varlaam, Carol, Leighton, Patricia, Pearson, Richard and Blum, Scott (1990) *Skill Search: Television, Film and Video Industry Employment Patterns and Training Needs: The Final Report*, University of Sussex: Institute of Manpower Studies.

Windlesham, Lord and Rampton, Richard (1989) *The Windlesham/Rampton Report on 'Death on the Rock'*, London: Faber & Faber.

Wyndham Goldie, Grace (1977) *Facing the Nation: Television and Politics 1936–76*, London: Bodley Head.

Index